HOGS IN THE SHADOWS

HOGS IN THE
SHADOWS

Combat Stories from Marine Snipers in Iraq

MILO S. AFONG

BERKLEY CALIBER, NEW YORK

THE BERKLEY PUBLISHING GROUP
Published by the Penguin Group
Penguin Group (USA) Inc.
375 Hudson Street, New York, New York 10014, USA
Penguin Group (Canada), 90 Eglinton Avenue East, Suite 700, Toronto, Ontario M4P 2Y3, Canada
(a division of Pearson Penguin Canada Inc.)
Penguin Books Ltd., 80 Strand, London WC2R 0RL, England
Penguin Group Ireland, 25 St. Stephen's Green, Dublin 2, Ireland (a division of Penguin Books Ltd.)
Penguin Group (Australia), 250 Camberwell Road, Camberwell, Victoria 3124, Australia
(a division of Pearson Australia Group Pty. Ltd.)
Penguin Books India Pvt. Ltd., 11 Community Centre, Panchsheel Park, New Delhi—110 017, India
Penguin Group (NZ), 67 Apollo Drive, Rosedale, North Shore 0632, New Zealand
(a division of Pearson New Zealand Ltd.)
Penguin Books (South Africa) (Pty.) Ltd., 24 Sturdee Avenue, Rosebank, Johannesburg 2196, South
Africa

Penguin Books Ltd., Registered Offices: 80 Strand, London WC2R 0RL, England

The publisher has no control over and does not assume any responsibility for author or third-party websites or their content.

PRINTING HISTORY
Berkley Caliber hardcover edition / December 2007
Berkley Caliber trade paperback edition / December 2008

Berkley Caliber trade paperback ISBN: 978-0-425-22382-6

The Library of Congress has catalogued the Berkley Caliber hardcover edition as follows:

Afong, Milo S.
     HOGs in the shadows : combat stories from Marine snipers in Iraq / by Milo S. Afong.
        p.   cm.
     Includes bibliographical references.
     ISBN 978-0-425-21751-1
     1. Snipers—United States—Biography.   2. Iraq War, 2003—Personal narratives, American.
3. United States. Marine Corps—Biography.   4. United States. Marine Corps—History—Iraq
War, 2003–   I. Title.
     DS79.76.A34 2007
     956.7044'342—dc22   2006102094

PRINTED IN THE UNITED STATES OF AMERICA

10   9   8   7   6

Dedicated to those who have served in the community
Past, Present, and Future

Contents

1

Way of the HOG

"If you want to quit, all you have to do is stop and get into the Humvee!" yelled a sergeant from behind me. The temptation crossed my mind. I was tired, hungry, and already drenched in sweat. But knowing that I wouldn't be able to live with myself if I quit, I let my mind drift to happier times while misery set into my body.

At four in the morning on the island of Okinawa, Japan, the humidity was in full effect and the sun hadn't even risen. Our morning exercise was an eight-mile run and twenty-two marines, including myself, each carried an M16 and a pack filled with a sandbag and other equipment. In two columns, we ran on a paved road as the sound of insects chirping filled the jungles around us.

"I'm done with this!" I heard a marine say from the front of the formation, and he slowed to a walk while we passed him.

"Another one bites the dust," said one of the sergeants leading the run.

At least he's going to get some sleep today, I thought. As for the rest of us, the day had just begun.

We were five days into the battalion scout/sniper platoon indoctrination, with one week to go. Thirty-nine marines had arrived with the intention of being in the platoon, but over a five-day span, seventeen decided that it wasn't important. It was easy for me to understand why they quit, considering that we hadn't gotten more than four hours of sleep each night. And we spent half the day doing exercises. We ran everywhere we went, took tests every morning and evening, and this was the easy week, because the next week would be in the field.

Back on the road, one of the sergeants barked, "I don't want to hear anyone's boots hitting the ground. That's a target indicator and it'll give your position away to the enemy!" Hearing that, I knew that my understanding of tactics needed to change. In the infantry we moved in thirteen-man squads and were taught never to run from the enemy. But in a scout/sniper platoon, we operated in two- or four-man teams, and we might one day find ourselves escaping from a numerically superior force.

One week later, fourteen of us were selected into the scout/sniper platoon. Out of the thousand-plus marines in the battalion, we were the eyes, ears, and trigger finger for the battalion commander. Most of us thought the hard part was over, but little did we know that it was just the beginning.

Like so many other marines, this was my first experience of scout/sniper operations. It had begun with indoctrination and once passing, living the miserable life of a PIG. Then there were the hundreds of hours spent training and preparing for scout/sniper school with one goal in mind, to become a HOG. And finally the triumph of graduating sniper school, with hopes of performing in combat. All together it's a continuous cycle with subtle changes, but in the end the process remains the same.

Marines who desire to become a scout/sniper in an infantry battalion first go through a screening and then a selection process. The screening is a set of basic requirements, and as a whole, the Marine Corps has set standards about who is eligible to be in a scout/sniper platoon. Individual battalions may or may not be lenient in the requirements, depending on the need for personnel. Also, the prospective sniper must go though indoctrination.

Indoctrination, otherwise known as an "indoc," is a selection process that the current snipers hold to select the next group of potential snipers. The length of the indoc may vary from battalion to battalion, but one thing each has in common is that it is a very grueling process. For potential candidates, an indoc may be the toughest thing they have done while in the marines, but to those who get selected, it's just the beginning. During this time, the potential candidates are up hours before the crack of dawn and are released hours after sundown. In between are physical exercises and tests. The tests are daily, and the process is very physically and mentally demanding. Once most individuals get the sense of how a sniper operates, they realize how unglamorous the job is and choose not to go any farther with the indoc—rather, they drop out at their own request.

Because a marine has no training as a sniper, during indoctrination he is known as a SLUG, an acronym for Slow, Lazy Untrained Gunman. The time spent as a SLUG is overwhelming for many, and those who fail an indoc carry the name back to their platoons. Those who are selected to join a scout/sniper platoon are given another name—PIG.

Once in a scout/sniper platoon, the marine receives the honorable name of PIG, meaning Professionally Instructed Gunman. The name explains that the marine is worthy to receive the training to become a sniper. Being a new PIG is probably the worst time physically and mentally for a potential sniper, because he has an enormous amount of information and tactics to absorb and will probably learn most of it through pain and repetition. Every marine who becomes part of the scout/sniper platoon has spent time as a PIG, but in the sniper community, he is not yet considered to be a marine scout/sniper. Although there are PIGs with more experience and knowledge about sniping than some school-trained snipers, every PIG aspires to become a HOG.

A HOG is a Hunter of Gunmen and is the only one of the three designations to be considered a marine scout/sniper. To become a HOG, a PIG must attend and pass a marine division scout/sniper school, and for verification, the school keeps a record of every class and marine who has passed. Marine scout/sniper school is so difficult that it's not uncommon for a marine to keep the title PIG his entire time in a platoon, because he may never pass the school or may never have the opportunity to attend one. Once a PIG graduates scout/sniper school he receives the title of HOG and the current military occupation specialty of 0317, which is the only designator for scout/snipers. (The previous MOS was 8541.) He also receives a 7.62 mm bullet as a necklace. This bullet is known as a HOG's tooth and is to always be on the sniper. It is a charm, meaning that it is the only bullet meant for that marine, and in combat, no other sniper will have a bullet for him. The new HOGs will operate in the battalion as the snipers and spotters. They gain valuable experience by performing missions for the units they support.

Marine snipers are known to be some of the best in the world at their profession, and marine scout/sniper school is a major reason for that claim. There are four recognized schools: First Marine Division, Second Marine Division, Third Marine Division, and Quantico scout/sniper school.

Before a marine can graduate from scout/sniper school, he must master land navigation, shooting stationary targets and moving targets at distances from 100 to 1,000 yards, and stalking. Stalking is the art of moving undetected from a certain distance to within 200 meters of the instructors and firing two shots. The student is being watched by instructors with high-powered optics the entire time. If a sniper instructor can detect him at any point, the student fails.

The student must also master calling mortars, artillery and air support, patrolling, use of equipment, and mission planning, which is a key element in sniper operations. He must also pass the final week, which is a culmination of all. The schools are known to have students from the U.S. Navy SEALs, Army Special Forces, FBI, Marine Special Operations, and other armed forces from countries around the world. Because the time spent as a PIG is so instructional, the student should be prepared to attend this school; however, it's not uncommon for a marine to fail scout/sniper school at least once. The school itself is considered to be one of the hardest in the Marine Corps.

It's during this training that I believe a sniper develops his ideas about killing. Marine snipers have a tremendous reputation that carries over from past generations. With such an illustrious history in combat also come expectations. Because of the countless hours spent training, most snipers feel a desire to "get a kill." Others who haven't spent as much time training to do so might wonder at the importance of this. But from the very beginning of a sniper's training, his entire goal is to do just that.

The organization for a scout/sniper platoon differs from the order of a line company from which most scout/snipers come. The platoon is commonly made up of five four-man sniper teams. The platoon commander is usually a first lieutenant who is also the sniper employment officer and is responsible for the platoon's overall employment as well as the administration and logistics. The platoon sergeant is a staff or gunnery sergeant and preferably a HOG. He advises the platoon commander and is responsible for overall coordination and planning. The third in command is the chief scout/sniper or "chief scout." He is the most experienced HOG and is the liaison for the other HOGs and PIGs to the platoon sergeant and platoon commander. The team leaders or TLs are typically HOGs and are directly in charge of planning for the sniper team's missions. Also, it's not uncommon for a senior PIG who has been to sniper school, but has failed, to fill the billet of a TL. The ATLs or assistant team leaders are typically HOGs or senior PIGs and are directed by the TLs.

For operations, the teams primarily support the battalion but can also be tasked out to assist the companies within the battalion. One team is usually held in reserve for Surveillance and Reconnaissance Center, SARC, which helps the teams in the field to relay information and radio transmissions back to battalion intelligence. A sniper team consists of two shooters and two spotters. Usually teams are made up of four men and can be split into two two-man teams at any time.

A sniper's relationship with his weapon is very special. He

is the ultimate caretaker of his rifle, and in return the weapon keeps him alive. A sniper has to give constant attention to his rifle, as if it were a baby. He cleans it, dresses it with spray paint, feeds it with ammo, sleeps with it, carries it, protects it from the elements, never loses it, and always guards it with his life. A marine sniper's weapon is the M40A3, called the "40." It's essentially a Remington model 700 with specific modifications, and until recently, a Unertl ten-power fixed scope was attached. The new scope is made by Schmidt and Bender and is a variable three–twelve by fifty. The rifle will fire accurately to 1,000 yards (ten football fields), but there are instances where marine snipers in Iraq have shot past that distance.

In Iraq, most snipers also carry an M16 to patrol with, so they can have the semiautomatic firepower as opposed to the bolt-action 40. The spotters can carry an M16 or an M203 grenade launcher. A SAW (squad automatic weapon), a light machine gun, can also be used. Most often, both the sniper and spotter will also have a sidearm 9 mm Beretta. When a sniper really needs to reach out to extreme distances, he can opt for the "50." It's the M82A3 50-caliber sniper rifle made by Barrett called the SASR, meaning Special Applications Scoped Rifle. It, too, has specific modifications. It's capable of penetrating armor and other tough obstacles like car doors, windows, and the biggest obstacle—distance. This weapon can reach out to 1,800 meters (over eighteen football fields) but snipers regularly shoot past that distance. However, one of the drawbacks to this weapon is its weight. Fully loaded with a ten-round magazine, the rifle weighs in at 32.5 pounds.

The equipment used by the sniper teams is selected depending on the mission. But the essentials are two radios, night vision and thermal devices, global positioning devices, flares, a laser range finder, as well as ammunitions and explosives. If on observation missions, snipers can carry cameras and laptops that have the capability of sending information and pictures back to the supported unit from the snipers' position.

During the invasion of Iraq in 2003, marine snipers fought side by side with infantrymen because of the speed involved in the attack. However, since the war was declared over, and infantry units have gone to security and stabilization operations, marine snipers have been primarily conducting defensive operations. This is something most snipers don't prefer because it drastically reduces the opportunity to hunt. More often than not, sniper missions in Iraq involve keeping essential roads clear of improvised explosive devices or IEDs, also known as "roadside bombs." Entire scout/sniper platoons have been tasked with these missions, leaving little room for conventional sniper missions.

For snipers, it's sometimes a challenge to determine who is planting the IEDs. There are many different methods that the enemy is using to place the bombs and with each counter that Americans use, the enemy adapts as well. In one instance, marines encountered insurgents using children to cover their activities. The sniper came across a car pulled to the side of the road, loaded with a family. The father appeared to be changing a tire with his children surrounding him watching, but in reality he dug a hole, and when night fell another person planted and covered an IED. Another technique that insurgents have used is to modify their vehicles. On one occasion, insurgents cut a hole in the floorboard of a van and were able to pull over, dig holes, and cover their IEDs. This happened all within minutes and without anyone exiting the vehicle. With countless methods and techniques of planting IEDs, it's become a challenging task for all coalition units in Iraq to stop these bombs.

Whether in combat or not, shooting is the primary facet that people focus on when they think of a sniper. Although shooting is only 10 percent of sniper operations, snipers shoot thousands of rounds, and once a sniper is very familiar with his rifle, he will know exactly where that round will land. A marine sniper focuses on "one shot, one kill" so much that it's unbearable to the sniper if he misses in combat—but it's also hard to believe that every sniper makes every shot he takes. In a sniper's opinion, every shot is significant, because the more enemy personnel killed equals the more lives saved for friendly troops. Some people say they are haunted by the people they have killed but in my experience, it's the ones I have missed that do the haunting.

A common misconception is that when someone is shot by a sniper rifle he immediately drops dead. However, many snipers in Iraq have reportedly shot people in critical areas on the body but the targets didn't stop.

Another misconception is that all snipers in Iraq will get a kill; for many, the opportunity to do so may never be presented. For those who do get the opportunity, they only claim the kill if they and their partner can confirm a hit and watch the individual die. Unlike in Vietnam, the snipers today do not have a military record of their kills, but most feel the need to keep a personal record. City environments such as the ones in Iraq make it hard to claim kills. On many occasions there have been snipers who have engaged moving targets and confirmed a hit, but the target moved out of sight. Also in Iraq, the locals try to collect their dead for burial before sunrise, making it hard to confirm at night. When a sniper has shot an individual but because of conditions can't confirm the kill, it's called a "possible."

One of the more difficult challenges in Iraq is to identify the enemy. The fact is that enemy fighters have no dress code and most American troops are uneducated on the differences in Middle Eastern culture. This makes it hard for snipers to identify the foreigners from locals. Some of the fighters are Mujahideen (referred to as Muj), which is translated in the West as "Holy Warriors." These Islamic extremists are mostly Arabs from surrounding countries who are drawn to Iraq for the chance of fighting the "Infidel Crusaders." There are also many local Iraqis who are fighting against coalition forces. Often, these groups work together, and they can easily slip in and out of the local population unnoticed by the average American.

In Iraq, American troops are finding that the enemy can be both anywhere and anyone. Because of that, snipers treat everyone as a potential target. But when a sniper shoots, he has to know that the person he is targeting is absolutely violating the rules of engagement. However, there are times when snipers have to distinguish the intent of people's actions instantly, and when doing so, they must try not to think of their fellow marines who have been injured or killed by IEDs, suicide bombers, mortars, or by shootings. This makes the decision to take a person's life unsettling for some, but for others it's an adrenaline rush. Nevertheless, a sniper has to have the maturity and integrity not to be overcome by that power, especially when emotions are involved. Because a sniper has the ability to provide highly accurate rifle fire and has the ability to identify targets more so than anyone else, he has a greater responsibility for his actions.

2

Ambush in Ramadi

Name: Sergeant S., Romeo

Billet: Scout/Sniper Team Leader

Area of Operations: City of Ar Ramadi, Al Anbar Province,
Operation Iraqi Freedom II, February 2004–September 2004

Numb, Romeo pulled the bolt out of his sniper rifle and slid it into his pocket, remembering what he was taught. "If at any time you feel like you're gonna die or gonna get overrun, do other marines a favor, take the bolt out of your weapon, and throw it. Smash or shoot a hole in the scope—but whatever you do, do not let the enemy have control of your rifle!" Romeo wondered how this could have happened. He didn't want to smash his scope just yet, because maybe what he saw wasn't what he thought it to be.

It was mid-March of 2004 in the scorching desert of western Iraq and the capital city of Al Anbar province, Ar Ramadi, had been turned over to the "Magnificent Bastards" of the Second Battalion, Fourth Marines. After relieving the Eighty-second

Airborne in late February, the battalion commander made it a point to make their presence known in the city, but with a population of over 400,000 in Ramadi, he knew right away that his 1,000-man unit faced an enormous challenge. Still, the marines mounted a strategy of continuous foot patrols, which was a tactic that the army hadn't used and in a sense it was proving to be successful because insurgents were surprised by all of the marines on the ground.

The battalion's scout/sniper platoon had been split up and most of the teams were attached to the companies spread throughout the city. Sergeant Romeo and his four-man team were assigned to Echo Company based out of an old Iraqi military maintenance facility called Combat Outpost on the eastern side of Ramadi. The compound sat along the city's main road, Route Michigan, and was a group of concrete buildings surrounded by a wall with guard posts. For the sniper team, being with Echo Company made coordinating and getting supplies easier because the PIGs in the team knew the marines in the company.

A few months before the battalion deployed to Iraq, the scout/sniper platoon received the marines that were chosen from the indoc; but they needed to be trained—and fast. They endured a tough time and the HOGs knew they were capable and ready. After all, if they had stayed in their infantry platoons, most of them would have become squad leaders or section leaders. Finally after months of rigorous training, the team leaders selected the marines that they wanted in their teams.

Romeo was the team leader for "Headhunter Two," and he chose the outcasts of the platoon. Corporal Ferguson from Philadelphia was the ditsy one. He's the blondest black man that you could meet, and was very respectful. Corporal Stanton from Virginia, who was full-blooded Thai, had an attitude, but Romeo liked his sense of humor and heart. Corporal Stayskal from Southern California was the workhorse of the team and was laid back. Other team leaders thought he had an attitude as well, but Romeo saw his strengths. Romeo had been in the platoon for four years and was a HOG for almost as long. A short and muscular Filipino, he was always mellow and knew how to get along well with his teammates. He didn't use his rank or status to intimidate or belittle them, either. It didn't take long before the team was working well together, and they came to understand their roles. They had to. Their lives depended on it.

Shortly after arriving at the combat outpost, Romeo and his team started to run "overnight IED" missions. A northern road on the outskirts of town was becoming increasingly littered with roadside bombs, and the battalion was catching the brunt of them. The road, Route Nova, wasn't far away, and after sundown the team left the outpost on foot. They patrolled through the suburbs of the city to find an observation position along the road. Every night they watched a certain area, and before dawn the team walked back to base. The problem with this was that no matter where they positioned themselves, IEDs were found or detonated on a section of Route Nova that they couldn't see. And when they did move their hiding positions to compensate, the IEDs were found elsewhere.

Even though they operated strictly at night, it wasn't hard to believe that someone knew where they were hiding. When they left the outpost, kids and teenagers followed close by. Dogs revealed their presence by barking as they passed, and the locals stared with looks of amazement toward these crazy Americans walking around after dark—and just the four of them. Soon the marines considered that the IEDs were being planted during the daytime and not at night. At the time, Romeo's team hesitated to operate during the day because of the chance of compromise and because patrols from the infantrymen were continuously on the roads. But they couldn't be everywhere.

Romeo understood the situation and knew that if his team were to catch the people planting bombs, they needed to stay out longer than just overnight. Before long he went to the Echo Company commander and told him that he wanted to carry out a twenty-four-hour IED mission. His team fully understood the consequences involved. Being out in the daytime meant a greater chance of compromise, especially being in a city with the population of this size. Even so, the team would take its chances; they knew that killing bad guys planting IEDs outweighed the risk.

Another motivation for the team to stay out longer came days earlier when a squad from Echo Company got in the battalion's first engagement. The squad caught insurgents planting IEDs on Route Michigan. Because of that, everyone in the battalion was itching to get combat action.

During his mission planning, Romeo received an intelligence report: "A few days ago American contractors were ambushed and killed in the city of Fallujah, located forty miles east of here. Two of the four men's bodies were hung from a bridge. Insurgent activities had been increasing in that area and our battalion intercepted reports that insurgents might be planning something in our area as well."

The marines knew that they weren't wanted in Ramadi. They could tell by the locals. When they patrolled, most people seemed to have animosity toward them, and although some were friendly, lately the attitude seemed to grow worse. Also, the kids weren't following the patrols like they usually did, and Iraqis ducked into their homes as the marines passed by.

Romeo briefed the team, and afterward everyone began to prepare for the mission. Stanton, the assistant team leader, arranged the patrol route, Romeo checked the radio frequencies, and the rest of the team situated the equipment they would need. When everything was done, Romeo held a team gear inspection ensuring nobody forgot anything, and as usual, everything was good. As darkness slowly fell, the team cleaned their weapons and discussed any last-minute details about the mission. Just as they normally did, the team waited an hour or more after sundown to depart friendly lines. Romeo gave a radio check to Echo Company as they left.

"Porky, this is Headhunter Two," said Romeo.

"This is Porky. Send it."

"Headhunter Two departing friendly lines."

"Copy that, Headhunter Two. Good hunting."

"Thanks. Headhunter Two out."

In order to get to their position, the team would have to move 1,000 meters through a housing area. They had done this before, and they spread out across the road to begin patrolling in a staggered column. Stayskal walked point, Romeo was second in the formation, followed by Ferguson, and Stanton brought up the rear. It was dark as the team walked under streetlights and through back alleys. Kids were following again, and the team tossed them some candy to do their part in winning the "hearts and minds" of the locals.

As they headed north, Romeo whistled and Stayskal looked back. Romeo signaled for a "long halt" with his hands, and then passed the signal back to the other two. The team was already through the housing area, and the kids had disappeared. They were close to the outskirts of town when they found a temporary place to harbor. The vegetation in the palm groves proved to be suitable to hide in while the team waited to move. Stopping like this would also make it easier to see if anybody was following them.

"Porky, this is Headhunter Two," whispered Romeo through the handset of his radio.

"This is Porky. Go."

"Stand by to copy pos rep."

"Send it when ready."

Romeo scrolled through his global positioning system and relayed the coordinates on the screen to the marine on the radio from Echo Company. This would tell them where the team was located. The rest of the team formed a circle, each facing outward while lying on their stomachs, not saying a word. They stayed there for a few hours, and every so often Romeo whispered a radio check. Occasionally he would touch everyone's leg to see if anyone had dozed off. No one did.

The area was quiet and there were no locals in sight when Romeo decided it was time to move. Traffic had completely ceased on the roads, and the moon hadn't come out yet. It was a perfect time to patrol. There was no ambient light to expose them, and a small breeze swayed the palm tree branches causing them to ruffle. This would help to mask the team's sound as they walked.

Romeo knelt and scanned the area with his night vision goggles. All clear. He signaled the rest of the team to get up and move. Starting with Stayskal, one by one, they stood up and patrolled north. The team was a little more comfortable now that they were in a vegetated area.

The terrain around Route Nova is mostly farmlands. The road is close to the Euphrates River, and some parts of the road are no more than 100 meters away from it. Because of that, the road is elevated three or four feet above the rest of the area so that when it floods, people can still travel on it. Much of the fields are ankle-high grass, and the bushes in the area are slightly higher than that. Lines of perfectly planted palm trees, known as groves, grew overhead, with small vegetation at the base of the trees. The palm trees produce dates, a major trade item for Iraqis. The bad part about palm groves is that they're known areas for insurgents to gather and escape the eye of unmanned aerial vehicles.

The team moved north to the road and bounded over Route Nova so they could travel next to the river. An hour of patrolling passed when Romeo signaled Stayskal again for a "short halt" to check his global positioning system. Looking across the road, Stanton could vaguely distinguish a few demolished and destroyed tank hulks through his night vision goggles. He knew they were getting close to their observation position, because they had been there before.

Shortly after they started walking again, Stayskal could see two mud huts called "pump houses" fifty meters ahead. This was going to be where the team would be located. These huts are known as pump houses because they hold the engines that pump water from the Euphrates River to the fields. The size of one pump house is as big as two outhouses. These two were spaced about ten meters apart, and the river lay only a few meters behind them. At the base of the pump houses, there was a drastic slope going down to the river.

Stayskal signaled to move up to a few bushes close to the houses. There the team kneeled down, and everyone faced outward in order to have security in every direction. They had to make sure the area was clear before they could move up.

"Stayskal, let's go. I'll cover you," whispered Romeo as he stood up to start walking toward the houses.

"Hey, we're here. Stayskal and I are gonna check it out," Romeo said to Stanton, still whispering. Stanton and Ferguson knew to stay in place to provide rear security. The slope and the houses were clear.

It was around 1:00 a.m. when Romeo radioed Echo Company to let them know the team was in its final position. Because it was night, the team split into two elements to watch over more of the road. Romeo and Stayskal, making up Headhunter Two Alpha would hold in this position facing south and cover their immediate front and to the east. Stanton and Ferguson, making up Headhunter Two Bravo went to a pump house 150 meters to the west, just until the morning. As Bravo team moved out, Stayskal and Romeo put their packs behind the pump houses and climbed on top. They made sure to grab some warm clothes from their packs, before their sweat soaked cammies began to get cold.

Romeo attached the Simrad night vision device to the M40A3 and set his DOPE (data on personal equipment, referring to the scope adjustments) at 200 yards, which was about how far he could make out a human silhouette. Stayskal was peering through his PVS 14s when their handheld radio cracked up.

"Alpha, this is Bravo. We're in position," whispered Ferguson.

"Okay, give radio checks every half hour," said Stayskal.

"Tell them to go fifty/fifty," said Romeo, "One man up and

one man resting." And with that, Romeo took the first watch. Every half hour the two marines rotated watching and sleeping. On the hour, Headhunter Two Alpha sent radio checks back to Echo Company and just like many of the nights before, everything was uneventful.

While on watch, the cool chill of the night and the sound of the Euphrates behind him took Romeo back to Camp Pendleton, California, where he had been stationed. He remembered being an infantryman patrolling the riverbeds and thickly vegetated hills while on training missions, then making it to the scout/sniper platoon and doing even more training. All the cold nights and all the field training hardly applied to the city environment that he was now in. He stared into the darkness where the road was and occasionally searched through his night vision goggles. A smile washed over his face as he thought of his recent wedding and of his wife. His missed her and his kids—actually the kids were his wife's, but since their father wasn't around, Romeo treated and raised them as his own. Spinning his wedding ring on his finger, Romeo was aware that he might never see them again.

As planned, before the sun rose, Bravo team gathered at Headhunter Two Alpha's position and disappeared down the slope behind the pump houses. The morning sunlight proved how good the hiding spot was. Bushes surrounded the slope on both sides, and a few overhead palm trees grew behind them, making the pocket perfect to hide in. Just before the sun peeked over the horizon, Alpha team pulled off the roof and sat in the pocket as well. Now that they were consolidated, the team could take turns observing. When not on watch, two were able to rest and eat. The other two kept their heads over the top of the slope to watch the road only sixty-five meters away. Laying their weapons beside them, they replaced their Kevlar helmets with boonie covers. Romeo set the sniper rifle on the slope next to him. The only problem with the position was that from their viewpoint at the base of the pump house, it was impossible to see over Route Nova. It was also hard to see farther west of the road because of the way it was slanted and vegetation blocked their view.

Romeo shook Stayskal awake. "You and I are gonna go on patrol," he said. "We can't see over the road, so we're gonna go check out the other side."

The two put on their flak jackets and grabbed their M16s. Romeo slung the sniper rifle on his back, just in case. The patrol lasted less than an hour, and the two didn't go farther than 200 meters away. Bushes in the area made it easier for them to hide, and the only thing they thought suspicious was a small car that drove by packed with Iraqi males. Some time later, the empty car traveled back toward the way it came, and when it came back again it was full of people. This happened a few times. When the two went back to the pump houses Romeo asked the others if they saw the same thing. "Yeah but they didn't appear to have weapons," replied Stanton, and they left it at that.

It was Stayskal's turn on watch when he spotted a boy walking from the east. He traveled slowly on the side of Route Nova and was walking toward their position, toward the pump houses. Stayskal thought the boy would bypass them, but he didn't.

"Hey, there's a kid coming our way," he whispered to the team.

"Is he looking over here?" asked Romeo.

"No, but he's getting close," he said.

Minutes later, the boy was only a few meters away and was still walking toward them. Stayskal kept his eye on the kid until the last second then dropped his head, trying not to be seen, but it was too late. The kid walked up and peered at the team. Stayskal instantly thought of shooting the kid with his pistol but didn't. The wide-eyed boy stared at the team for a few seconds, said something, and then ran. By now it was late in the morning and getting close to the afternoon. The team couldn't believe that they had become compromised, and they discussed what to do next.

"We should move."

"And risk getting even more compromised?"

"We don't know that the kid's gonna tell anyone."

"Are you kidding me? Haven't you seen the movie *Bravo Two Zero*?"

"Hey, listen," said Romeo, "we're not gonna move," hoping that nothing would happen and knowing that if they did move, they were likely to be compromised and by someone who probably would do something about them being there.

Soon it was Ferguson's time for watch. A few minutes later he noticed an older man and woman in the distance heading in their direction. They were walking furiously toward the pump houses. Ferguson alerted everyone, and they all grabbed their weapons. The woman was first to reach their position and she immediately started screaming at them. Ferguson kept his eyes on the road, hoping that nobody would drive by and see what was happening. He couldn't believe it himself. Nervous, Romeo held his M16, waiting for the man to reach for a weapon from under his clothes. As he glanced at the others they, too, had their weapons ready. The two Iraqis didn't speak English but they understood body language. While the woman was still screaming, the man looked at the four marines, all with weapons, staring back. He pulled the woman by the shoulder and turned to walk away.

The whole situation had lasted less than a minute. They thought seriously about moving but didn't, and decided that the best idea would be to move once nightfall settled.

An hour passed when Romeo thought he needed to see more of the road west of them. It was about noon, and they hadn't observed it since early in the morning.

"Stayskal, you're on watch. I'm gonna go to that pump house to the west and observe for a while."

He didn't plan on staying long, so he took his M16 and a few magazines and left his equipment. His pistol was in the drop holster that was always attached to his leg. Stayskal got up as Romeo grabbed his handheld radio and stuffed it in his cargo pocket.

Being short has its advantages, especially in the field. This made it easier for Romeo to bound from bush to bush. Once he got close to the pump house, he crawled on his hands and knees to the entrance. It was no trouble for him to move unseen because of the tall grass, and once inside, he sat on the engine and cracked the front door. This gave him an excellent line of sight up the road. There were also holes in the walls of the pump house that helped him to see different angles around it for security.

Soon the team could hear gunfire in the city. It appeared to be coming from Golf Company's area. The team was used to hearing shootings, but they themselves hadn't been involved in any of it.

"Damn, what are we doing wrong, Stayskal!" said Romeo.

"What do you mean?" replied Stayskal on his handheld radio.

"Why don't we ever get any action, man?" said Romeo.

"I know. This sucks! We're never anywhere near the action, either," said Stayskal.

The other two teammates were asleep.

"Hey, maybe they'll give us a call when they need more ammo," Romeo agreed with a chuckle.

The heat of the day was in full effect. With a cool breeze blowing through the crack in the door and thirty-minute watches all night, Romeo was tired. He knew that if he stayed in the pump house any longer, he might fall asleep. He decided to join the rest of the team, but just as he opened the door, a gut feeling told him to see what was on the other side of the road. "I'll investigate it before I go back," he said to himself.

In front of the pump house, to the left, was a small ditch leading up to a patch of bushes next to Route Nova. Romeo low-crawled 75 meters in the ditch until he reached the bushes. Once inside, he sat up, and with the four-power ACOG (advanced combat optical gunsight) scope on his M16, he inspected the area across the road from left to right. Directly beyond the road was an open field. Farther back were the ruined tanks and then palm groves that were about one hundred and fifty yards away. Shade filled the palm groves, making it difficult to see inside, but he could make out homes farther in the distance. Around that area he watched civilians walking and cars driving by. He sat back down, and seconds later he scanned again. The last time, he sat up higher and caught a glimpse of two farmers with shovels running from an alley into the palm groves. Others followed behind them. "I wonder what those guys are doing," he thought, as he followed them with his scope.

A gleam of light broke through the overhead canopy and lit a small area of the ground within the palm groves. The man he was watching ran into the light and Romeo saw perfectly that the farmer's shovel was actually an AK-47. Immediately he scanned back to the others and realized they had rifles, too. He watched more people with weapons pouring from the alley into the palm groves. He could tell they were men by the way they were dressed—most were in robes but some had pants on. Many of them had head wraps covering their faces. He could tell that they were talking and pointing, and they were spreading out on a horizontal line facing him. Shocked at what was going on before him, Romeo knew all too well what was happening. He came from an amtrack company and they were doing what he was trained to do once he exited the amtrack. They were getting on line to assault through an objective area. He did a hasty count of the men and stopped at fifteen. He flew out the back of the bush while digging through his pocket for his radio.

"Hey, get your gear on! Get your gear on!!" he yelled.

"What?" asked Stayskal, who couldn't understand him.

"Get everyone up!" Romeo yelled.

"What? I can't hear what you're saying," said Stayskal.

Frustrated, Romeo stopped talking as he ran back to the team. *The Iraqis don't seem to know exactly where we are,* he thought, so he ran bent over, trying not to be seen over the road.

Once Romeo reached the others, he slid down the slope. *"Get up and get your gear on. We're in trouble!"* he said, out of breath.

The other teammates didn't know him to lie or joke in the

field, but they were confused, not being able to see what was happening on the other side of the road. "We're about to get some right now! I counted fifteen guys and more behind them, all with weapons, coming this way. We need to get ready!" he said. "They're gonna come over that road in a minute! Hurry!"

Everybody scrambled to get their flak jackets and helmets. All at once they lined their gear at the base of the slope and grabbed their weapons. They were surprised, wondering if what Romeo said was true. As a team, they had trained for something like this but never thought it would happen—nor wanted it to.

As they finished putting their gear on, they lay on the slope creating a half circle. Everyone kept a different sector, including the flanks. They began to pull their magazines out of their pouches and lay them on the slope next to themselves, making a magazine change easier. Romeo pulled the bolt out of the 40 and stuffed it in his pocket. Then he told the others where he put it, just in case he didn't have time to get rid of it. They all knew that they wouldn't need the bolt-action rifle. The road was only sixty-five meters in front of them. Romeo decided that before they were overrun, he would throw the rifle and radio in the river. They quickly discussed an escape route.

"We might have to swim for it."

"I'm not swimming for nothing," said Ferguson. "You know I'll drown."

Romeo wanted to laugh but couldn't. He remembered during the indoc that Ferguson could barely swim twenty meters in the pool.

The team didn't know exactly where the insurgents were going to come from, so they didn't want to move.

Maybe they'll go in a different direction, Romeo thought.

He never thought his first combat action would be like this. He always imagined himself looking through the scope of a sniper rifle at a gunman with an AK, and then sending a 7.62 mm bullet through his heart.

The team knew there was no way to escape without being seen, so they resolved that they were going to have to fight it out. But they wouldn't start shooting unless they were shot at, thinking that maybe the men wouldn't find them and bypass them. Romeo grabbed the radio and called back to Echo Company.

"Porky, this is Headhunter Two!"

"Headhunter Two, you're coming in broken and barely readable. Say again."

"Porky, this is Headhunter Two. We're gonna need a QRF [quick reaction force, in place to immediately help a sniper team]. We have fifteen or more locals, coming toward our position, all with weapons and appear to be hostile!"

"Headhunter Two, say again. You need a QRF?"

"Yes, send the QRF!"

"Copy. What is the sit—" Romeo put the handset down before he could finish.

Ferguson had the M16 with the grenade launcher attached. He loaded a 40 mm grenade and slammed the barrel shut. He had to make each shot count, because he only had two more. A minute or so passed as everyone lay in position with their weapons up, searching for the men coming their way. Romeo spotted one. He watched a man stand up and look over the road. Romeo could see a red-and-white checkered cloth wrapped around his head through his four-power scope. At first, the man was looking in different directions trying to find exactly where the

marines were. Romeo had his sights on the man's head. When
the man looked in their direction he stopped, then disappeared.

Ssssssip! Boom! A rocket-propelled grenade sizzled over the
team's head, impacting and exploding in the palm tree growing
behind them. The sound was deafening. Shards of the tree landed
on them as they opened fire and went into survival mode. Gunmen with sandals and head wraps flooded the road, shooting
their AKs wildly at the team. M16s were roaring when another
RPG hit the pump house in front of the marines, dazing them.
More grenades flew by and exploded in the river. It took only
seconds for the insurgents to realize that they could flank the
four-man team, and two of them crossed the road to the right.
But Stanton, holding the right flank, shot them both before they
could find cover. Bullets were throwing dirt in Romeo's face as
he tried to take aim, and when he leaned back, a few landed in
the dirt where his head had been. More landed at their feet, as
they realized that someone was on their left flank in the bushes.
Stayskal, holding the left flank, unloaded into the bush and the
shooting stopped. Bullets were flying in every direction, and the
team needed to gain fire superiority or they would be overrun.

The insurgents were bad shots, but sheer numbers make a
difference. The team was getting only a few shots off when Ferguson launched a grenade. It landed on the road knocking over
a few of the men and stopping the others for a second, giving
the team time to aim in. The team started to suppress and were
soon taking well-aimed shots. No one tried to cross the road
again. The insurgents resorted to holding their AKs over their
heads and shooting recklessly, only exposing their weapons.
Occasionally one of them would stand up to shoot but would

only take a shot or two before retreating for cover again. The team knew that the QRF was coming, and all they had to do was buy time. Miraculously no one in the team was shot, but everyone was down to their last magazine. In the fight for their lives, the shooting seemed to last only seconds, but it had been twenty minutes.

The gunfire from the road ceased, and the team looked and saw the QRF Humvee packed with a squad, racing down the road from their left. As planned, Stayskal threw a smoke grenade to mark their position and prevent friendly fire. In the Marine Corps, machine gunners are taught to shoot a six- to ten-round burst, but no one was going to correct the marine in the back of the Humvee who had a steady grip on the trigger of his M240 Golf machine gun, spraying back and forth at the insurgents.

"Get ready. When the QRF gets closer, we're going across the road to assault through," said Romeo. "Leave your packs here."

When the Humvee was within 100 meters, the team got up and hustled to the road. The squad was already dismounting as the team got on line and started to climb to the top of the road with their guns up. When they reached the other side, to their surprise nothing but a few pools of blood and sandals remained.

"Where the hell did they go?" asked Stanton.

"Look," said Ferguson.

In the distance, the Iraqis were running into the palm groves. Seconds later, the team could hear bullets snapping over their heads.

"Spread out to the right. Stay on line," said Romeo. The squad was on line as well, covering the left flank.

The marines safely pushed forward, avoiding the few stray bullets coming toward them, but when they reached the palm groves, mortars and machine-gun fire opened up on them. The insurgents had waited for them to reach the palm groves and prepared a counterattack. The mortars were landing in the distance and had no effect, but machine-gun fire was tearing into the trees around them, causing them to stop, when a marine from the squad got hit. When he went down, the squad didn't want to advance without him, so they held their position and fired back. The insurgents were shooting from buildings on the other side of the palm groves, and it was hard to get any good shots on them through the trees.

Romeo's world was moving in hyper speed. Every noise was elevated. He could hear the sound of marines yelling and of bullets hitting the trees around him. A few zipped close by. Everything seemed surreal. He glanced at the marine who was shot and lying on the ground. He was out of the way of the enemy gunfire, and his squad was unleashing their arsenal but still couldn't advance. They were pinned down just fifty meters to the left of Romeo's team and someone in the tank hulks was taking well-aimed shots at them.

"Move up, move up!" yelled Romeo to his team. *"We're gonna envelop the tanks!"* and they started to shift. The squad knew what the four-man team was doing. It was simple infantry tactics. The squad was suppressing the target, keeping the enemies' heads down, while the sniper team was going to come from the side to finish them off.

The team was quickly advancing to the tank hulks from the right when Stayskal yelled, *"I see him. He's right there. He's right there!!"* As Stayskal was pointing and yelling, Romeo looked over at him just in time to see a bullet impact his upper torso.

Romeo was stunned; he watched his partner fall to the ground and heard him moaning, his legs kicking wildly. Romeo reassured himself, "Okay, he's all right. He's still moving and yelling."

The team had already established a standard operating procedure that if one of the teammates had been shot in action, because there were only four of them, the rest of the team would carry on with the fight until they could help that member.

Romeo didn't want to, but he left Stayskal and kept going. The other two teammates were holding in position and were providing covering fire for Romeo, who looked back at Stayskal. He stopped moving.

Damn it, thought Romeo as he turned and ran to him. He knew Stayskal was dead.

"*Ahh!* My back! My back!" moaned Stayskal as Romeo reached him.

Romeo could see blood on his shoulder and told him, "It's nothing, just a little blood, man. You're fine!"

"No, it's my back. Cut my gear off me!" Stayskal moaned in pain.

Romeo wondered how he was going to cut his gear, and then he remembered that he had a knife in his pocket. After he sliced through Stayskal's flak jacket and just as he started to roll him on his side to check his back, Romeo suddenly remembered where Stayskal had been pointing and looked up toward that area.

Through the palm trees, Romeo saw a man about 100 meters away, behind one of the demolished tanks. He was dressed in all black and was sitting in such a way that the squad couldn't see him from their angle. He was also looking over his shoulder at Romeo and was in the process of swinging his Dragunov SVD sniper rifle toward him. A Dragunov SVD is the sniper rifle of choice for many snipers around the world and because of that marine snipers intently study the weapon and its capabilities, making it easily recognizable if spotted.

Stanton and Ferguson were both shooting when Stanton felt something knock him down. He didn't feel any pain and Ferguson checked his body for a wound. All he found was a small hole in his fatigues by his shoulder. He didn't have any signs of bleeding so Ferguson told him he was okay, and Stanton got back up and started fighting again.

Romeo yelled for Stanton to check on Stayskal while he picked up his M16 and began to squeeze off bullets toward the man who was now facing him. With his adrenaline pumping and the insurgent who just shot his partner in his view, Romeo assaulted toward the enemy sniper alone, but he had tunnel vision and was unknowingly running through the squad's line of fire. He was moving fast from palm tree to palm tree trying to make himself a hard target. Romeo heard his bullets dinging off the back of the tank and could see them hitting the dirt around the other sniper. The enemy sniper kept his head down and wasn't able to shoot because of Romeo's bullets, which provided Romeo with enough time to close in on the man to within fifty meters.

When Romeo stopped and brought his scope to his face, he could see the man, now lying on his stomach, beginning to pull his rifle into his shoulder to aim at him. Immediately Romeo rested his sights on the man's chest and squeezed the trigger. His heavy breathing threw the shot off, but he watched the man flinch in pain as the bullet entered his hip. Part of the robe around his waist sprang up, revealing to Romeo where the bullet had impacted.

Standing between the palm trees and with no cover, Romeo knew that one bullet wasn't going to kill the gunman; at best it would only temporarily disable him. With his sights higher on the man's chest he squeezed the trigger again, sending another bullet into his stomach. The man flinched and his robe sprang up again, but he was still moving. Romeo used Kentucky windage and estimated his sights to where they needed to be to shoot the man in his chest. He squeezed off one last bullet and hit the man in the chest. The man collapsed to the ground as the sniper rifle slipped out of his hands. He was dead.

The squad had shifted their fire when Romeo ran through their kill zone. They were concentrating their shooting on the houses in the distance now, and the enemies' bullets were starting to fade. The corpsman was tending to the wounded squad member, and Stanton was helping Stayskal while calling in a medical evacuation from the battalion.

When Romeo reached the dead gunman, he grabbed the sniper rifle from the first man that he had ever killed. He'd heard stories of what it was like to kill and read about others who did so and how they felt at the time. He had thought about this moment many times before and wondered what it would feel like. But he felt no emotion of joy or excitement, and he didn't feel sorry, either. He just felt that he did what he was trained to do.

After evacuating the wounded, Headhunter Two gathered with a platoon for resupply. They were immediately directed to support a squad of marines that was isolated and being attacked in the city. Unbeknownst to them, almost every marine patrol in the city was ambushed. The firefights lasted throughout the next few days, killing many insurgents and a few marines.

Stayskal was shot in the shoulder. The bullet shattered his collarbone and exited his back, missing the spine by less than an inch. Stanton didn't know it, but he was also shot in that firefight. He ducked down and a bullet entered under his flak jacket by his neck and grazed his flesh three inches before exiting. There was no bleeding because the bullet had seared the skin.

3

East Side of Hit

Name: Sergeant Clifton, D.

Billet: Scout/Sniper Team Leader

Area of Operations: City of Hit, Al Anbar Province,
    Operation Iraqi Freedom II, August 2004–March 2005

"Clifton, are you good to go out?" asked Gunny urgently.

"Well, I'm still on bed rest, Gunny," Clifton replied.

"Damn it!" Gunny yelled and slammed the door.

Clifton wondered why he was so angry. Gunny knew that he was unable to operate and it wasn't like they were doing anything important. They'd been in Iraq for two months now and still no action. Clifton thought that he was going to be in gunfights every day, but so far it was just boring missions, and that definitely wasn't what he came back into the marines for.

He was the team leader of "Shadow Six", a scout/sniper team with the proud First Battalion, Twenty-third Marines, a reserve battalion based out of Texas but currently stationed in western Iraq. The unit deployed to Iraq for seven months, marking the first time the battalion had been activated since World War II. Most of the marines from 1/23 were temporarily residing on an air base called Al Asad, which had been home to the Iraqi Air Force before being captured in mid-2003. It's the second largest air base in Iraq used by coalition forces and is located in Al Anbar province about 110 miles northwest of Baghdad. The base is mostly secured by its isolated location but is heavily fortified around the populated areas, and it now belonged to the First Marine Division, specifically Regimental Combat Team Seven and its air wing counterparts.

The First Battalion, Twenty-third Marines were to help with security and stabilization in the region. The scout/sniper platoon was tasked with helping to keep the essential supply routes free of IEDs. This meant, to the snipers, watching certain roads for days at a time, hoping to catch insurgents planting bombs.

Clifton got out of bed and put his shoes on. He wanted to see why Gunny was so upset. The heat of the Iraqi desert instantly swept over his body when he stepped out of the "can." It felt like being in an oven. His "can" was similar to a boxcar, except that it had been turned into a two-man living quarters. It came complete with beds, a door, electricity, and air-conditioning.

He couldn't help but dwell on how disappointed he was with his situation. Only four months earlier he was in Huntington Beach, California, and was on his way to becoming a fireman. But when he heard that friends from his old unit had died or had been injured in Iraq, he felt a conviction to do his part in the war on terror. He dropped everything in his personal life and rejoined the marines just to go to Iraq. A friend told him about a unit from Texas that was activating for a year and would be deploying to Iraq. He was told that the scout/sniper platoon needed HOGs, but what appealed to him most was the fact that he didn't have to reenlist.

In Iraq he was hoping to see action, but instead, he had seen nothing. The bulk of his missions had been watching roads to prevent IED emplacement, and to make matters worse, he found a cyst in his butt cheek after arriving in Iraq. It had had to be surgically removed, putting him on bed rest.

On his way to Gunny's can, Clifton moved slowly and with a minor limp over the loose rocks in the area. The surgery had left him unable to leave the base, but he didn't mind. He would rather stay back than go and sit in the sand to watch roads in the empty desert where nothing happens.

When he reached Gunny's can, also the scout/sniper office, he opened the door and stepped inside to find organized chaos.

Most of the platoon was there. The team leaders were gathered around a map talking quietly with the chief scout and Gunny. A few assistant team leaders were working on the radios, gathering extra ammo and explosives. Others were organizing equipment and taking it outside. It was obvious that something was happening. There usually weren't this many people in the office.

He asked another team leader what was going on.

"A colonel was driving up Route Bronze coming to Al Asad. Once they got to the city of Hit [pronounced "Heet"] they were ambushed, but they were in AAVs [Amphibious Assault Vehicles], and no one on our side was hurt. We're probably going into the city, but all the team leaders are going to a brief in a few minutes."

Clifton wanted to be on this mission. With no combat so far, he thought that this might be his only opportunity for action.

Gunny was upset because he needed all the teams for this mission, but since Clifton had already told him that he was on bed rest, Gunny wouldn't let him go. Unfazed, Clifton convinced the platoon corpsman, Doc McBride, to persuade Gunny that Clifton was good for the mission. The corpsman's concern was for Clifton not to tear his stitches.

At the brief, the team leaders learned the whole situation: "At 1300 this afternoon a convoy of AAVs from Ar Ramadi was traveling on Route Bronze coming to Al Asad. The convoy was supposed to turn off Route Bronze onto Route Uranium, ten miles before Hit. The convoy commander failed to make the turn and continued up Route Bronze toward the city. Before reaching Traffic Circle One in Hit, the convoy was attacked. The ambush was initiated by IEDs, followed by rocket-propelled grenades and machine-gun fire. It was a well-planned attack. The convoy returned fire, and the engagement lasted twenty minutes. A few vehicles were damaged, but no marines were killed. Shortly afterward, the battalion received reports from local sources within the city that one to two hundred masked and armed gunmen were witnessed setting up roadblocks and defensive positions. A few civilians were pulled from their vehicles; some were suspected of aiding American forces and were killed. A police station on the east side of Hit was attacked, and the Iraqi police officers who didn't escape were executed. The police station was reported to be held by insurgents.

"Now, the scout/sniper platoon will insert this evening to report on any activities on the west side of the city, around Traffic Circle One. The platoon will hold in position, report on any activities, and engage any threat to themselves or to civilians.

"Bravo Company will be tasked with traveling south to

Ramadi, crossing over to the east side of the Euphrates, then traveling north to the east side of Hit. They will conduct a raid on the police station to regain control, then move to and hold the east side of the Hit Bridge. Two two-man sniper teams will be attached to the company to provide support.

"Once in position, marines from RCT-Seven will move into the city and conduct a sweep from north to south. Bravo Company will block and intercept any insurgents fleeing to the east. The entire mission will take forty-eight hours.

"Sergeant Clifton and Sergeant Allison will be the team leaders attached to Bravo Company. The two of them will have to coordinate with Bravo Company's commander immediately."

After the brief, Clifton and Allison found Captain Dumas, Bravo Company's commander, and provided him with a plan on how the sniper teams would support them.

This was the plan: Once the convoy reached the east side of the city, Clifton's team would break off and take up a position south of the Hit Bridge. At the same time Bravo Company would conduct a raid on the police station. Allison's team would support the company as it raided the building, and immediately afterward, his team would move to a position north of the bridge. The sniper teams would observe the east side of the city for enemy activity or personnel. When they felt it was safe for Bravo Company to move up to the bridge, they would radio them. The company was to take its position only after the sniper teams had called for them. Both team leaders reiterated to the captain that he should only move his men when they confirmed that it was okay for him to do so.

After coordinating with the captain, Clifton briefed his partner, Corporal Stokley. Corporal Stokley was also a HOG.

He had graduated Quantico sniper school just months before shipping out to Iraq. He had never been on active duty until now, which gave the two something to playfully argue about. Stokley was short and one of the most physically fit marines in the platoon. Running was his specialty, and he also had a sense of humor, just like Clifton. They made a good team, even though they hadn't been operating together for a long time.

"Finally, maybe we'll get some action!" Stokley said. The two began to plan for the mission. They made sure to pack over twenty-four hours' worth of chow and water. Stokley prepared the radios and gathered the ammunition while Clifton cleaned his M40A3, then packed his gear. He decided to use the drag bag for this mission. The drag bag would allow him to carry his sniper rifle and the rest of the equipment on his back, freeing up his hands so he would be able to patrol with his M16.

As the sun went down, the convoy departed Al Asad. Everyone knew it would be a long ride to Ramadi, then back up to Hit.

Hit is a city of 200,000 people located eighty-five miles northwest of Baghdad. It is within western Iraq's Euphrates River Valley in Al Anbar province, which is the largest province in Iraq. The province is known to be the heartland of the insurgency, which made it difficult for U.S. forces to gain control of the region.

First Battalion, Twenty-third Marines was spread throughout the area and was responsible for four cities and many more small towns within the province. Hit wasn't regularly patrolled at this time, only the roads on the outskirts. Route Bronze, which was used by coalition forces, is a two-lane highway that runs north to south on the west side of Hit. Cafés, restaurants, and garages lined Route Bronze within the city. On the other side of town, the Euphrates River flows roughly north to south and is the border of the city, but one bridge connects to a small community on the eastern banks of the river. Also during this time, it was reported that the insurgents were warned that American forces were planning a major assault on Fallujah, which was to happen one month later in November of 2005. Because of this, there was a surge of population traveling north to Hit, Haditha, and Haqlaniyah, where American presence in the cities was relatively nonexistent.

The ride on the seven-ton was long and Clifton could feel every bump and vibration through the flimsy metal seat. His backside was throbbing, but he ignored the pain while he and Stokley discussed the mission again. They verbally rehearsed everything that was to happen when they left the vehicles. Stokely had the radio and every so often heard the vehicle commander counting down until the time of arrival.

"Thirty minutes out!" he said, and Stokley relayed it to Clifton.

Clifton was thinking about his father. He was a marine in Vietnam—an infantryman, too. He seldom heard stories about the war from his dad. The first time Clifton even heard his father talk about Vietnam was after he graduated boot camp. He wondered what his dad would be like in combat and thought back to when he was nine years old and telling his dad he wanted to be in the army.

"Why do you want to be in the army, son?" his dad asked.

"I think it will be cool," said Clifton after watching an episode of *G.I. Joe.*

"Don't you want to be a marine?"

"What's that?" asked Clifton.

His dad then proceeded to tell him about the Marine Corps, and Clifton was sold. After that it was no more playing army. It was always playing marine.

"Five minutes out," said Stokley as he tapped Clifton on the shoulder.

They both began to position their packs and rifles so they would be able to exit the seven-ton fast. Clifton put his night vision goggles around his neck.

It was 1:00 a.m. when the marines came upon the city. Lights from Hit could be seen in the distance to the west. They drove into the area with no headlights, in order to use the element of surprise. They would need it, if they were going to take the police station back. The community seemed empty and Clifton started to get anxious as the convoy slowed. The other sniper team, Shadow Four, wished them luck when they came to a halt.

"This is us; let's go," he said to Stokley, while he climbed over the side of the vehicle.

The fall from the seven-ton seemed longer than the old five-tons that he was used to. His suspicions were confirmed when his feet hit the pavement. The impact felt as though he had torn the stitches, and pain surged through his butt. Disgusted, he didn't say a word, but he remembered Doc's final command not to tear the stitches.

Good way to start a mission, he thought, just as Stokley landed next to him.

They quickly put on and adjusted their equipment. Once their packs were on, Clifton grabbed the handset that dangled from Stokley's back and gave a radio check to Bravo Company. The radio check was good, and the team dashed off toward the palm groves.

The mission depended on the team's getting into position with enough time to report on any activities for the company. From the map study, they knew to go west. They ran south next to the paved road and were moving fast. A palm grove was to their right, but they couldn't get into it because a fence was blocking it off, so they continued south. Clifton came upon a small hole in the fence, and they both crawled through. Once on the other side, they found a trail that headed west. Running on the trail, Clifton's magazine pouches were slamming into the body armor on his chest. He came to the realization that he and Stokley were being loud, and he immediately slowed the pace to a patrol. Soon they could hear Bravo Company in the background. Their vehicles seemed noisier than usual and must have caught the attention of stray dogs, because they were barking wildly.

Clifton's senses had him at full alert as he took point on the trail leading through the palm groves. The path was a jackpot. It was dirt, making the patrol quieter compared to walking on the leaves and palm branches lying off the trail on either side. It was pitch black. The palm trees smothered the sky and no light appeared. The only sound coming from the two snipers was their boots softly landing on the path. As they made their way farther west, lights from the city shone briefly through the trees, and soon they could hear the trickling of the Euphrates River. Clifton felt his heart pounding through his chest. He was nervous and anxious, and was thinking of what could potentially happen. He wondered if there would be as many Muj in the city as were expected. If so, there would be plenty of kills.

Once at the edge of the palm groves, the team stopped. Clifton used his night vision goggles to examine the area. In front of them was an open field. It went from the edge of the palm groves to the river, which was only twenty meters away. Across the river, he could see the east side of the city. To the north was the Hit Bridge. There was also a pump house to his right, standing a few meters away from the river. He decided that's where they would observe from.

As they began to cross the open area toward the pump house, they heard a loud voice that surrounded them. The team had been caught off guard and they immediately thought that someone was talking to them. Stokley thought they were compromised, but then they both recognized it as the city's prayer speakers. Every few hours the city was filled with a voice that led the people in prayer. But it was two o'clock in the morning and they usually don't pray at this time, Stokley thought.

The pump house was made of clay and wood; the roof had a few small holes in it. A piece of wood emerged from the front of the roof, making it easy to climb onto.

"Stokley, hold security until I get up," Clifton whispered.

Clifton put his drag bag on the roof, then his M16, and climbed on. He then took security while Stokley made his way up.

The shed was flat on top, making it great to lie on and shoot from, but after doing a hasty search they noticed a problem. They would have to leave the pump house once daylight came. The area they were watching was directly across the river and was built on a hill. All the buildings were significantly higher than the team's pump house. This would give anyone who was in that area the advantage of occupying the high ground, and come daylight, anyone from the city would be able to see the sniper team easily. From doing a map study, Clifton knew the area they were observing was going to be elevated, but he hadn't realized to what extent.

On the roof, the team began to set up their position. There was nothing in between them and the city, so they needed to be as silent as possible. Clifton pulled the sniper rifle out of the drag bag, yanked the bipods down, and pointed the rifle toward the city. He reached for the night vision attachment and slid it over the scope. The clicking sound meant the scope was on, and he tightened it down. Stokley was beginning to set the spotting scope up, and the radio was next to them in the pack.

The city was quiet; no vehicles were roaming the streets, and nobody was outside. They made a hasty search around the bridge and into the city, and then began to unload more equipment. They decided that once completely unpacked, they would do a detailed search and then radio the company to move up. Clifton was removing his flak jacket and Stokley was reaching in his pack when a deep and long burst from a machine gun broke the silence of the city. The sound echoed throughout the area.

They both looked toward the bridge as green tracer bullets sliced through the darkness like lasers, coming from the city. A heavy barrage flew relentlessly down the path of the bridge. Clifton originally joined the marines as a machine gunner and immediately noticed the green tracers, because he had never seen any before.

"That's got to be a 50-cal," Stokley said. It was louder than any small arms.

The team could hear the bullets impacting metal, and they realized that Bravo Company had moved up to the bridge. The bullets were digging into the armor of the Hummers and seven-tons.

"Shadow, take the shot! Shadow, take the shot!!" someone yelled over the radio.

Clifton was partially amused when he heard that. Whoever was yelling must have thought that the snipers were just waiting with their sights on the machine gun, but really they weren't even set up yet. Clifton scrambled to get behind the sniper rifle, thinking that the company shouldn't have moved up to the bridge without their advice.

It didn't take long for the marines to answer back with their own weapons, but as they did, bullets from AKs and other small arms began to rain down on them. Red tracers from the marine's machine guns smashed and tore into buildings and occasionally flew aimlessly into the sky, hitting nothing.

Clifton was behind the rifle trying to locate the source of the green tracers, but through his scope he wasn't able to see any muzzle flash or the source of the bullets. The tracers appeared to be coming from nowhere.

It wasn't long before the two of them could hear the whistling of incoming mortars on their side of the river. One explosion shook the trees behind them.

"That one was close!" said Stokley.

A mortar landed seventy-five yards behind them in the palm groves and caught a small patch of vegetation on fire, but it eventually burned itself out. Clifton could hear small arms fire coming from behind them, but thought that it was the marines from Bravo Company who had dismounted and started firing into the city.

He searched for the source of the green tracers for minutes but couldn't find it. He could see other targets moving around, so he stopped looking for the machine gun. But he needed distances to the targets before he could shoot.

Clifton and Stokley decided to use the most prominent building as a target reference point and they briefly discussed the distance to it. Agreeing that it was 500 yards away, Clifton adjusted his scope. He would have to hold higher or lower to hit his targets depending on where they were in conjunction to that building. As he was searching, he realized that the city was too bright for his night vision. His ability to see was being flooded with light, so he removed the attachment. He was trying to remain calm so he could find the enemy, but the insurgents were shooting and moving smartly. Once he would spot muzzle flash from an AK, it would disappear after one or two shots, making it frustrating to get a fix on any targets. Meanwhile, Stokley was scanning with his ACOG. It was more maneuverable than the spotting scope.

"If you see someone, get me on 'em," Clifton said.

Clifton started to search under the streetlights. He looked toward the light of the building they ranged. The light was on the main road that ran through the city. The road curved slightly north on the city side, making it impossible for Bravo Company to see that area. Clifton, however, could see it perfectly because of his position.

Everything seemed to be happening fast. The machine gun firing green tracers was letting off bursts; small-arms fire and rocket-propelled grenades were still impacting on the marines' side.

Bravo Company wasn't giving up without a fight. They unloaded everything they had, and it sounded as if they were firing in every direction.

Clifton was about to scan a different location, but he caught sight of a man running from an alley and into the middle of the street before kneeling down. He started to aim an RPG. Clifton felt lucky; the man ran right into his vision. Without hesitation, Clifton adjusted his sights making them rest directly center on the man. He wanted to take a deep breath, then exhale to get his natural point of aim, but there was no time. This was his chance. Everything he was taught came down to this single moment. Concentrating as much as he could, Clifton slowly squeezed the trigger. He held his breath, trying to steady the crosshairs, and nothing but making a fundamental, clean shot went through his mind. In a split second the bullet was fired.

The rifle bucked momentarily. After the recoil settled, Clifton saw the man lying on his back and the RPG was on the ground above his head.

Excitement filled Clifton's heart. He was glad he'd finally completed what he was trained to do. He realized this was just the start of the action, and there would be plenty more people to shoot. Then greed set in. He began to fantasize about all the kills he would get. His mind raced as Stokley asked him where he was shooting. It wasn't proper etiquette when Clifton shot without orienting his spotter on target, but if he had, he wouldn't have had time to engage.

"By the building we ranged," Clifton said. "I got 'em. He's down on the main street."

As soon as those words left Clifton's mouth, another man ran into the road to take the RPG. Clifton's eyes lit up with joy. He started to see the numbers now. He quickly aimed at the insurgent and tried to concentrate again, but the man was moving swiftly. Just as the man stopped to pick up the RPG, Clifton sighted in. He could see cloth wrapped around the man's head, and he squeezed the trigger, knowing immediately, however, that it was a miss. When the rifle settled, Clifton watched the man run out of his sight.

I shouldn't have shot! Clifton thought. At the last moment, the man had moved from his crosshairs. In his mind he visualized the last place that the crosshairs sat before the trigger squeeze, they were just over his target's left shoulder.

I shouldn't have rushed the shot; it wasn't clean. I wasn't relaxed, he thought, beating himself up for shooting when he knew better.

"Did you get him?" Stokley asked, now scanning where Clifton was shooting.

"No, he was moving too fast," Clifton said, aggravated.

Clifton couldn't fathom missing a shot in combat. He was getting down on himself. He was taught never to miss. He couldn't believe it.

He looked back to the area where the dead man was lying. The RPG was gone.

"Damn!" he said to himself.

While watching the same area he saw another guy with an AK dash across the road and then behind a building. Clifton kept his crosshairs on the edge of the building waiting for the hajji to come back around the corner. He watched that area for a few minutes, which felt like an eternity, when he could have been finding other targets. But his patience paid off when the insurgent turned his head around the corner. He appeared to be looking for the marines on the other side of the bridge. Clifton waited to see if he would step into the open. He did. The man slid around the corner with his back against the building. He apparently wasn't going to make the same mistake as the dead guy lying only a few yards away. Clifton was excited again as he watched the man shuffle against the building with an AK in hand.

That dude thinks no one can see him, Clifton thought, and he cleared his mind, forgetting about his last shot.

The man was moving slowly at an angle toward them, but his silhouette was great.

Clifton had time to use the fundamentals. He calmed his nerves and slowly inhaled, then exhaled. He led the man with his crosshairs. He was going to let the insurgent walk into his death. His sights were in front of the man's chest when the bullet sped from the barrel. It felt like a good shot.

Clifton ripped the bolt back, then slammed it forward to chamber another round. He caught sight of the man and watched his body slump down the wall. The weapon fell from his hand. This shot helped to make up for the miss.

With a taste for blood, Clifton feverishly began searching for more targets, but soon the shooting started to fade from both sides. The team wanted to move positions. They'd fired three shots and didn't want to become a target themselves, but after checking the area around them, there was nowhere to move. If they went back into the palm groves, they wouldn't have the view they had from atop of the pump house.

They agreed that in all the commotion no one had seemed to notice them, so they stayed in position. It would be hard for anyone to see them at night anyway.

"Get on the radio and see what's going on with Bravo," Clifton said to Stokley.

Stokley tried to make contact, but there was no reply. He tried to reach the other Shadow team but, also, no reply.

Minutes later Clifton found a muzzle flash from a window.

The shooter fired twice and then nothing. Clifton didn't think it would happen again, but it did. As he took aim at the window, he nestled into a good shooting position, and because the window was farther away, he held his crosshairs high. He could see light flash from the barrel of a weapon one last time, and he squeezed the trigger. Both he and Stokley waited a few minutes to see if anyone would shoot again, but nothing. There was no way to tell if Clifton had scored a hit, but the shooting stopped.

Soon, Shadow Four came over the radio.

"Shadow Six, we got air on station," said Sergeant Laursdorf, the other sniper team spotter. "We'll handle it."

For the next few hours Shadow Four directed air attacks on various targets. Clifton and Stokley witnessed firsthand the destructive power of America's air machines. AH-1W Super Cobras attacked possible enemy positions, but only after F-16s swooped in and demolished entire buildings did the enemy machine guns and small-arms fire finally stop.

With the stars beginning to fade and the glow of morning sun quickly lighting the sky, Clifton and Stokley needed to move or they would be exposed.

"Pack up, we're out of here," Clifton said.

Stokley gathered a few items still unpacked. It didn't take long for him to be situated, and he climbed off the roof. Clifton put all his gear away and was placing the rifle in the drag bag when suddenly bullets hit the roof beside him. Someone from across the river opened fire. Chips of the roof kicked up next to him, and the supersonic crack of bullets whizzed by his head causing Clifton to flinch. Instinctively he rolled toward the edge of the roof leaving his rifle and drag bag but as he was falling, his body jerked. He was stuck on something. Clifton couldn't believe what was happening. The same piece of wood he had used to climb up on the roof had snagged his high speed gear as he tried to get down! His body armor carrier was caught, leaving his upper chest and head exposed to the shooter. Clifton squirmed to get free while a stream of bullets impacted around him.

Stokley looked up at Clifton. His legs weren't moving. He wondered if Clifton was dead.

Why me? Clifton thought. He stopped moving briefly, trying to gain his composure for a last-ditch effort to get off the roof.

He frantically wiggled himself free, and after what seemed like minutes (but was only seconds), he fell to the ground unhurt—but he still had to get his rifle. Stokley was amazed that Clifton wasn't shot. Stokley was trying to find where the shots were coming from. Clifton knew the rifle was lying on the drag bag, and if he could grab the bag, it would all come down. It was within jumping reach. He leaped, trying to grab the bag while more bullets zipped by. Suddenly they both cringed at the whistling of incoming mortars, and one splashed into the river just a few yards south of them.

Clifton finally got hold of the drag bag as another mortar landed in the palm groves behind them. It was so close they could feel the concussion.

"We need to get going!" Clifton said, as he pulled the straps on the drag bag, cinching it down on his back. Before Stokley could reply, another mortar exploded just yards away from them. The soft dirt of the palm groves caught most of the explosion, but they both were thrown off their feet and into the pump house.

Clifton was dazed and his ears were ringing while he

checked his body. Amazingly, he still wasn't injured. He looked at Stokley, who was struggling to his feet, uninjured as well. Wide eyed, they looked at each other, astounded at what had just happened, and momentarily laughed. They needed to get away from there before more fell. "Yeah, you think we should go?" Stokley answered sarcastically.

Clifton was on his feet now. He hoped that the zero on his sniper rifle was still good. As they ran for the palm groves, they could hear the shooting pick up around them while crossing the open area. It was a short distance from the pump house to the palm groves, and in seconds, they were concealed by trees and bushes, but they were still running. They needed to link up with Bravo Company.

Moving swiftly through the palm groves, Clifton thought about a scene from the movie *Born on the Fourth of July*—the part where Tom Cruise shoots one of his own men in the heat of battle, while the guy was just trying to get back to friendly lines. Clifton wasn't going to be the one who came running through the palm groves toward friendly lines while a young trigger-happy private behind a machine gun was on watch. No way.

They stopped. "We need to get in contact with Bravo," he said to Stokley. "Tell them we're coming from the south."

Stokley radioed the company. The team waited a few minutes before they left, giving the company enough time to spread the word that the two-man sniper team would be coming from the south.

Minutes later, while patrolling, they reached a clearing. Stokley saw the marines from Bravo Company on vehicles only a short distance away. Clifton smirked at the young marine manning the 50-caliber machine gun as they walked into friendly lines. He was oriented in the direction from which the snipers had arrived.

Shadow Four was waiting for them. Clifton asked why the company had moved up to the bridge without their advice. It was a question that could not be answered.

Allison explained to Clifton what happened.

"The company sent four marines to secure the bridge when the machine gun opened up on them. Then gunfire opened up all around them from the palm groves and from the east."

"From our side of the palm groves, too?" Clifton asked.

"Yeah, from everywhere!" replied Allison.

Clifton realized that the gunfire in the palm grove behind them during the night wasn't from the Bravo Company marines; it was from insurgents. Luckily, he hadn't shot many times because doing so might have given their position away to anyone behind them. He wondered if they had made chance contact with insurgents if they would have changed positions. He also thought about the trail he found, and how loud it might have been had they walked on either side of it. There is no telling how close they came to death that night, but that comes with the territory when you're in a war zone.

The fight in Hit lasted five more days. For the next few days the two sniper teams formed and operated as a four-man sniper team. They were sent to clear the palm groves around the company and they also engaged enemy snipers in the palm trees. Clifton hoped to get more kills, but the rest in that engagement would be unconfirmed. In the end he was happy to make it out alive.

After clearing the city, marines found a 12.7 mm machine gun in a building across the bridge from the company's position. It was placed in the back of a room and aimed directly down the bridge and positioned in such a way that the only angle for it to be seen firing was from the bridge. That was why Clifton couldn't get a shot on it.

4

Airfield in Baghdad

Name: Corporal Mulder, O.

Billet: Scout/Sniper Assistant Team Leader

Area of Operations: Kuwait to Baghdad,
    Operation Iraqi Freedom I, March 2003–September 2003

"Sierra One in position," whispered Mulder over the radio. He dropped the handset and put his head behind his spotting scope to begin searching the area for targets. He held the AN/PVS-7B night vision goggles behind a twenty-power spotting scope to maximize his visibility for night observation. It wasn't a perfect fit, but he could see farther. His partner, Sergeant Hamblin, was already scanning the area through his AN/PVS-10 day/night scope mounted on the M40A3 sniper rifle. In the middle of the night, the two-man scout/sniper team had slipped unnoticed onto a one-story abandoned building in the Al Rashid Airfield.

Corporal Mulder expected another long and boring night, no different from any of the other previous missions, with one exception: His unit was now roughly seven miles away from their objective, downtown Baghdad.

A month earlier in Kuwait, Mulder had relinquished his billet as a team leader to operate as an assistant team leader to his best friend, Sergeant Hamblin. Initially they were part of a four-man team, but before crossing the border, the team had split into two two-man elements so they could provide more support for their unit. In Kuwait, the team trained hard every day. They hiked and patrolled, practiced shooting and land navigation, and rehearsed their reaction drills for any situation they might find themselves in. When the four-man team split, the other team took the SASR 50-caliber sniper rifle. Mulder and Hamblin took the two 7.62 mm sniper rifles. For them, hunting in Iraq would be the proving grounds for all of their efforts.

Mulder grew up hunting varmints on a farm in the small community of Worthington, Minnesota. He wanted to be the first marine in his family and explained this to his parents one day. They agreed with him and laughed innocently, but in a patronizing way. Mulder instantly knew that he was going to do it. Not only did he want to be a marine, he wanted to be a scout/sniper. When he turned eighteen, he joined the marines and after boot camp, while he was attending the School of Infantry, an instructor found out that he wanted to be a sniper. The instructor enlightened young Mulder on how hard the process was and said that it would be impossible for him to become a sniper. But Mulder was determined to prove him wrong. Mulder knew that eventually he would be part of the best shooters in the world.

After arriving at his duty station, Mulder learned that he would have to spend at least nine months in a weapons platoon to become familiar with the "fleet," before he was eligible to take the scout/sniper indoc. Waiting was hard for a motivated young marine like he was, but soon he was signed up for Third Battalion, Seventh Marines scout/sniper platoon indoc, which is where he met Hamblin. The indoc was one intense week, and out of about thirty marines, only seven were selected. He and Hamblin were part of the seven, and for the next four years they would share the experience of becoming snipers.

Hamblin was from Kansas. Mulder was impressed with his intelligence and toughness. Hamblin had been in martial arts from the age of five, but Mulder noticed that even with all the training, he was a mild-tempered person who didn't flaunt his skills. Soon they both graduated the First Marine Division scout/sniper school together. After graduation they returned to their unit and instantly became team leaders, because all of the senior HOGs were discharging from the marines.

A few years later, word spread that a war against Iraq was imminent. Mulder was at home when he received a phone call telling him that his unit was going to the Middle East. There had been rumors that his unit was going to be deployed and that they could possibly go to war. This phone call solidified the rumors. After hanging up the phone, Mulder celebrated the good news, while his father asked him what had happened.

"We're going to *war*!" Mulder yelled excitedly. His dad looked at him like he was insane. He didn't understand that Mulder was getting what he had prayed for.

Just before combat operations started, Mulder and Hamblin both decided to use sniper rifles. Mulder carried an M40A1 with the Unertl scope and Hamblin carried the M40A3 with the AN/PVS-10 day- and night-capable scope. Mulder would have to spot for Hamblin during night operations, because Mulder didn't have night capabilities for his rifle. But when it came to shooting during the day, they both agreed to trade off spotting for each other.

When Operation Iraqi Freedom I started, the team's unit was in support of Regimental Combat Team Seven and after crossing the border, the team began moving nonstop. Soon they learned that in order to see combat, they had to be up front with the lead vehicles of the convoys. If not, the enemy would have either been dead or would have surrendered by the time they got to the fight. They resorted to catching rides with various sections from their unit. But the lead element was constantly changing, making it harder for the team to stay up front. It didn't help the team's ability to remain on the lead vehicles when they operated continuously for three or four days before they realized that they needed rest.

Initially they were hardly involved in any of the fighting, and during the few occasions they did shoot, the situations made it impossible for them to confirm anything. This wasn't good enough for Mulder. He and Hamblin had spent years training to kill, and he wanted all of his hard work validated by seeing the bodies personally. He wanted the satisfaction of knowing without a doubt that he had a kill. Even though they were with the lead elements, they still had trouble getting to the action. However, one instance made them vow never to be far from it again.

The team had spent twelve boring hours in a no-name city. After hearing that another platoon was fighting in a different sector of the city, the two-man sniper team charged to their position. Once they reached that platoon, the snipers discovered that they were too late. The platoon commander explained that Iraqis with rocket-propelled grenades and small arms were weaving in and out of the crowds around them. The platoon had machine guns and M16s but nothing precise enough to kill the men without any collateral damage. Had the snipers arrived earlier, they would have definitely seen action. Mulder and Hamblin hated hearing that, and from then on, they swore to always be up front.

Finally on the afternoon of April 7, they reached the outskirts of Baghdad. Their unit secured the Al Rashid Airfield, which was in a suburb only eleven kilometers from downtown. The airfield was a target for coalition forces and after being secured, the battalion set a perimeter around it. Sierra One informed their commander that they would find a position to observe, and that night the team crept onto a one-story building in the northern edge of the perimeter. It was midnight when Mulder radioed his position back to higher.

From the roof, the team could see the buildings of Baghdad; some were still ablaze. Occasionally the faint sound of gunfire echoed in the distance. Their viewpoint from the roof was great, and so was the night illumination. Only 200 meters directly in front of them was an interstate overpass. They could see 750 meters beyond the overpass, down one street, and about 600 meters down another street.

So far, no one in the scout/sniper platoon had any kills. Most of the platoon had been in engagements, and although some operators had possibles, no one could confirm their kills. This made getting a kill within the platoon a competition; everyone wanted to be the first.

On the roof, Sierra One had been observing for a few hours

when a truck turned a corner in the distance. It traveled in their direction on the street in front of them. Once it got close, Mulder noticed through the spotting scope that four men were inside and they were carrying AKs.

"Do you see that?" asked Mulder, referring to the weapons.

"Yeah, I do," said Hamblin.

"Should we shoot?" asked Mulder.

"They meet the rules of engagement. Let's shoot 'em," replied Hamblin.

The team waited for the truck to get closer. Moments later the driver parked the vehicle on the left side of the road, facing the team. As they parked, Mulder and Hamblin discussed what dope to dial on the rifle. Neither of them had a range finder, so they would have to estimate the distance to the truck. They agreed that it was about 500 yards away. Mulder watched as men sprang from the back of the truck, and one handed the others their weapons. Mulder could hear Hamblin begin to control his breathing in preparation to shoot.

"Which one you going for?" asked Mulder behind the spotting scope.

"The one who has his back turned," answered Hamblin.

The man was standing alone on the left side of the truck, facing away from the snipers, making his profile the most prominent. He was the only full-value target.

"Fire when ready," said Mulder.

Hamblin had already pushed the safety forward and was confirming his natural point of aim. He let the crosshairs settle on the center of his target's back and fired. The man's black silhouette contrasted with the green background through Mulder's modified night vision spotting scope. He could see the

Iraqi's head snap back as his lifeless body dropped to the ground in one motion. The shot was loud and it rang out through the night. Hamblin instinctively chambered another round. Mulder enthusiastically reported to Hamblin his kill and was surprised when the other Iraqis didn't scatter. *They must be used to hearing gunfire,* he thought. It seemed to him that it was a normal noise within the city.

"Are you gonna take another shot?" asked Mulder.

"I don't have a clear one," replied Hamblin.

The other three hajjis were standing on the opposite side of the truck, toward the back. Moments later, one of them walked to the same side of the truck as the dead man. He stopped and looked confusedly at his buddy. Mulder thought the man was probably wondering why his friend was on the ground.

"He sees his friend. You need to shoot him," Mulder said.

Hamblin was already centering the crosshairs on the man, but with only a side view, Hamblin needed to be as steady as possible for accuracy. Seconds after he shot, Mulder watched the man fall to the ground. He noticed that this hajji's head did the same as the last one, and it occurred to him that they must have been closer than 500 yards. Hamblin was shooting them in the head.

Their gig was up. The Iraqis on the other side of the truck watched as a bullet separated their friend's brains from his skull.

"Sierra One, what's your situation?" came over the radio.

Mulder couldn't answer. His hands were full with the optics, and Hamblin was already trying to acquire another target. But the remaining men ducked behind the truck. Within seconds, a man scrambled into the cab and was driving the vehicle. He moved the truck to where it blocked the bodies from the snipers' view. Hamblin didn't shoot again, and as the Iraqis drove off, Mulder saw that the bodies were gone. While the truck was speeding away, the eerie sound of the nightly prayers blared throughout the city.

Mulder radioed the situation to higher and although this wasn't the team's first firefight, it was the first time they were able to confirm kills, and they were excited. Mulder and Hamblin had an agreement that the shooter would switch with the spotter after the first kill; that way they could both get some action. It was Mulder's turn to shoot, and as soon as he took over the gun, he was glued to it.

Hamblin was the first to get kills, and Mulder was happy for him. He was glad to be there to watch it, but envy and jealousy momentarily set in. He wanted a piece of the action, too.

A few hours passed when Hamblin noticed something. He directed Mulder's attention to a small mud hut a few meters beyond the overpass in front of them. In one of the windows two small dots were moving up and down. It was a man with binoculars looking toward the airfield. The first thing that passed through Mulder's mind was "forward observer."

Days before, in another city, when their unit received artillery fire, the battalion commander issued an order that anybody observing them with optics was fair game. However, that was earlier, and the current rules of engagement didn't allow for people with binoculars to be engaged, so they radioed to higher to see if they could shoot. They got approval to do so.

Mulder dialed 200 on his scope. He steadied the sights between the dots and squeezed off a shot and the object disappeared. He felt good about the shot, but wasn't completely

satisfied that it was a kill. There was no way to positively identify that the target was dead.

As the sun began to rise, the team knew they needed to find
ranges to different target points in their sector, and they decided
to zero their rifle on a car. Mulder shot at a section of the vehicle and adjusted his scope until he was on target; the vehicle was
350 yards away. From that car they were able to tell the distance
to other points beyond it.

Soon afterward, Mulder noticed a man with an AK-47
walking toward them. He quickly adjusted the rifle and dialed
on a dope when the man disappeared into a building. *That was
my only opportunity,* Mulder thought. He didn't want to be
pessimistic, but he realized that nothing else was going to happen. He was positive that his destiny in the war was to watch
his best friend get two kills.

After spending most of the night staring through a scope,
Mulder's eye was fatigued. He rolled off the glass and let his
partner take over observing. Hamblin was behind the sniper
rifle for a few seconds when two Iraqis, one with an AK-47 in
hand, walked into the snipers' view. Mulder shook his head in
disbelief at his bad luck. The men appeared from an alley and
were at the same distance as the car they had just zeroed their
rifles on. The Iraqis were oblivious to the fact that a marine
sniper team was watching them. No Americans had entered
Baghdad yet. This helped the sniper team, because the locals
had no idea they were there.

The Iraqis walked across a street, unaware that Hamblin
was aiming in on the man with the weapon. Seconds after the
men stopped in the street, Hamblin squeezed the trigger. Mulder confirmed a stomach shot but surprisingly the man didn't

fully realize that he was hit. In seconds the pain set in because the man dropped his weapon and put both hands on his now-bleeding stomach. Mulder watched the AK bounce off the pavement and as the man crumbled to the ground, his friend panicked. He scooped up the AK and ran off before Hamblin could shoot him. *What a friend*, thought Mulder and he and Hamblin turned back to the dying man who was crawling to the side of the road.

Ten minutes passed, and Mulder began to wonder how long it would take for the Iraqi to die. The man was obviously in a lot of pain, and every so often he yelled out and hopelessly tried to move, but found that he couldn't. The team didn't want to shoot him again and risk giving their position away. One problem was that they were lying on the roof with no cover and concealment, but with the naked eye it would be hard to spot them at that distance. Finally, after some time, the man stopped moving.

Moments later a Nissan truck stopped next to the body and two men got out. Mulder could tell by their body language that they were upset. They stared for a second, said a few words to each other, then got into the truck and sped off, leaving the body behind.

Mulder congratulated Hamblin on his third kill, but by now he was anxious to shoot. He got behind his rifle. This would give them both a fair chance at the next kill. Mulder told himself that he wasn't going to miss another opportunity even if it meant staying awake for two days.

It was late in the morning, and the team was searching for targets. They could see rows of old sandy buildings made of concrete and bricks. Trash littered the streets and a few people were on the sidewalks, but no military-aged males with weapons. Mulder found the pools of blood from the men Hamblin had shot the night before. Suddenly Mulder noticed the Nissan truck with the same two men in the cab. It turned a corner farther back on the street directly in front of them. Only this time it had many more people; six men with rifles and rocket-propelled grenades were in the back. A flat-bedded diesel followed close behind them. Three men were in the cab, and at least five men with the same type of weapons occupied the back.

Instantly Mulder's adrenaline spiked and he knew that he was going to get some kills. Both he and Hamblin were behind their rifles as the Nissan stopped next to the dead body on the left side of the street facing the snipers. The diesel truck stopped on the right. This made it easier for the snipers to choose targets. The diesel truck was Mulder's and the Nissan was Hamblin's. Mulder quickly adjusted his dope to 350.

Neither of them said a thing to each other. It was clear what had to happen next.

Mulder formed a plan; he wasn't going to spoil this opportunity.

You have to wait until all of them get off the truck. Otherwise they're gonna drive away, and you're only gonna get one! he told himself. *You wanna get all of them!*

Mulder was a left-handed shooter and was well into the habit of manipulating the bolt with his right hand and squeezing the trigger with his left, giving him an advantage over right-handed shooters, when it came to engaging multiple targets. He could work the bolt faster.

As it would happen, Mulder's plan didn't last long. He slowed his breathing, calmed his nerves, and put his crosshairs where he thought the men would eventually jump from the bed of the truck. He waited. The first man dropped off the side of the truck. Mulder had tunnel vision. He adjusted his sights and squeezed the trigger, hitting the first Iraqi in the chest and causing him to tumble onto his back.

You blew it! You just couldn't wait, could you? he said to himself.

But surprisingly, the truck didn't drive away, and the rest of the men were rushing to dismount the vehicle. Seconds later Hamblin was shooting at targets. But Mulder didn't have time to look in his direction, because a hajji was trying to help the man who was on the ground. Mulder aimed and fired, knocking that man to the ground as well. He worked the bolt and chambered a round with his face never leaving the butt stock. Another hajji was trying to drag the man whom Mulder had just shot. Mulder sighted in on him and fired. He went down. Mulder worked the bolt again. One Iraqi stayed behind the truck, and Mulder could see his head peeking around from the back. Mulder lined him up and squeezed the trigger. The Iraqi had stayed in place long enough for his head to catch the bullet.

Mulder began firing at other men who were now scrambling for cover. When he didn't have a shot on them, he fired into the men lying on the ground to make sure they were dead. When the trucks first rounded the corner, he had a fresh twenty-round box of ammo, but by now he had already gone through half of that. He emptied all of the bullets in the internal magazine and was reloading one by one as he had been taught.

I cannot reload fast enough! he thought. He was irritated that there was nothing in the weapon for a few short seconds before he could shoot again. He didn't want to give the enemy any time to move.

Luckily for the team there was no wind in the area, because in all of the excitement they hadn't made a wind estimation. But they were only 350 yards away, and a little wind wouldn't have thrown the bullet off target by much.

One of the Iraqis made it into the passenger's side of the cab before Mulder could shoot him. Mulder knew that he was going to try to drive away. He sighted in above the steering wheel and waited. If the man was going to start the vehicle, that's where he would end up.

Mulder controlled his breathing. He had to make sure that his next shot was precise because he was going to be shooting through the windshield. He positioned his sights by taking a deep breath and relaxing. Where the crosshairs lay would be his natural point of aim, and if the crosshairs were off target, he would adjust and do it again until he was on. The sights settled above the steering wheel, right where the unlucky Iraqi just happened to stick his head up.

Mulder thought back to what he was taught. He was going to be shooting through glass, and his bullet would be deflected if not shredded. He decided to shoot anyway, to see what would happen. The man leaned forward, putting the key into the ignition while Mulder cut the slack from the trigger. The bullet punched through the glass and hit the man in the face. He died instantly.

Mulder caught sight of his body slamming against the seat, then slumping onto its side. Blood splattered the back window. Mulder was glad they had zeroed their rifles at that range.

Another man scrambled into the cab. He pushed the body out of the way and was smart enough to keep his head below the steering wheel. Mulder's fun was over because he couldn't get a clear shot. The Iraqi started the truck and turned it around.

Mulder reloaded and scanned Hamblin's area just in time to see him smoke one of his targets.

"A guy in the diesel truck is getting away," he said to Hamblin. Together they turned their attention to the truck. It was barreling down the street away from them.

"He's gonna have to turn," Mulder said, knowing that the street merged right, farther back. Having set the back street as a target reference point they quickly adjusted their scopes to 750 yards. Sure enough, the truck slowed down to make the turn, and as it did, Hamblin and Mulder put a lead on the cab. They didn't expect to hit anything but they still unloaded every round left in their rifles. To their surprise the truck started to drift, halfway into its turn. *That's just plain luck,* thought Mulder. They were never trained to shoot moving vehicles—especially while they were turning. Suddenly a machine gun from a Humvee opened fire on the truck as well. The marines in the Humvee had heard the shooting and drove over to the building that the snipers were on. The flatbed truck burst into flames, and then drifted out of sight. From their position, the team could see smoke floating up from behind a building in the distance.

Mulder reloaded again then scanned the area. Finally he took his head off the rifle and looked at his partner, who was also looking at him. They were both in awe of everything that had just happened. Scanning over the dead bodies, Mulder hoped to finish off any survivors. Both he and Hamblin found a man trying to start the Nissan and without speaking, they shot through the windshield. The man died in seconds as bullets riddled his body, shaking him in his seat.

The team called over the radio to higher and updated them on their situation.

Bodies were scattered on both sides of the road and blood drenched the sidewalks and streets. The dead were wearing red-and-black head wraps. Some had ski masks on, but none wore military uniforms. In fact, none of the people that the team had ever engaged wore the full green Iraqi military uniform.

After a few minutes an old man and his family came out into the street from a building near the Nissan. The kids began playing around the bodies and stripped them of anything valuable. Mulder was astonished.

You know that you're in a hard-core country when the kids don't think anything about playing around or stripping a bunch of dead bodies! he thought. The old man looked toward the sniper team and waved. Mulder and Hamblin should have moved positions but they were on the building with the best view of the area. Although they knew the old man would probably tell someone their location, they stayed in place.

There wasn't much action for anyone else in the area this early in the day, so when the sniper team used the radio to report the situation, marines came to their building to get a glimpse of their handiwork. The situation got so out of hand that even the battalion commander came up to the roof. This wasn't a good thing for the snipers, especially if any enemy snipers were trying to locate their position.

A couple of hours had passed when a forward observer came to the snipers' position. Having heard the situation, he was there just in case anything else should happen, and they needed to call for mortars or direct air support. He also brought a laser range finder and they found the actual distances to the areas around them.

The battalion was spread throughout the airfield, mostly

holding perimeter security. The line companies were spread to the flanks of the snipers. M1 Abrams tanks were in support as well, but they were coming and going throughout the airfield.

Later in the morning, more people began to come out of their homes. The bodies lay on the street for a short time, until a few people eventually dragged them into a nearby alley. Soon stray bullets sounded to the flanks of the snipers, near the infantry. The snipers heard the shooting picking up, and quickly the shooting became large gunfights.

Mulder noticed something peculiar. A vehicle full of males drove into the alley where the bodies had been dragged. When the vehicle left, it had only the driver. It dawned on Mulder that the vehicle was dropping off fighters into the alley. They didn't appear to have weapons, which led Mulder to believe that they were being supplied by a weapons cache. The team radioed the information back to higher.

"If a vehicle comes around more than two times, light 'em up!" was the reply, and for the next couple of hours, the team shot vehicles. They aimed for critical areas, the wheels and engines, and hit more than a few causing most of them to turn onto backstreets and alleys.

Meanwhile the Nissan truck was still parked next to the road with the bodies and weapons of the dead Iraqis still in it. The team kept an eye on that area and when a man came walking by the truck, Hamblin hawked him through his scope. The man stopped to look inside. He reached for an AK, and once he stood up with the intent to take the weapon, Hamblin took his life. The old man who had waved at the team earlier saw this. He came out from his house, and before anyone else could take any weapons from the truck, he tried to stop them.

Late in the evening, a man came into the snipers' view. The team watched as he broke into a bus and tried to steal it. He shattered a window to get in, but once inside he couldn't start the vehicle, so he left it. As he walked away from the bus, he caught sight of the Nissan and went to look inside. The old man hurried to stop him from doing something foolish but was pushed aside. Mulder, watching this from his rifle, shot the rearview mirror as the thief reached into the truck. Mulder wanted the man to know that the next bullet wouldn't miss. Throughout his entire time in Iraq, Mulder only gave one person a warning shot; it was this thief. But the man just smiled and waved toward Mulder. Even with the dead men in the cab, he reached into the truck and grabbed an AK.

Darwinism at its finest, Mulder thought. The Iraqi didn't know that he was seconds away from death. Mulder had the crosshairs on the thief's head but the man moved at the last second and the boat-tail bullet tore into the back of his neck, severing his spine. On the ground, the man's head twitched but his body wasn't moving at all. His neck was broken, and he eventually died. Hamblin called for one of the tanks to come up and destroy the truck. They didn't want to shoot people who only wanted free weapons. After blasting the truck to pieces, and leaving only the bed intact, the Abrams stayed next to the team on the ground, which was comforting to them. They took comfort in the extra security, especially because more people had an idea where they were.

As the day came to an end, Mulder and Hamblin reflected on what had happened, but it wasn't over yet. There were firefights all around. The team wanted to change positions, but it wasn't feasible to get as good a vantage point from anywhere around them. Mulder found some sandbags from inside his building. They filled them and used them as cover to shoot behind. They also placed their flak jackets in front of their bodies. The body armor would stop any bullets or shrapnel. Mulder stayed awake all night, and because the team had been in the same position all day, he was paranoid that someone might try to sneak up on them. He remained behind the optics, constantly searching, hoping to get the drop on anybody trying to shoot at them. But the night was uneventful.

Early the next morning, on the second day, a machine gunner came up on the roof to replace the forward observer. After being in position for over thirty hours, Mulder felt the effects on his body. He was tired and his body ached, his knees were swollen, his eyes wouldn't focus, and he had a screaming migraine from looking through the optics. He rolled onto his back to stretch and let the machine gunner observe through his rifle.

"Hey, I got someone," said Hamblin.

Mulder turned over and grabbed his spotting scope. He couldn't believe his eyes. A man who was obviously in the Iraqi Army was walking toward them on the street. He wore a green uniform, a helmet, rifle, and rank insignia while walking toward the sniper team as if to come to the airfield. Nobody had told him that the Americans held the base.

"I'm gonna take this guy," Hamblin said. "Let's just see how close he gets."

As the Iraqi soldier came down the street, the old man ran out to tell him that the Americans were there. The team could tell that the old man was gesturing the soldier not to go toward the airfield, but the soldier wouldn't listen and it cost him his life.

As soon as the Iraqi got to the 350-yard mark, Hamblin shot him square in the chest. The man fell to the ground and moments later began to crawl toward a gutter by the sidewalk. The machine gunner, who was behind Mulder's rifle, was excited to watch. He couldn't resist the temptation and asked Mulder if he could shoot the soldier with the sniper rifle.

"No, we'd kinda like to save our ammo. Just let 'em bleed out. He'll die," said Mulder. The machine gunner gave him a look of disgust and shock.

"That's pretty cold," he said.

Mulder stopped. He never thought about the amount of pain the individuals he shot were in. "You know what? Go ahead," said Mulder.

The machine gunner sighted in on the man, who was now closer to the gutter. He aimed at the man's ribs and shot. The bullet tore into the Iraqi's buttocks, and he rolled around on the ground in pain.

"You're jerkin' the trigger," said Mulder calmly, spotting for him. "You have to watch your trigger pull, just like the M16 on the rifle range."

Mulder chambered another round for him and coached him to aim center mass and not to pull the trigger but to squeeze it.

The machine gunner aimed but hit the man in the leg.

"You're still pulling the trigger. Just squeeze it slowly," Mulder said.

The machine gunner shot a few more times but wasn't able to kill the man. The Iraqi kept crawling and eventually made it into the gutter where all that was visible of him was his feet.

Get off my gun, Mulder was thinking, wanting to finish the Iraqi off.

The word was out that the snipers were there watching the area. Some people held up white pieces of cloth when they passed through. Some men even took their shirts off and held them over their heads gesturing signs of peace. A few men tried to hide weapons while walking across the streets. They covered them in their clothes, but the shape of the rifle under their clothes easily gave them away, and Mulder killed a few men who tried it. When the snipers shot people, the bodies would lie in the street, and typically, the area was non-eventful. If, however, the bodies had been cleaned up, other gunmen appeared in the area. Usually the bodies didn't stay out for long before someone dragged them into a building or an alley.

Sometime later, the snipers noticed a truck in the distance. It had been parked there the whole time, but they wondered why so many people were going to it now. It was close to the turn at about 700 yards. After observing the truck, they could see that there was a wooden ammunition crate in the back. Two men approached the vehicle. One man reached into the back of the truck. Hamblin already had the man in his sights, and as the Iraqi turned away, Hamblin fired. The bullet impacted, causing the ammo crate to slip from the man's grip, and he collapsed. The Iraqi shook violently on the ground for a moment, then stopped. His partner, standing next to him, ran before he could be shot.

By the end of the day, Mulder recognized that the time had flown by. The more he kept shooting, the more the moments, faces, and targets seemed to blend together. It was before sundown when Hamblin was off his gun, resting. He let the machine gunner observe for him. Mulder was scanning vehicles when he spotted weapons in the cab of a truck turning onto the road in front of them, but before he could adjust his rifle and shoot, the truck drove into an alley. Mulder told the machine gunner to fix his dope to his, and the two waited for the truck to come back out. When it did, Mulder initiated the fire, and they both unloaded on the truck. The person driving stepped on the gas and sped up. The truck made its way toward the turn at the end of the street. Both Mulder and the machine gunner were shooting for the back. Mulder was surprised when it burst into flames and traveled out of sight. Surprisingly, ammunition in the truck began to detonate. They all watched as RPGs flew into the air and ignited. The heat from the truck caused bullets to go off, and they could be heard exploding in every direction. A cloud of smoke filled the air above the truck. Mulder thought that something like this could only happen in movies. At twenty-three years old, Mulder wondered how many people experienced things like this in their lifetime.

Soon the team received information over the radio that the battalion was moving farther into Baghdad. They had to be packed and ready to leave immediately. The team was staged in the back of a Humvee when they were told that marines patrolled the area where Mulder reported the weapons cache. They found massive amounts of explosives and small arms. When the cache was blown, the explosion was large enough to destroy the building. As the convoy drove into Baghdad, Mulder watched the smoke from the demolished building drift into the sky.

5

April in Fallujah

Name: Lance Corporal A., Cody

Billet: Point Man

Area of Operations: City of Fallujah, Al Anbar Province,
Operation Iraqi Freedom II, March 2004–September 2004

Lance Corporal Cody was thrilled to be in Iraq even though he was sweating profusely in the back of an armored Humvee speeding through the open desert. Since leaving California two weeks earlier, he was anxious to start combat operations, but his unit, "The Professionals" of the Second Battalion, First Marines, first needed to retrieve their vehicles in Kuwait. From Kuwait they had the tiresome task of convoying to the city of Fallujah, over 450 miles away. Once there, the battalion would replace elements from the Eighty-second Airborne Division and take command of that area of operations.

Cody was right where he wanted to be. Ever the patriotic Texan, he joined the marines straight from high school, and a fascination with sniping from a young age drove him to want to become one. His recruiter told him that in order to become a marine scout/sniper, he would have to enlist into the infantry. Before long he passed the basic rifleman training at Camp Pendleton, California, and was soon on his way to fulfilling his dreams. The very week he was assigned to the battalion of 2/1, he found that the scout/sniper platoon was holding an indoc. He signed up, and when the two weeks of hell was over, he was selected to be part of the platoon.

Cody didn't know it, but he was one of the few marines who hadn't spent any time in a line company prior to being chosen for a scout/sniper platoon. And he had only been in the corps for six months. But with such limited experience, he would have to learn quickly how to operate in a sniper team, because his unit was deploying for Operation Iraqi Freedom II in six months.

Although the dusty drive from Camp Udairi (pronounced "U-dar-e"), Kuwait, was long, Cody was happy not to be struck by any car bombs or IEDs. He did get nervous when a few oblivious civilian vehicles slipped into the massive battalion convoy, causing the threat status to elevate temporarily. Finally after three days of driving, the battalion reached Camp Baharia (pronounced "Baha-re-ah"), just two miles southeast of Fallujah. The camp was once a Baath party retreat used by the sons of Saddam Hussein. The property was lavish and secluded, but after U.S. forces occupied the country, the estate became home to U.S. military units serving in the area.

Soon after Cody's unit settled in, the sniper team leaders began to go on missions with the army snipers. The left seat, right seat ride along helped them to transition better by having someone show them the area.

The thought of soon hunting insurgents motivated Cody,

and he felt privileged that on his first deployment, he was in a combat zone. And with confidence in his team, he wasn't worried about having the most dangerous job. He was the point man and would lead the team on all patrols. But because the point man is always exposed first, Cody knew that his life depended on the critical factor of constant vigilance.

His team's call sign was "Grim Reaper One." The team leader was Sergeant Shuhart, the assistant team leader was Corporal Curnell, and the radio operator was Cody's good friend, Lance Corporal Posten. Cody and Posten were the PIGs in the team. As a whole, everyone was more than confident when it came to operating in Iraq.

Before the marines arrived, the top American commanders in the area met regularly with the leaders of the city every Thursday. The marines planned to accompany the soldiers during the next visit, and the sniper team leaders would accompany their army counterparts as well.

On the mission, the sniper teams took positions on rooftops outside of the city. The army snipers informed the marines that they had never received contact in that area. Soon afterward, a rooftop close by was hit with a single mortar, injuring the soldiers and marines on it. That day, the snipers began their long tour in Iraq by racking up four kills.

Once the battalion fully relieved the army and assumed responsibility of the city, the sniper teams began to conduct overnight missions.

Unknown to Cody, the insurgency in Fallujah was escalating. With a population of over 200,000, it was hard to believe that several small groups of anticoalition and insurgent fighters could take control of the city. However, by avoiding prolonged clashes with U.S. military and persuading any opposition with ruthless acts of violence, the insurgents indeed took power. For months, the city had been unstable and U.S. military units could trust that roadside bombs and hasty ambushes waited for them while they traveled through the area.

The mounting pressure came to a pinnacle when four Americans with the contracting company, Blackwater Security, were ambushed and killed while traveling though the city. The men were dragged through the streets after having been badly burned and mutilated, and two of the four were strung from the "Brooklyn Bridge." Video footage of the attack aired in the Western media, prompting outrage from the United States. U.S. commanders, aware of the insurgency within Fallujah, knew that something needed to be done to quell the bands of fighters who held the city.

Immediately after the incident, the battalion of 2/1 entered Fallujah to apprehend the insurgents responsible for the attack. For the operation, Cody and his team were side by side with the grunts, because the battalions wanted to prevent as much friendly fire as possible.

When word reached the teams that they were going into the city, Cody wasn't totally convinced. But the lieutenant gathered the platoon and informed everyone they had to write a letter to their loved ones, just in case they didn't make it back. It was their death letter. That's when Cody knew that the attack was true. Cody's letter was short. He found it awkward and unnatural writing to his family and explaining to them that he was dead and that he loved them.

In the days before the siege, the teams were given instructions on what to pack. The gear list had already changed multiple

times, but the final say came down to packing three days' worth
of chow and water. The snipers also had to carry their weapons,
optics, and radios, but they were short on weapons. Both Shuhart and Curnell had M40A3 sniper rifles, but the battalion had
no M16s available for them. The two snipers would be stuck
patrolling into Fallujah with bolt-action rifles while insurgents
carrying fully automatic AKs waited in ambush. They were told
that the 9 mms would suffice just fine. Cody carried the M16
with an ACOG four-power scope, as did the radio operator,
Posten. Cody packed extra socks, batteries, night vision equipment, and optics. The day before the offensive, the teams were
ready. Someone passed around cigars for a platoon smoke. They
all knew that this could be their last time together. The sniper
teams would be attached to different elements within the battalion as they entered the city the next morning at 0300.

Grim Reaper One was going to be attached to Echo Company, and hours before they were scheduled to depart, the
snipers went to their staging points and rested in the back of a
seven-ton until it was time to go.

Cody was nervous. Not long ago, war was just a thought for
him, but now, he was on the verge of being in full-fledged combat. On the short ride to the staging point on the outskirts of the
city, Cody wondered what to expect. As they stopped, he saw the
city lights and heard dogs barking in the distance. He searched
with his night vision goggles hoping to see anything, but found
nothing. Before morning his team discussed their plan. Having
the freedom to move among the platoons, the snipers were aware
that they could position themselves anywhere necessary for
shooting. Their priorities were to provide covering for the infantry during the assault and to kill as many insurgents as possible.

Only a few hundred meters outside of Fallujah, the marines waited in darkness for the word to go. Looking around, Cody could tell that some of the marines were apprehensive. Still more were excited. This is what they had been waiting for their entire military careers. Others seemed as if they just wanted to get it over with. Cody was nervous and anxious, but he definitely wanted to be a part of this.

Hours later, the marines were told that it was time to move forward. Three companies from 2/1 began to patrol in toward Fallujah. As the formation started to move, Cody saw that Echo Company's most senior marine led the movement. He was the company first sergeant and was also a HOG who had once been in charge of the First Marine Division scout/sniper school. It came as no surprise to Cody that when the first sergeant spotted the sniper team, he told them to fall in behind him. Cody knew that the old man was a hard charger but leading his company into an attack on one of the country's most dangerous cities proved his courage as well. As they got closer, Cody felt a little more comfortable when he saw that M1 Abrams tanks and CAAT (combined anti-armor teams) vehicles were positioned on the roads with their main guns directed toward the city. They were an impressive show of force, and it was good to know that he wasn't on the receiving end of them.

Now, just a few hundred feet from the buildings on the outskirts of the city, Cody paid little attention to the marines behind him. He was focused on searching for anyone trying to ambush them and couldn't help but wonder if he would make it out of this alive.

As daybreak began, all was still quiet. The sniper team let Echo Company marines clear a few houses before they made their way onto a rooftop. Squads of marines left and right of the snipers were swarming buildings. The attack had begun, except that there hadn't been any shots. Cody was expecting to receive fire immediately, from the way that the battalion had explained how many insurgents there were in the city. He was told that intelligence reports suggested that thousands of fighters would be waiting for them.

Cody went into a house that was already cleared, but the building was only partially constructed. Wooden beams were in some places where the ceiling should have been, and the team would have to cross those beams in order to shoot from the solid part of the roof that was already built. As he skirted across a beam, Cody hoped he wouldn't fall; his heavy pack was causing him to lose his balance. Halfway across he noticed that two IFAVs (Interim Fast Attack Vehicle) used by marines had stopped next to their house. They were parked only a few yards away. Suddenly from across the street, two rocket-propelled grenades flew toward the vehicles. Hearing them hiss, Cody looked in time to see that they had missed their marks and exploded. Immediately marines unleashed hell on the gunmen, but the insurgents also returned fire until moments later when the tanks and CAAT vehicles began to wreak havoc. They blasted the buildings that insurgents were in. Soon, it seemed as though everyone around the snipers were firing except them.

Ready for action, the team hurried to shoot. They scrambled across the beams and set up to search for targets. But the situation was under control because when Cody scanned through his ACOG, he found empty windows and abandoned rooftops. Shuhart and Curnell searched from behind their scopes, but no one exposed themselves. Their view was limited because other buildings didn't allow them to see farther into the city. Eventually, as the insurgents retreated, the marines pushed deeper into the city.

"Let's go! We're moving," said Shuhart.

Cody heard the traffic over Posten's handset as he prepared to exit the house. Rushing outside, he scanned across the street for a place to take cover. As they moved, he kept his weapon at the alert while trotting quickly through the dangerous streets, cautious not to trip on debris. Occasionally squads of marines entering houses and buildings appeared at their flanks. Moving through streets and courtyards was intense. In the back of his mind, Cody knew that at any moment they could be ambushed or accidentally targeted by jumpy marines. When Cody came across the next squad of marines he made his way into the house with them. Inside was the first sergeant who was eager to join the sniper team, but moments later he was needed elsewhere.

The team set up on the roof but couldn't see much. In the distance they heard multiple explosions and gunshots and before long it was time to move again. Cody prepared to lead the team. Every time he exited a building, he felt vulnerable to being shot. He made his way through alleys and pathways, looking back at the team every so often. Soon they could hear marines yelling nearby. Shuhart guided them to the next building, and they found another squad in a house. Cody entered and moved from room to room as marines from the squad were busy searching everything. The house was being demolished from the inside. Marines smashed mirrors and windows, while pictures fell from walls, and doors were being kicked in. But the process had to happen in order to secure the building. There was no telling what type of explosives the insurgents would use on the marines, and they could come in any way, shape, or form. The first sergeant was with the squad, and he followed the team to the roof just as the house was deemed clear.

On the roof the snipers went to work.

"Cody, you're holding rear security," said Shuhart.

Cody took the orders in anger. He hadn't shot his weapon yet, and it looked as though he wasn't going to. He posted himself by the doorway while Shuhart and Curnell searched for targets. Posten had the radio and planned to spot for the two snipers if they were to shoot. Cody noticed that the first sergeant had a personal scope on his M16; it was a Leupold. He could also tell that the first sergeant was happily in his element.

Smoke billowed in every direction as the assault came to full force. Firefights raged all around. Then, without warning, bullets hit the house the snipers were on. Cody instinctively ducked, but the team wasn't exposed; the walls around the roof covered them. The team found where the fire was coming from, and Cody was annoyed when everyone else started shooting, except him.

Soon Shuhart gave the order to move forward again. Cody was surprised when the first sergeant not only joined them but took point. He led them from one pile of rubble to another, constantly moving. Cody wondered where they were going, but trusted that the first sergeant knew.

One thing that stood out to Cody was all the civilians. As the snipers moved throughout the city, he wondered why they were still around while insurgents and marines traded fire, but he soon found out why. The team met up with a squad who was interrogating detainees. There were also other marines in a nearby building, and the first sergeant disappeared with them.

As the team talked with the squad, they were told that civilians had been observing them and after the Iraqis left the area, the marines came under small-arms fire. It was obvious that some of the civilians were insurgents acting as scouts.

After hearing gunshots elsewhere, the team pushed forward. Cody took point again. He scanned every doorway, window, and rooftop as they patrolled. He expected the enemy to be any-where and everywhere. The team moved swiftly and with more caution and soon they were alone.

Hours after the assault began the team found a three-story house still under construction. Piles of bricks and mortar lay inside, and the windows and doors had no materials in them. The walls and ceiling were the only things built. After the team moved in, they cleared the two bottom rooms and a small bathroom by the steps leading to the second deck. Cody scanned the second level as he moved up the stairs. Once they cleared the rest of the house the team moved back to the second level. They didn't want to establish a pattern by always setting up on the roof.

It was past noon, and with the blistering sun, the heavy packs and gear began to wear on the team. They chose to hold up in the house and observe from there. After dropping their gear, Cody and Curnell decided to secure the area around the house and they moved cautiously downstairs. Looking through a win-dow, Curnell caught sight of someone outside. He alerted Cody, who then aimed toward a window that the man would walk by next. Before the individual came into sight, Cody's heart raced knowing that this might be his first kill. But moments later he relaxed, seeing that it was only a child. Still, he wondered why the kid was out of his house, especially with the fighting.

Back in the room, Cody noticed only one window to observe

from. It was two feet from the floor, centering the far wall. Outside of the house below the window was a paved street. Across the street were a row of buildings that appeared to be businesses. The buildings on the other side of the street were close, only thirty-five meters away. Cody was near the door, holding rear security on the stairway. Curnell and his radio were by the window, and the other two were resting. The team hadn't been in the room long when they received a sudden onslaught from an enemy machine gun. A cascade of lead ripped through the window, strafing the window ledge and impacting the back wall. Everyone instantly hit the ground.

"Does anyone see anything?" yelled Shuhart.

But no one risked picking his head up with bullets pouring through the window. Soon they heard explosions from across the street. Cody had a burst of adrenaline. This was it! He was finally going to get some action! He and Posten had the M16s and they low-crawled to the window to return fire. The bolt-action sniper rifles wouldn't have been the weapons of choice on a machine gunner who was already spraying their position. Cody was on the left side of the window and Posten was on the right. They could hear the sound of two different weapons shooting from across the street. AKs and M16s were exchanging fire, but the machine gun was still hitting the window ledge and wall in front of them—except now, it was less accurate. During a lull in the fire, Cody peeked through the window to find the enemy machine gunner. Seeing the building that he was on, he instantly thought of the auto store called Pep Boys. The roof had mufflers strewn about with two large blue doors in front of the building. It was a "Hajji Pep Boys."

Cody saw the machine-gun barrel only thirty-five meters

away. In one motion he got up on a knee, picked his rifle up, and began to shoot at the gunner. Posten was on the other side of the window, and he began to fire as well. In order to throw the enemy off, Cody and Posten switched off shooting. Cody was excited, shocked, nervous, and anxious all at once. Being in the midst of the action, his senses took over. He was in combat! Leaning back against the wall, he watched Posten throw a three-round burst. When Posten leaned back, Cody turned to shoot, but before he could lift his rifle over the window ledge his world went pitch black.

Instantly Cody lost awareness of his surroundings and found himself alone with his thoughts, wondering if he were dead. He knew that something had hit him, because the last thing he felt was his head snap back. Confused, he reasoned that he was alive since he was thinking, but he couldn't hear or feel anything. If this were death, he expected his life to flash before his eyes.

It seemed as though hours had passed when Cody felt something hitting his feet. He slowly opened his eyes to see Shuhart kicking him.

"What happened?" Cody mumbled, still lying on the ground.

"Dude, you got shot in the head!" Posten replied.

As Cody became more conscious, he felt pain in his head.

When he had been about to shoot, a bullet had penetrated his helmet. It hit him while he was kneeling and he naturally fell in the fetal position. His teammates heard him let out a yelp, and it sounded as if he got the wind knocked out of him. He was out cold for ten minutes.

When he went down his teammates searched for blood. They couldn't help him, because they would have become targets themselves. They knew that the shooter might have been another sniper trying to bait them. Everyone was told that the new Kevlar helmets were able to withstand a bullet from an AK or machine gun, but didn't think they would ever witness it, especially on one of their own.

Cody lay on the ground still feeling drowsy and weak. The goggles on his helmet had exploded when the bullet impacted, causing the plastic part to hang down on his face. As he came to and fully realized what had happened, he cried tears of both joy and pain. He couldn't believe he had gotten shot in the head and lived.

"Are you all right, Cody? Man, you scared us!" someone said.

"Yeah, I scared ya'll?" he replied.

When the gunfire ceased on their building the team crawled out of the room. They tried to make radio contact with anyone in the area but weren't able to. Even though he was a little shaken, Cody knew he had to get back into the game, when his team leader told him to take point again. His legs were heavy as he led the team downstairs. Once more they attempted to make radio contact but came up empty. Shuhart knew that Cody needed to be examined by a corpsman. Cody's teammates were fumbling with the radio when he noticed someone walking up to their building. He saw a shadow of a man moving closer and closer from the main doorway. He was filled with anxiety thinking that it was the Iraqi who had shot him, coming to the house to confirm his kill. Just as the man reached the door, Cody flipped the selector lever on his weapon to semiautomatic and gripped the trigger with his finger while turning the corner and punching the barrel of his M16 into the man's chest. He didn't shoot when he saw it was a scared old man. Someone dragged the man into the house and Curnell held his 9 mm to the hajji's head.

"He's a scout. Let's kill him," he yelled.

Moments later three more men came from the same direction. When they reached the doorway, Shuhart jumped out and yelled for the men to get into the house.

Now the team had four Iraqis; Shuhart and Curnell tried to calm two who were begging and crying, while the other two stared on, emotionless. Posten was on the radio attempting to contact other units, and Cody needed to see a corpsman. The situation was way too complicated. They decided to leave the men in the house and head to the rear. Elements of Echo Company would be around there, and the snipers were bound to find a corpsman. But the team needed to move fast, because they were at risk on the street and in such small numbers.

Elsewhere in the city the fight still raged. Tanks and air support destroyed vehicles carrying enemy fighters and reduced houses to rubble. On the ground, marines fought small groups of insurgents. Coordination was a big factor when the marines moved through their sectors, clearing houses and buildings. The insurgents, however, moved freely throughout the city. Some caught rides from taxis, and once they got the courage to actually shoot at the marines, they usually withdrew, just to repeat the process.

The team traveled for a few blocks before they ran into a squad of marines who were resting. When he sat down with the corpsman, Cody had a dip of tobacco in his mouth and a cigarette on his lips as he nervously explained what happened. The marines were amazed that Cody had been so lucky, and the corpsman told him a story about another squad that was farther ahead.

"The squad heard machine-gun fire and moved into a nearby building. On the roof they saw a machine gunner surrounded by mufflers and shot at him. As they were shooting they spotted a guy in a house across the street. Someone in the squad took him out with a head shot."

Suspicious, Cody questioned where the squad had been when they did the shooting. When he found out they were in the same area as the sniper team, it was clear that Cody had been shot by someone from the squad. He was furious when he thought about almost being killed by another marine. He wondered how they hadn't seen his helmet, but there was nothing he could do about it now, and he had to forget about it.

Soon, the sniper team and the squad were directed by higher to fall back and link up with the rest of Echo Company outside of the city. When they reached the location, Cody was sent to the forward operating base, but against his will. He wanted to help his team but effects from the bullet on his body were making him a liability. At the base, a 5.56 mm bullet from an M16 was found lodged in his helmet. It was two inches above his right eye.

On April 5, the marines reentered the city for an offensive on the insurgents in Fallujah, dubbed Operation Vigilant Resolve. Four marine battalions backed by air support, tanks, and artillery would take part in the attack, each sweeping through separate sectors of the city. When Cody recovered, he returned to his team inside the city. By then, the battle-hardened marines of 2/1 occupied fighting positions in the northwest areas of the city. During this time Grim Reaper One was with Echo Company in the Jolan district. They, and other sniper teams, were hunting from rooftops by the notorious Jolan graveyard.

Cody made friends with the infantrymen from Echo Company and enjoyed getting to know them. The time in the city was exciting for him because he was guaranteed to shoot his weapon at least once a day. Attacks on their position from insurgents seemed to happen on a schedule—usually after the morning prayers and as the sun went down. The snipers quickly memorized the schedule, as did the rest of the platoons, and during those hours the rooftops were filled with marines waiting for their opportunity to kill. Most nights, AC-130 gunships flew over the city, raining destruction on packs of unsuspecting insurgents who believed that they moved unseen. By now being in firefights had become routine for Cody; even using the sniper rifle was common.

Because the sniper team had been in the area so long, Cody needed to be implemented for watch on the rifle. One day, during a firefight, Cody was on the sniper rifle when he spotted a man trafficking guns from a mosque to a car. He was 400 yards away. The man disappeared, only to come back into view minutes later. Behind the rifle, Cody could tell that the man thought nobody could see what he had done. The Iraqi stepped into the open and stopped. Cody thought of all his fellow marines who had been shot and killed by rifles just like the ones this man was moving. Cody aimed for the man's chest. He felt no emotions as he killed the man, who stood just a few feet away from his wife and child, nor did he have time to think about what he had done, because another firefight erupted.

Exactly one month to the day from when he got shot in the head, Cody and his team were scheduled to set out on a patrol with a platoon from Echo Company and a few Delta Force operators. The marines had been receiving sporadic small-arms and indirect fire from a certain house across the graveyard. They planned on raiding and possibly occupying that house and the one next to it.

On April 26, 0400 came early as Cody got up and packed his gear. He was excited to be going on the patrol and even told his teammates that he hoped to get into a crazy firefight like in the movies. The assault men had already blown a hole in the wall in the front of the house for the marines to proceed through. The patrol moved quickly through the graveyard, taking into account that prior to theirs, every patrol that went out was attacked. But Cody felt comfort in knowing that their movement was being covered by the rest of the company and the other sniper team.

After arriving at the target house safely, Cody's team helped to search the building. Inside they found weapons, drugs, money, and arms paraphernalia, but no insurgents. Once the sun came up the snipers discovered a hole in the wall on the roof. While looking through the hole, they could see their old position across the graveyard. A palm tree near the house had hidden the hole from the marines. It was an impressive shooting position obviously used for sniping.

In the morning, the sniper team set up on the roof with two machine gunners and a grenadier. One squad stayed downstairs, holding security while the other marines went to a house just across the street to cover more of the area. After the morning prayer bellowed throughout the city, marines from the house across the street went on patrol.

From the rooftop the sniper team could see across the grave-yard to where the company was. On the other side of the roof, houses spread out for miles and were built nearly right on top of each other. Some of the buildings had rooftops that were slightly higher and some lower. The neighboring building was so close that if you leaned out one of the windows, you could touch it. Looking down from the rooftop Cody saw a network of courtyards and walls sprawling throughout the area, with the occasional palm tree and shrubbery.

Cody and his team went to work on top of the building. Metal rails lined parts of the roof wall and the gaps in the metal would have allowed anyone from adjoining roofs to see the marines. Cody covered the rails with carpets; the other walls surrounding the roof were made of concrete, so the team made three holes facing the road running toward their house. Two of the holes were for the snipers, and one was for the machine gunners.

The team began to find target points to specific landmarks through their holes. This would make it easier to engage rapidly any oncoming hajjis trying to shoot and move. After they were finished working on their position, they waited patiently for insurgents to find out that they were there.

Cody was on the spotting scope at first but soon he and Shuhart traded places behind the sniper rifle. They rotated every half hour. Through the scope Cody hoped to see anyone with a weapon, but the neighborhood was empty. When the sun was overhead and blazing down on the marines, Shuhart told Cody and Posten to go rest downstairs and be back up in a half hour. It didn't make sense to keep everyone on the roof with no action, and he didn't want everyone up there, just in case they got hit. Cody and Posten left their packs, and Posten left his M16 on the roof for Curnell. Cody asked Shuhart if he wanted his M16 as well, but Shuhart replied, "No, you might need it."

When they walked down to the second level of the house,

Cody and Posten went into a room filled with mattresses. As they walked in, a window sat on the wall directly in front of them, with the neighboring building just outside of it. Cody put his weapon against the wall next to the door, and they both stripped off their helmets and flak jackets. Their desert cammies were still damp from sweating in the sun. Finding two suitable mattresses, they joked with each other while resting. Cody lit up a cigarette, and the two made small talk for twenty-five minutes, until Posten mentioned they should be getting back on the roof. As soon as they stood up multiple explosions shook the house.

"What the hell was that?" questioned Cody.

Suddenly the area went from complete serenity to utter chaos. RPGs flew into the walls of the houses and courtyards that the marines occupied. RPK machine guns launched a series of vicious barrages from the mosque and other structures in the distance. After the initial volley the marines returned fire with all they had. Bullets flew in the window next to Posten, hitting the wall by the doorway. More explosions and screams rang out from the rooftop. Posten immediately dove for the M16 next to the door. He threw Cody his gear and picked up the M16 to return fire through the window.

"Throw me my gun!" Cody yelled, once he had his equipment on. When Posten tossed him the weapon, Cody wasted no time shooting. He was hardly aiming while squeezing the trigger as fast as he could. This provided enough covering fire for both him and Posten to exit the room. Blasts from all sorts of weapons echoed throughout the house. From the hallway he could see the marines from the roof coming down the stairs. They were bloodied and shell-shocked.

Shuhart, Curnell, the machine gunners, and the grenadier had been lying on the roof while talking and keeping watch. All was quiet until two rocks landed on the roof—except they weren't rocks. They were grenades. One rolled by the M240 Golf. The marine manning it instinctively rolled onto the gun to protect it. The blast from the grenade blew his arm off. Another grenade rolled behind the snipers, causing shrapnel to pepper them and the other machine gunner. All of their weapons and gear were destroyed almost immediately. After the grenades exploded, insurgents emerged from the surrounding buildings and shot from rooftops, doorways, and windows. Both houses came under intense fire. Bullets from machine guns and rocket-propelled grenades flooded the marines' positions and the insurgents had momentarily overwhelmed the marines by sheer firepower.

Nobody had known that the houses next door were full of insurgents who waited for the opportune time to ambush them.

In the hallway, Cody and Posten met the others coming down from the roof. Shuhart was the first down with only his 9 mm strapped to his leg, followed by the grenadier who was limping. Curnell was next to come off the roof. His face was cut from shrapnel, but in one hand he held Posten's M16. He was also helping the marine who had lost his arm.

Downstairs the squad was shooting everything. One marine was down with a gunshot wound to the back. He had been in the process of shooting a hajji clutching an RPG when he was struck. Another marine took his turn at the insurgent but with a 40 mm grenade launcher. The round smashed into the insurgent's head and instantaneously vaporized it.

Cody was shocked, seeing that everyone from the roof was

injured. He started to help with medical aid when two of his buddies from the squad pointed out that they needed to get all the gear off the roof and salvage any weapons if possible. Cody slapped a fresh magazine in his weapon and told them that he and Posten would provide covering fire while they dashed up top. As they rushed away, Cody moved up the stairs and began shooting at the insurgents who were next door. When the marines disappeared onto the roof, the enemy fire noticeably roared. Cody was concerned about the marines upstairs; one of them was a senior machine gunner whom Cody had gotten to know really well. Moments later a corpsman approached him. He clutched a 9 mm and a handheld radio.

"I need backup! Someone's down up there!" said the brave corpsman.

Cody knew that he had to help and without hesitation he, Posten, and the corpsman charged upstairs. On the roof they ran into a hail of bullets; Cody saw Iraqis shooting weapons, but he stopped in his tracks once he noticed his friend. Time slowed, and he lost focus of everything around him. The senior marine who had befriended him, taught him, and had taken him under his wing was down on the ground. Cody saw that his skin was pasty white. The machine gunner had taken three bullets to the chest and all of them missed the SAPI plate. The other marine was holding his arm. He, too, had been shot. The corpsman went to work while Cody gained his composure and began firing. Just as he was about to shoot, another marine came up the stairs and ran right by his muzzle. Cody almost shot him.

The rooftop was overwhelmed by small-arms fire from adjacent buildings. Heads and AKs darted over walls from houses farther off, sending bullets flying in every direction. Cody was in the fight of his life. Only twenty feet away, on the roof next door, insurgents let loose on him and the others. When Cody started shooting, his training kicked in and his body reverted to muscle memory. All he could do was make snap shots and try not to get hit. Bullets impacted the concrete that he leaned against while shooting. He watched as some of the insurgents put their rifles over walls and squeezed the trigger, praying and spraying. He thought back to wanting to be in a ferocious gunfight and now regretted saying that. Soon one of the Delta operators came on the roof. He was a medic and was able to get an IV into one of the marines. Cody looked around while changing his magazine. Curnell's 40 had been damaged badly. It was in flames. In fact, all of the packs were in flames. The radios, optics, and night vision were all damaged and bullets that were in some of the packs were beginning to cook off.

The corpsman yelled that they needed to get the wounded down. Cody told the others to go while he and Posten covered them. When the others were off the roof, Cody and Posten started to pull back as well. Posten searched for anything still useable. Shuhart's sniper rifle was the only thing left, and he grabbed it on the way down. Cody was the last one on the roof, and he was still shooting while he moved off.

The two houses full of marines had held out long enough, and soon air support arrived. Cody was happy to see helicopters laying lead on the buildings around them. Tanks showed up for the fight as well, and because the enemy fire was so intense, the tanks needed to drive directly up to the houses and provide enough suppressive fire for the marines to make it out of there. With no armored vehicles in support, they would have to walk back across the graveyard. It was only 300 meters away, but bullets were still flying past the marines. As the tanks pulled up, Cody helped to carry his friend who had been shot back across the graveyard. When they finally reached the other side Cody gathered more ammo to go back and help the others make it across safely. But everyone had already made it back. Cody left his friend with the corpsman and looked down at his blood-soaked cammies. It was the last time Cody would see his friend alive. He took seconds to think about what he had just been through, but didn't have much time to reflect, because the fight continued.

6

April in Fallujah II

Name: Corporal P., Ethan

Billet: Scout/Sniper Team Leader

Area of Operations: Cites of Umm Qasr, Al Basra Province, and An Nasiriyah, Dhi Qar Province, Operation Iraqi Freedom I, February 2003–August 2003; City of Fallujah, Al Anbar Province, Operation Iraqi Freedom II, March 2004–September 2004

After the Blackwater Security contractors were killed in late March 2004, the battalion of 2/1 responded and entered Fallujah to catch the culprits. However, from the amount of resistance on that day, it was clear that more time and improved planning were needed to find and kill all of the men responsible. But in that attack, one of the battalion's senior HOGs, Corporal Ethan, began a killing spree that would ultimately topple thirty-two enemy fighters.

Ethan's time in the marines began in October 2001. Originally, after high school he wanted to play college football, but his lack of interest in college studies squashed the dream. Instead he joined the marines as an infantryman.

He easily passed all of the basic training and upon reaching the fleet, he spent four months going through extensive infantry training with his battalion. When it was over, a corporal let him know that as far as infantry was involved, Ethan had seen the best that it had to offer. He also told him that if he wanted to do something harder, he should try out for the scout/sniper platoon indoc because it was coming up soon. Ethan had seen the snipers around, and couldn't forget where they lived. In big red letters the stairs leading up to their barracks read PAIN, SUFFERING, 8541. Even though he had an idea of what the snipers did, during the indoc he came to realize exactly what those words meant.

The one-week indoc was unimaginable, but Ethan was one of the four out of twenty-five marines selected to the platoon. From there he fell into the role of a PIG, and was the only one in his team. The other three members, all HOGs, were seasoned operators compared to him, and he tried to learn as much as he could. Just over six months later, Operation Iraqi Freedom started.

He was with the Second Battalion, First Marines, who were the battalion landing team, or BLT, for the Fifteenth Marine Expeditionary Unit based out of Camp Pendleton, California. When the MEU arrived in the Middle East they were attached to the British Royal Marines, specifically the Three Commando Brigade, and saw their first action in Iraq's southern seaside port of Umm Qasr. For the coalition, the city held a strategic importance, because it would allow military and humanitarian supplies to be transported directly into Iraq.

On March 18, 2003, Ethan was miles ahead of his battalion, in a Kuwaiti police tower reporting on an Iraqi compound. Two more sniper teams from his platoon were in the towers to the left and right of him. One thousand meters away, the Iraqis ran vehicle patrols on the border, and one thousand meters beyond that, they had a compound and a tower of their own.

After three days of collecting and reporting, the snipers were given the order to call in artillery on the Iraqis. Ethan's team had an exact distance on their target, but still, he was intimidated when his team leader told him to call in the strikes. Only nineteen years old and just two years out of high school, Ethan helped to direct fire on the Iraqi compound. He knew that his uncle, a marine sniper in Vietnam, would be proud. British artillery ripped into the concrete structures and even scored a direct hit on one of the towers. Glass fell from the windows, and part of the building collapsed. A short time later the British Royal Marines crossed the border, after creating three breaches. It was weird for Ethan to know that he was part of history and that everyone in the world was watching the war. But he was there.

Hours later in Umm Qasr, Ethan spotted a kill for his partner. The team was attached with Fox Company to help overrun another compound. The snipers were in an apartment complex 200 meters in front of the infantry and were cleared to engage any vehicles traveling into the compound. Soon a red truck, loaded with people and weapons, drove into the area. At 800 yards, Ethan's partner shot a man riding in the back of the truck. After the man fell, Ethan's partner shot one more round into the cab, but the driver was able to put the truck into reverse and flee the area. Later the truck was found with bloodstains in the cab and bed. Ethan thought it was great that his partner got a kill, but he couldn't wait until the day that he was behind the sniper rifle.

After Umm Qasr fell to the coalition, Ethan's unit traveled north to An Nasiriyah. By that time most of the action in the city had died off. The only eventful mission that took place was a raid on an Iraqi Army officer responsible for enforcing an attack on an army convoy earlier that month. Ethan's team was to confirm that the man was in his house and if so, the raid force would swoop in and snatch him.

From a schoolhouse nearby, the team was able to positively identify the man, and the battalion moved in for the raid. As the marines approached, Ethan and his team leader joined them, while the two other snipers stayed at the school. When Ethan entered the house, he saw the man bolt for the stairs. In pursuit, Ethan and another marine trapped him on the roof, but to their surprise, he jumped off. Unfazed, the man ran into another building but was soon caught. After interrogations, it was discovered that he had tied dead American soldiers to his vehicle and dragged them through the streets.

After this deployment, Ethan's unit returned to Camp Pendleton and the HOGs were discharged. Then, Ethan was given the chance at First Marine Division scout/sniper school. Although the school was challenging, most of the curriculum that was taught Ethan had already done in combat, and he graduated on his first attempt. It was also his turn to run an indoc because his platoon had lost many marines. After a fine selection of new PIGs, the platoon began training, and less than a year later they were headed back for Iraq.

On the opening day of Operation Vigilant Resolve, Ethan

listed two kills. The push into the city was an unexpected treat for Ethan. He was bored with the essential, but dull, IED missions outside of the city. Although the news about the contractors was tragic, he knew that all the action was inside Fallujah.

The action started when his team followed a squad. The routine for them was to occupy rooftops after the squad cleared a house, but the buildings were so close together that eventually the snipers moved from rooftop to rooftop. It wasn't long before firefights broke out, and Ethan was thrown into battle.

The snipers had entered the city from the north, and from atop a building his team scanned directly to the south. Searching the clustered buildings, walls, and streets, Ethan caught a glimmer of muzzle blast and the dust cloud that followed. The shooter was an Iraqi man on a rooftop. He was wearing a dirty white gown. Phil, Ethan's spotter, carried the laser range finder and ranged him near 500 yards while Ethan worked the scope, anxious to fire.

A sniper's first target in combat can be stressful if he reads too far into the shot. When Ethan first sighted in, a hint of uncertainty rattled his confidence, and he remembered his mind-set as a PIG and thinking that a lot of things could go wrong. But his doubts quickly disappeared when he focused on the reticle in his scope, and in fact, during the days to come, the crosshairs would be his safe haven and confidence for all his shootings. They reminded him of the knowledge and experience he had gained while passing sniper school and some of the hardest shooting courses, including the Special Operations Training Group's urban sniper course.

The trigger squeeze was quick, and Phil reported that the bullet floored the insurgent. But because Ethan had put his rifle on the hard surface of the wall, the recoil knocked him off target. As he refocused, the man was out of sight. The joy of his first kill wasn't overly satisfying, because Ethan wanted to make sure the man was dead. That satisfaction, however, would come hours later after they had moved to another position.

Later that day, a raid was planned on the house of an insurgent who had taken pictures of the mutilated Americans. Ethan led his team to a building near the target house to initiate a decoy for the raid force, but they received fire on their way. Taking to a rooftop, they searched the area where the shots originated. In the distance they caught sight of a few men poking their heads over a wall. Phil lazed the wall at 450 yards. As the primary shooter, Ethan told his men that if his shot was on, they could open fire with their M16s. Everyone waited to see if the men would come over the wall, and soon they did.

As planned, Ethan fired first. His target was a man sliding over the wall with a rifle in hand. When the man was on top, Ethan shot for his ribs. The man fell while hunching to his side, and soon afterward, the spotter, Phil, opened fire, killing another man. Later, a squad from Echo Company came across the bodies and searched them.

That evening, the battalion pulled out of Fallujah but held a position north of the city at the town dump. The smell of the trash was horrible, but to Ethan the weather was worse. He couldn't remember Iraq being this cold his first time around.

After a resupply, the word was passed that it was only a matter of time before they went back into the city. Ethan and his team waited with anticipation, completely sure that Fallujah was a dream world for snipers and that plenty more action waited inside. Once Ethan learned they were going back in, he started planning.

Realizing that the battalion was going into the Jolan Heights and having been in that area, Ethan knew that the opportunity for hunting was perfect. There, roads and alleyways funneled to certain locations. His plan was to find a position where his team was able to key in on roads that insurgents needed to pass in order to make it to other areas. After a detailed map study, he found a likely site and notified his team.

As far as sniping was concerned, Ethan's teammates were inexperienced. Ethan was the only HOG. As a twenty-one-year-old, his maturity and seriousness surpassed his age, but his teammates were also mature. The assistant team leader was Lance Corporal Jentry, who was thirty-two years old and a former cop. His spotter, navy corpsman "Doc" Phil, was twenty-eight, while the youngest member and point man was Private First Class Wittage at nineteen years. When the team split, Phil paired with Ethan while Jentry and Wittage made up the second two-man team. Ethan soon learned that Phil was not only very capable of operating, he was also a killer.

On the morning of April 5, the marines entered the city once more and began Operation Vigilant Resolve. Ethan and his team were again attached to Echo Company. For hours they cleared houses and buildings, fighting door to door. Insurgents were on the retreat, but the intense fighting was slow and wore on the marines loaded with heavy body armor and equipment. As night fell on the first day, the marines gained a small foothold on the northwestern part of the city, and they set up defensive positions in buildings until the next morning.

That evening Ethan and his team came upon a three-story house. After clearing it they made it to the roof, and to their delight a six-foot-tall concrete wall surrounded the top. Before morning, Ethan and his partner knocked two holes in the wall with a hammer. From the fighting, most buildings in that area had similar-looking holes, which allowed Ethan and his partner to blend in. Together, they backed away from their holes about ten feet. With the naked eye it would be almost impossible to find them. They knew that the area was where they wanted to be, but after sunrise they realized just how great the position was.

On the northwest side of the city and from the roof, they had eyes down a crucial street leading southeast. The fifty-meter-wide paved road ran from the foot of their building to an intersection 900 yards away. Smaller streets and alleys north and south of the road merged onto it. Because it was the primary road in the area, enemy fighters attempting to escape from the north would have to retreat across it, and if the fighters were to attack the marines in that area, they would have to pass over that road from the south.

As morning swept over the city, Ethan selected target reference points and began to get the distances to them. He started at 300 and ended at the back wall near 900 yards. Realizing that he probably wouldn't have time to dial his scope to each particular range, he put his dope on 550 and from there he would either hold high or low.

Early that morning, Ethan sent Lance Corporal Jentry and Private First Class Wittage with a squad to flush out insurgents. Acting as the sniper overwatch, the two marines set up on a rooftop to cover the squad. Because of miscommunication, when Jentry opened fire, another squad shot at him, thinking he was an insurgent. In the confusion, Jentry was hit and needed to be medically evacuated, after a bullet severed part of one finger and split two others in half.

Down to three men, Ethan decided to keep his team on the roof. Hours passed before the marines in the area began to take random fire, and even the wall in front of Ethan was hit a few times. Peering through the hole, Ethan came across a bald Iraqi in a man dress standing 300 yards away. He was talking to somebody in a house and pointing toward another marine position. When he left, shots rang out toward the other marines. Clearly the Iraqi was giving away their locations. When the man returned, Ethan aimed in on him in case he did anything suspicious.

"Hey, I'm gonna take this guy out if he points again," Ethan warned his spotter. As the Iraqi walked away, Ethan followed him with his scope. Suddenly the man stopped and began to point again. Standing sidewise, Ethan aimed below the Iraqi's shoulder. His intention was to shoot the man in the upper chest, but while he rolled the safety off, he was reminded of his first kill ever.

When it came to hunting, Ethan was no stranger. He was born and raised in Missouri where hunting and fishing is a tradition, and his father had taught him to use both guns and bows. His first kill came after tracking a deer into a clearing where it stood eating acorns. Because the deer stood facing away from him, it would have been hard to drop the animal with his first shot. Holding his bow in place, Ethan hoped that the deer would spin. Just as the thought crossed his mind, the deer turned, allowing Ethan to kill him on the spot.

Now, as Ethan was about to shoot, he hoped that the Iraqi also would spin. While Ethan was still lingering on the thought, the man turned and Ethan took full advantage. He drilled the man in the chest, sending him to the ground. Sprawled out on the side of the street, the front of his man dress turned red, while his legs kicked and his body twitched before the movement faded away. Earlier, Ethan had carried a rice bag upstairs and used it to rest his rifle on. Because of the stability, he was able to witness the entire event.

Later, in the distance, men began to dash across the road from the south. Ethan reported that they were moving to a weapons cache, because he noticed that they reappeared with rifles and RPGs.

Soon afterward, groups of enemy fighters rushed toward the marines. They moved like rats through alleys and pathways. As they began to rally, Ethan focused on the openings leading to the road, knowing that it was where the gunmen would have to shoot. The enemy attempted to get as close as possible before attacking with waves of RPGs followed by machine-gun fire from roofs farther off. As explosion after explosion ripped into buildings, Ethan and Phil searched to find the RPG gunners, but they seemed to be too late to engage any. The insurgents using these weapons slipped around corners and quickly fired before returning for cover. Because of the heat of the day, Ethan noticed that dust swirls remained in the air after the men shot. He kept his sights on the area of the next swirl he found, positive that an insurgent would shoot from there again. Moments later a man with an RPG turned the same corner, but Ethan didn't give him a chance to fire.

Zipping through his spider hole, Ethan's bullet flew into the man's upper chest. After he was struck, the RPG fell from his shoulder. The impact put him on his back, but before Ethan could fully celebrate, his partner was guiding him onto another target. The next was a gunman glancing around a corner. Ethan was amused at the black ski masks that were meant to terrorize, because to snipers the black was great for target identification. He let the insurgent get comfortable, and before long the man was standing in the open. Rather than give the insurgent time to aim in, Ethan put one in his chest.

The shooting started after sunrise, and by noon Ethan had wasted six insurgents. Their bodies lay on the street at ranges from 300 to 600 yards. He believed that common sense told them to stay out of the area. Still, a white car with three men brandishing weapons turned a corner farther down the road and drove toward his position.

"I know they see the dead bodies," Ethan told his partner.

As the car approached, Ethan aimed above the steering wheel, intending to kill the driver, therefore temporarily disabling the vehicle. Because the car wasn't moving fast, it was easy to lead, and when it reached 300 yards, Ethan opened fire. After hitting the driver, the car instantly went idle, and Ethan shot for the passenger. When he did, the car swerved to the left, and the rear passenger jumped from the car after it smashed into a tree. Ethan couldn't see the man, but Phil was on target, and he pumped seven bullets into him with his M16.

When Echo Company's commander learned about the weapons cache, he sent tanks to destroy the building where it was located. Ethan was surprised to see his kill up close when the tankers carried the body of the driver back to their house. His bullet had ripped through the windshield and into the driver's chest, but the glass had shredded the bullet causing bits of metal to gouge a hole in the enemy's throat. Inside the car they found ammunition, weapons, and sophisticated binoculars.

As the day wore on, Ethan terrorized insurgents by sniping

anyone attempting to cross the road. Holding high or low to make quick shots paid off because throughout the area bodies began to add up. Some of the men he hit died instantly, others suffered and bled out. In time the insurgents began to try different tactics to cross the street.

Still unfound by the enemy, Ethan and Phil chuckled at the enemy's use of decoys. At one distance someone threw an object into the street in hopes of distracting Ethan so that further back, another person could run for it. But what they didn't understand was that Ethan could see the entire street, and when the men did run, their fate was usually a bullet. Of course Ethan couldn't always hit everyone—he missed a few—but as night fell twelve bodies were spread out along the road.

That evening, the company commander thanked Ethan and Phil for their work. Together, the two of them had forced the insurgents to change their tactics. Ethan and Phil realized early on that the insurgents attacked with RPGs, while gunmen attempted to close in on the marines. But with Phil guiding him on target and Ethan's precision fire, they were able to push the insurgents back enough that their RPGs couldn't score direct hits, allowing the infantry to counter-ambush.

Although it's uncommon to make a corpsman a spotter, Ethan was glad to have Phil. Usually the doc's purpose is not to participate in the killings, but Phil not only guided Ethan onto targets and spotted his kills but he also shot and killed a few men himself. Ethan wasn't surprised that Phil performed well in combat with his military heritage and all. Phil's father had completed three tours in Vietnam as a Green Beret. His grandfather was a marine during World War II, and for his heroics he was awarded the Silver Star.

That night Ethan learned that his Simrad night vision for his sniper rifle was broken. Every time he shot, the device slipped off his weapon. As much as he wanted to hunt at night, he didn't have to worry, because the enemy knew that the night belonged to the United States.

That evening, and every night, PsyOps (psychological warfare operations) flooded the city with music. Air support reigned supreme, destroying houses and leveling entire buildings. Any insurgents caught on the street were hit either by bombs or machine guns.

The next day Ethan and Phil made it a point to demoralize enemy fighters. Although some of the bodies had been dragged away during the night, when Ethan spotted others attempting to recover more, he shot them as well. A few insurgents played the hero role and dashed for their mortally wounded comrades who were screaming in pain, but they also fell victim to Ethan's bullets. Ethan didn't hesitate to shoot anyone even moving toward the bodies, because their weapons were lying nearby. By noon the street was teeming with swollen and maggot-infested insurgents. The count totaled over seventeen.

Behind his trusted M40A3, Ethan kept watch over his bodies. He tried not to stare at the dogs and cats eating the flesh from the corpses. But when the animals had their fill, he noticed that parts of bodies had been eaten clear to the bone. And for him it was satisfying to know that insurgents were nearby, behind cover, helplessly watching this happen.

The entire day, Ethan killed men trying to maneuver on them and trying to drag bodies away. By nightfall on the second day, over twenty bodies lay on the street but because of the shooting, he had used up all of his match-grade ammunition and was forced to use the less accurate machine-gun ammo.

On the third day, the company moved positions farther into the city. They occupied the buildings at the end of the street, 900 yards away. Ethan and his spotter counted the kills as they patrolled to their new position. On the road they passed twenty-two bodies. Ethan also noticed pamphlets scattered about. The papers showed pictures of the animals eating the dead and the writing translated, "This will happen to any foreign fighter or Iraqi who takes up arms."

When they reached the houses, Ethan received over 300 match-grade rounds of ammunition. Once on the roof, his team used the same tactic they had used before. They smashed a hole in the wall and backed off enough to see down an alley. This time the company first sergeant and a machine gunner team joined them and made holes of their own.

Within the hour they spotted a target. It was a man kneeling in a shadow, holding an AK. When they ranged the wall next to him, he was 500 yards away. The only problem was that everyone saw him except Ethan.

"I'm gonna take the shot on this guy," said Phil, who could see him perfectly. Just as he said that, though, the man stood up, and his head was positioned directly in Ethan's crosshairs.

"Oh, dude," whispered Ethan, delighted at the picture.

Phil knew from the implication that Ethan was going to shoot. Ethan had his rifle resting on a sandbag, and he squeezed the trigger. Everyone on the roof witnessed the round split the man's jaw while slicing through his head and impacting the wall behind him. It was a prime example of instant incapacitation; the man was dead before he hit the ground. Ethan couldn't wait to tell one of his instructors at the urban sniper course about the kill, because that instructor had frequently stressed these types of shots.

On the other side of town, other marine snipers were successfully killing insurgents in the same manner. Throughout the city the damage done by marine snipers was so great that when U.S. commanders discussed peace negotiations with city officials, the Iraqis first request was to call off the marine snipers.

In the city, Ethan was comforted and frustrated when two other sniper teams joined them on the roof. It was great to know that his brothers were there, but now everyone was gunning for the same kills.

For the next two days, Ethan and Phil moved positions to mislead the enemy. Insurgents still attacked, but it was harder to hit them, because the roads and alleys were narrow, and they had a shorter distance to run allowing them to be less exposed. Ethan let a few enemies shoot from their positions. When they were confident that they couldn't be found, he killed them.

Ethan rested while Phil took over the gun. Shortly thereafter, the corpsman got his first kill with the sniper rifle. It came when a car packed with armed gunmen parked in the distance. Phil's best target was the passenger, and he shot through the side window. Ethan saw the man slump forward after being hit, before the car sped off.

When the team went back to the original house, waiting upstairs was a Delta Force team. The team was there for support because at the time, everyone suspected that they were going to capture the entire city. It's known that Delta is the complete fighting package. Their proficiency in weapons, foreign languages, and operating in general is known throughout the world. For Ethan the first thing he noticed about them was their age. Every one of them was at least in his midthirties. Their team consisted of snipers, assaulters, and medics, and Ethan was honored when the man in charge, John, asked for him by name. Apparently John had heard about the marine corporal who was quickly adding to a phenomenal kill tally—and with a bolt-action rifle.

Knowing that these were the best operators that America had to offer, Ethan was humbled. He was also surprised that they were open to the snipers' opinions on tactics.

Delta had also brought with them an impressive array of weapons. These included several different sniper rifles and explosives, as well as night vision and thermal devices.

The snipers and Delta operators stayed at the same position, and Ethan was impressed with their experience and knowledge. One day he had the opportunity to prove his skill. It was afternoon when one of the operators found two men observing their position from a window. Only the men's heads were in view. Ethan and another Delta sniper were the only two engaging. Although nobody said it, it was a standoff to see who the better shot was. The distance was over 500 yards and after the wind call, Ethan adjusted his dope and took aim, but at the last minute he readjusted his sights. On command the two snipers fired, but both of their bullets hit the wall less than a foot below the men. Ethan was upset with himself, because he would have gotten a head shot had he left his initial dope alone.

After weeks in the city, the marines caused plenty of damage. Echo Company alone dropped a few 500-pound bombs, and so did the other companies and battalions. The air support was relentless, and on the ground, mortars and machine gunners tore into everything. But the fighting was taking a toll. Ethan wasn't able to sleep more than three hours a night, and he hardly ate anything. The need to hunt consumed him.

The company ran patrols out of their defensive perimeter, and one afternoon a squad was ambushed on their way back. Ethan regretted that he wasn't able to help them, and he promised himself to move and support the next patrol if it came under fire. A few days later he was put to the test.

On the morning of April 26, a platoon, a sniper team, and a few of the Delta Force operators set out across the graveyard to raid two houses. Ethan wished the sniper team luck. It was Sergeant Shuhart, Corporal Posten, Corporal Curnell, and Lance Corporal Cody. Hours later, Ethan was on his roof when all hell broke loose. The insurgents ambushed the marine patrol across the graveyard and the marines were stunned, under heavy fire. From the radio traffic, Ethan knew that some of them were injured and needed to get out of there. Soon his position was under fire as well. Searching for the shooter, Ethan found him in a minaret.

It wasn't surprising to the marines that in "the city of mosques," enemy gunmen used these religious structures to shoot from. But it was upsetting when footage of marines destroying these buildings was used against them.

Ethan tried to fire back but was forced to take cover on the roof while the machine gun honed in on them. Suddenly, bullets flew through one of the holes and one grazed the helmet of the marine next to Ethan. Instead of losing his composure, the marine just laughed it off. But the fire didn't stop. More bullets streamed through another hole and hit the sandbags inches away from Ethan. When he moved up against the wall to take cover, he felt the vibration from the bullets impacting outside of the wall. His natural instinct was also to laugh, but he was also overcome with anger. Although the insurgents had the advantage for the moment, Ethan was determined to make them pay.

Still under fire, but remembering his promise, he told his spotter and another marine to follow him. On his way out of the house, he told an officer that he was going to kill the insurgent in the minaret firing on their position. It was an aggressive move on Ethan's part because in the heat of the moment, they were sprinting down an alley while under fire. The marines ran 400 meters, unaware of what they were getting themselves into. At the same time, marines pelted the tower with 40 mm grenades and machine guns, allowing Ethan and his team to move. When they stopped, the team climbed to the roof of a building near the mosque. After he set up, Ethan realized that the machine gun had disappeared from the minaret and the gunmen were running out of the mosque. Just as he found the door, the man with the machine gun scurried out. Ethan held his sights on the door when another man came out and stopped facing away from him. Ethan aimed at his back and fired one shot, killing the man.

Over the radio, the team heard that the marines were moving back across the graveyard. Ethan and the others moved out of the house to join them. Once they linked up, he helped to carry a wounded marine back to the house. The marine was lying on a door that was being used as a stretcher. When Ethan grabbed the door, he had a flashback of sniper school and an eight-mile stretcher carry. At that moment, he was just as exhausted as he had been in sniper school, and he understood why he needed such strict training.

By the time they made it back to their building, the insurgents smelled blood and were on the attack. Although the marines had tanks and air support, intense RPG and small-arms fire rained down on their building. It was a shock for Ethan to see the other sniper team members injured. He was standing near the causality collection point and was grief stricken when he saw the other wounded marines. Phil and the Delta Force medic immediately helped the wounded and worked nonstop.

With RPGs impacting the building, Ethan sank back into kill mode. He had to pull Phil away from helping the injured, because they needed to get back into the fight. Instead of making for the roof, they decided to shoot from rooms. Once Ethan got a glimpse of what the insurgents were doing, he planned to bring his bolt-action wrath down on as many of them as possible.

For weeks he and the other snipers were able to keep the insurgents off the rooftops, but when the tanks rolled in, the insurgents flooded the roofs, desperate to destroy one. Ethan and Phil immediately started killing. After every shot they changed rooms, and in time Ethan was exhausted, so much so that his heart felt like it was going to explode. When he shot, he had to hold his breath in order to stabilize the crosshairs. Soon insurgents were in alleyways, and Ethan shot a man moving through one. Just as his partner tried to drag him out, Phil opened fire and killed him.

In the house, Ethan couldn't hear a thing. Marines shot from every room and machine guns rumbled on the roof. In one room, as Ethan was about to shoot, an explosion shook the wall in front of him and knocked him and Phil to the ground. The force was so powerful that it rattled dust from the wall, and both Ethan and Phil were covered in it. Slightly dazed from the blast, Ethan stood up while looking out the window and realized that a tank had fired its main gun just below their window. That's what the explosion had been. Overhead, AH-1W Super Cobras flew so close that the 20 mm cannons mounted under the nose dropped their shells on neighboring houses. When Ethan looked out the window, unexpectedly, everything stopped. In a matter of seconds the battle was over. No insurgents could be found and the shooting ceased.

After the commotion, Ethan and Phil slumped down a wall. Their cammies and skin were filthy with dirt and sweat. Resting in silence, Ethan was completely worn out and burning up under his flak jacket and helmet. One of the grunts appeared in the doorway and asked if anyone wanted water, but neither of them did.

"If your wife knew what I'm dragging you through, she'd kill me," said Ethan to Phil, and they both smiled.

With their bodies beginning to relax, Phil lit up a cigarette, but before Ethan could take a drag, he leaned to his side and vomited.

When they finished the smoke, Ethan and Phil moved downstairs where they found a pile of M16s from the dead and wounded. Ethan grabbed a few to take back to the company headquarters. Looking down, he noticed that the tape on one of the rifles' buttstock read the name of a friend who had died in the fight.

Back at their original position, the team moved back up to the roof. On top Ethan found John, the Delta operator. As the two warriors talked, Ethan asked John how the fighting compared to what he and his men were used to.

"In Iraq, this is it," he replied. "The action doesn't get any better than this."

Seeing the men operate, Ethan picked John's brain on how to be a part of Delta. He learned that there was a reason why the men were all in their midthirties. It was because operating is an older man's game. The men had been doing it for years and seeing them inspired Ethan to do it as well.

Days later, the snipers and Delta operators were on a rooftop discussing tactics on how to kill more insurgents. The company commander came up and delivered some bad news.

"Men, we're ordered to withdraw from the city," he announced sadly. The information was devastating for Ethan, and he felt betrayed. The chance to finish the fight was close at hand, but he would never know what that felt like.

In early May, the marines filed out of the city, handing it over to an Iraqi security force called the "Fallujah Brigade." Ethan and the others knew what the end result would be. The fighters would rebuild, regroup, and in the end, another unit would have to go into the city and finish the job.

When it was all said and done, Ethan had amassed thirty-two kills, not including the men that he couldn't see fall dead. This was an incredible feat, considering that it took him two weeks, while the finest marine snipers in Vietnam had accumulated roughly ninety in an entire year. His aggressive maneuvers and tactics were successful against the enemy, and his competitive nature drove him to operate the way he did. For him, sniping was extremely personal. He wanted to finish off as many men as he could. He felt lucky to have seen the action that he had—and in the first two months, because after that, action died off.

After the deployment was over, Ethan was assigned to the First Marine Division schools to instruct marksmanship.

7

Seminole on the Roof

Name: Sergeant Reyes, O.
Billet: Scout/Sniper Team Leader
Area of Operations: City of Fallujah, Al Anbar Province,
Operation Iraqi Freedom II, February 2004–June 2004

In the late evening hours of April 4, 2004, as Operation Vigilant Resolve was beginning, Sergeant Reyes and his four-man sniper team patrolled silently through the rolling desert en route to a soda distribution factory in the industrial zone of southern Fallujah. Hours earlier the team was eleven kilometers south with Bravo Company, First Battalion, Fifth Marines, but now they were a thousand meters from their objective. Reyes and his heavily armed sniper team had been tasked with finding a path to the factory for the company and reporting on enemy movements in that immediate area. Battalion intel suggested that the building would be full of insurgents with guards in the watchtowers that surrounded it. The battalion wanted the sniper team to confirm enemy activity, and if there was any, Bravo Company

Headhunter Two team picture before the overnight mission. *L to R:* Stayskal, Romeo, Stanton, and Ferguson.

Collection of Romeo Santiago

Romeo showing the knife that he used to cut Stayskal's flak jacket. On the left, Stanton, showing the scar on his shoulder from the bullet. *Collection of Romeo Santiago*

Clifton in a building hide.
Collection of Dayllen L. Clifton

Clifton watching roads in the open desert.

Collection of Dayllen L. Clifton

Mulder's view from his position. *Collection of Owen M.*

L to R: Hamblin; Gunny French, the team's platoon sergeant; and Mulder. *Collection of Owen M.*

Ethan from his first position, between engaging targets.
Collection of Ethan P.

The cemetery in An Najaf. *11th Marine Expeditionary Unit*

Jack and his team standing over the 74mm Recoilless Rifle. *Collection of Jack Avak*

Jack finding targets in An Najaf. *Collection of Jack Avak*

Jack on his way through Iraq during OIF 1.

Collection of Jack Avak

Memo and his partner engaging targets from the apartments in Fallujah. *Collection of Guillermo M. Sandoval*

Memo clearing houses. *Collection of Guillermo M. Sandoval*

Memo engaging targets with the MK 11 sniper rifle.
Collection of Guillermo M. Sandoval

Memo preparing to step out on a mission during his second tour.
Collection of Guillermo M. Sandoval

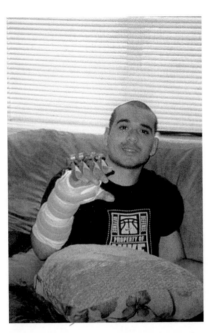

Final outcome of Longoria's surgery.
Collection of Jesse J. Longoria

May and his team conducting surveillance.
Collection of Lance D. May

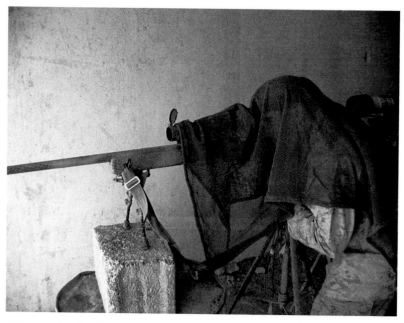

May in the final moments before killing another insurgent.

Collection of Lance D. May

May preparing to engage insurgents. *Collection of Lance D. May*

May defending Camp Gannon. *Collection of Lance D. May*

CJ with destroyed tank during OIF 1. *Collection of C. J. Quinlan*

CJ with his weapon of choice, the SASR .50-caliber sniper rifle. *Collection of C. J. Quinlan*

Decoy atop Sgt. Afong's rooftop. *Collection of Milo Afong*

After engaging the mortar men. *Collection of Milo Afong*

was going to raid the compound just after the snipers killed the guards in the towers.

Concealed by darkness, Reyes signaled the team to halt, and even though they were at a distance, they would be able to observe the building with night optics. The marines in the team were excited at the chance of finally making contact with the enemy. When they first arrived in Iraq, the battalion was based out of Camp Abu Ghraib just twenty miles west of the capital city, Baghdad. The camp received indirect fire constantly, and after the sniper teams settled in, they were assigned to counter-mortar missions. For days at a time the sniper team waited on the outskirts of the town Abu Ghraib, hoping to catch men sending mortars toward their base. Their persistence paid off, and eventually they did see insurgents. But to their disappointment, they were unable to engage because of the distance. It was during this time that the team began hearing rumors about a major offensive in Fallujah, which was twenty miles west of their base. Reyes was skeptical, but after a few weeks of hunting for enemy mortar men, the sniper teams were told to get ready, because they were going into Fallujah.

In position, Reyes looked around at the three other marines. He was confident in the abilities of his teammates. His spotter, and the team's point man, was Corporal Kowalski. The assistant team leader was Corporal Morgan. Morgan, Kowalski, and Reyes had been in the same class when they had attended and graduated the First Marine Division scout/sniper school. The three of them had been together for some time and knew each other well. Corporal Gravel, who was Morgan's spotter, had only recently joined the platoon and was the only PIG in the team. All together, the four of them had enough firepower for almost anything they could find themselves in.

Reyes and Morgan both carried M40A3s and M16s, but Reyes was the only one with night vision capabilities for the sniper rifle. Kowalski had the M16 with an M203 grenade launcher, and Gravel was carrying the SAW (squad automatic weapon). They all carried 9 mm pistols. The team was relieved to drop their heavy packs when they stopped. The radios, batteries, optics, claymores, flares, and ammo were spread among them. They also packed the basic load of twelve quarts of water, three days' worth of chow, and extra clothing. They knew to plan for the worst on this mission, because they weren't told when they would get resupplied.

Lying in the cold desert sand, the team observed the factory for three hours and reported that the building and watchtowers appeared to be abandoned. Bravo Company, who was now following the infrared chemlights that the snipers had left for a trail, told the team to find a way into the building. Reyes directed Morgan and Gravel to move up and look for the best entrance while he and Kowalski provided cover for them. The building was surrounded by a ten-foot wall, and when the two came back, they confirmed that the only way in was through a small gap. When the company arrived at their position, Reyes informed the company commander that the opening in the wall wasn't big enough for them to move through. The commander nodded and decided to make his own way in. The sniper team moved up close to the wall with a squad and waited a few seconds before they were told to get down. A SMAW (shoulder-launched multipurpose assault weapon) gunner took a knee and blasted a huge chunk of the wall to pieces, making a hole big enough for everyone to pass through. After the dust settled, the squad rushed through, followed by the snipers. Once inside the walls, the snipers broke away from the squad and set up in an elevated position on a building adjacent to the factory to provide covering fire. Just as the snipers had said, the buildings were clear of insurgents, and soon the company moved into the compound. Later the battalion would occupy the building and make it their headquarters.

After the company took the factory over, Reyes moved his team onto the roof for better observation, but they found they couldn't see past the walls. They weren't able to shoot from that position and soon the assault was to begin. Reyes knew the company commander wanted his team in an elevated position to support his marines by providing covering fire for them as they pushed into the city. The snipers had their work cut out for them, because there were many buildings to be cleared and roads to be crossed.

It had been planned that during the attack Bravo Company was to overtake the factory and clear buildings into the city according to their sector. By now the other companies in the battalion were on Bravo's flanks. Reyes decided that because he couldn't see from that rooftop, his team would follow behind a squad, just until they got into the first building. He coordinated to meet with a squad, but when his team went to link up, they found themselves alone. The squads had already started to push across the street and into other buildings. Reyes called back to his platoon sergeant and was told to get into the city and get to work.

Kowalski led the team across the main street in front of the factory and toward the tallest structure in the area. The squads had the meticulous task of clearing everything, and they were already in buildings. Gunfire rang out in every direction as the snipers crossed the street. The voices of marines shouting and yelling filled the air, and when the snipers entered their target building, a squad was on the way out. The adrenaline-filled infantrymen barely recognized the snipers as friendly. Like most sniper teams, Reyes and the others wore different gear than the grunts did. They needed to be able to move farther and carry more ammo and equipment than the squads. They also needed to be comfortable enough to deliver accurate rifle fire. But also, they needed the same amount of protection as everyone else. The military-issued gear didn't provide the comfort and protection necessary for the sniper teams. This caused most of them to buy specialized equipment. Luckily, the squads were using their night vision goggles and were able to distinguish the snipers and their weapons before shooting them.

Once the team made it to the rooftop, they found it was impossible to see forward of the buildings in the area. This meant they wouldn't be able to shoot in support of the advancing grunts. Reyes decided to keep his team moving from building to building until they could find a position to fire from. With all the shooting going on around them, he was surprised that they hadn't come across any insurgents. The scene was chaotic, and on one occasion the team came under fire from other marines. Reyes and his team dashed behind a wall after the bullets flew toward them. It was obvious that a squad was shooting because he could hear them yelling. It took a minute for them to stop, but they did when Reyes yelled over the radio for them to shift fire because they were shooting at friendly. No one in the team was injured, but it was a close call.

Early the next morning, Reyes and his team were on a rooftop when the battalion ordered all of the marines back to a certain area. Headquarters also wanted the buildings that had been cleared to be searched again on the way back. The snipers, however, made their way to the SARC (Surveillance and Reconnaissance Center), which was at the factory. From there, they were attached to weapons platoon from Bravo Company.

When the search was finished, the line companies established defensive positions in the southern buildings along Route Christina, which was a main road running east to west through the industrial area. The snipers made their way to the road and set up on a high, one-story building with the machine gunners. Grunts laid concertina wire and took up positions at the bottom of the building. On top, the snipers found a small concrete shed that was big enough to fit the four of them. The added height of the shed gave them an advantage because they could see farther north than anyone else. Also, a ledge stood up around the top of it, giving them something to hide behind. When the team needed to observe, all they had to do was rest their optics on the ledge.

On the shed, Reyes began to search for targets in the dark. Soon the marines came under sporadic gunfire. To Reyes the scene around them was often comical. At first, the marines took shots from unknown locations, and then the machine gunners and grunts would unleash a barrage toward the direction they thought the fire came. The sound of the machine guns echoed off buildings and walls, while red tracers cut through the night. Some hit their mark and disappeared, while others ricocheted off houses. This went on more than a few times before the enemy fire slowly stopped; however, not long afterward, mortars landed behind the marines. When the fire did pick up, Reyes anxiously scanned the area through his scope, but was unable to locate any gunmen. He and his team had yet to fire a shot.

When the morning came, the team started to make out the surrounding areas. Behind them was the industrial area with factory buildings that had already been secured. Route Christina was at the base of their building and directly across the street is where the housing area began. The snipers' viewpoint was great. They were on the highest building around and were able to see if anyone took to the square rooftops on the other side of the road. They could also see perfectly down the alley in front of them and had a direct line of sight to a school in the distance. Although they had a huge vantage area, there were still areas where the team couldn't observe.

Their main concern was a narrow alley in front of them. It had connecting alleys and roads leading to it, and Reyes knew that it could be used as an avenue of approach to their building and to the marines below. The alleyway had black power lines strung out in certain areas above it while concrete walls and metal gates formed its border. Three hundred yards up the alley, it curved to the right and then it went straight again. The machine gunners and grunts couldn't see past the curve, but they could.

By midmorning, insurgents began to come into view. Reyes and his spotter Kowalski were on the right side of the roof, while Morgan and his spotter, Gravel, stayed to the left. They had finished finding distances to certain reference points when men began to scurry behind walls and through back alleyways coming toward them. Some were masked and some weren't, but almost all of them carried weapons. The snipers tried to take aim but they were only able to see the men briefly, because they were moving fast. Reyes felt his adrenaline rising, knowing that he was about to shoot.

It didn't take long before the two sides were engaged in all out combat. It started with insurgents firing on the marines from alleys. This caused a firestorm from the infantrymen and machine gunners, but the insurgents only exposed themselves enough to shoot a sloppy burst of AK fire before ducking behind cover again. Reyes was busy trying to find his first target when suddenly Kowalski oriented him to the curve in the alley where three men stood shooting toward them. Reyes traversed the rifle in time to watch a man on his knee shoot an RPG toward their building while the two other men shot wildly with their AKs. The man with the RPG dashed behind cover and Reyes sighted in on one of the men with a rifle. The snipers had already marked this area as a target reference point, and Reyes knew to put his dope on 300. With his dirt-stained face resting on the rifle, Reyes set the crosshairs of his scope over a fat, middle-aged insurgent's stomach. He had been waiting for this moment for three years.

"Which one is yours?" asked Kowalski.

"The fat one," replied Reyes.

"Fire when ready."

Reyes flipped the safety forward with his thumb. A few black power lines were between him and the target but he paid them no mind, he focused on settling the crosshairs over the man. With the pad of his index finger he lightly squeezed the trigger and seconds later he was manipulating the bolt. The rifle stopped just in time for him to see his bullet strike the man's midsection.

Through the spotting scope, Kowalski followed the vapor trail from the bullet after it passed over the power lines until it impacted the insurgent.

"You hit 'em in the stomach!" said Kowalski.

But surprisingly, the bullet didn't instantly cut the man down. After being shot, the man looked at his stomach, then fell to a knee and began shooting his rifle again. Reyes lined him up one more time and squeezed the trigger, sending another bullet into his left breast. The impact of the round knocked the man to his back, killing him and forcing the gun from his hands.

Both Kowalski and Reyes were excited and wanted to celebrate Reyes's first kill, but the intensity of the battle was escalating and more targets were everywhere. Morgan's rifle thundered as Reyes looked toward the man he had just killed. Another bad guy was down beside him. Morgan shot the man in the chest as he tried to pick up the gun that the fat man had used. Reyes caught sight of another man in the area and quickly killed him as well. In a matter of minutes Morgan and Reyes left five insurgents dead in the alley, before the others began to realize that they needed to stay behind cover. Eventually, the enemy only exposed themselves momentarily while firing off their RPGs, which frustrated Reyes. This wasn't nearly enough time to acquire a target and take a well-aimed shot. The marines below them were still firing on other insurgents, and by now, it seemed as though hundreds of them swarmed the housing area. The machine gunners were taking fire as well. Bullets hit the building and passed overhead. This was a different kind of fight from the ones Reyes had been in during the invasion in 2003.

Reyes was a PIG then and the radio operator in the team. His unit was constantly on the move during that time, and the sniper teams saw firefights in the Saddam Canal and in Saddam City on their way to Baghdad. None, however, had been as sustained as this.

Back on the rooftop, the company was calling for Reyes and his team, whose call sign was "Seminole Alpha." The company had been receiving fire and wanted the snipers to search the area for the shooters. Reyes and Kowalski were already covering the alley, so Morgan and Gravel turned their attention to the section that the company wanted them to observe. The area where they were looking was left of the alley a few hundred meters. The neighborhood looked similar to the one in front of them, but there were still places where the snipers couldn't see. It had the same type of buildings, alleys, and roads. When Morgan and Gravel searched that vicinity, they saw that the enemy was moving around there as well.

One advantage that the insurgents had was their makeshift bunkers. Demolished vehicles that sat on the road made great shooting positions for the RPG gunners. They would typically move to the vehicle to shoot their grenades and then run away, which made it hard for the marines to get any shots on these men.

But Morgan made an exceptional shot there. He and Gravel were observing, when they caught a man running to one of the makeshift bunkers. Gravel used the laser range finder to get the distance. It showed 975 yards. Morgan adjusted the dope on his rifle. Only the snipers could see the man who was carrying the RPG at that distance. Also at that distance, the insurgent could only aim the weapon in the air and hope that it would arc down on the marines. As the man stood up and leaned on the car to shoot the weapon, Morgan fired. The bullet entered the man's shoulder and the weapon fumbled from his grasp. Seconds later he crawled from behind the vehicle toward the other side of the road, but now he wasn't moving fast at all. As he tried to slip away, Morgan finished the man off with another shot, and his body was left lying on the road.

By midafternoon it seemed that the entire city was up in arms. Marines held positions near the outskirts of the city, while insurgents moved about freely within it. Seminole Alpha had been shooting all day and tried not to waste ammo. Insurgents kept firing and moving, giving Reyes and Morgan only enough time to make snap shots. They were shooting selectively, and although a few of their bullets weren't deadly, they were precise enough to keep RPG gunners from landing grenades on the marines' positions. Reyes and his team soon found that the curve in the alley was empty except for the dead bodies. But back a little farther was another alley which the Iraqis began to move from, and just before night fell, Morgan spotted a few gunmen at that new shooting position.

Reyes and Kowalski watched as one of the insurgents stuck his head out from behind a wall. He waited for a moment, and when he felt that no one could see him, he walked from behind the wall into the alley. It looked as though he was trying to get a better view of the marines' location. The snipers had yet to be found, because the insurgents were focusing on the machine gunners and infantrymen below them. The other marines on the roof couldn't see that area, and when the snipers saw that the insurgent held a weapon in his hand, he became a target. Reyes made an adjustment and put his sights on the man and shot, hoping to hit him before he went back behind cover. It was a quick shot and the bullet landed slightly high, but it tore into the man's neck, causing flesh to spray out of the hole in the back of his neck. He instantly dropped his AK and fell. Reyes watched the area, waiting for someone to pick up his gun.

Usually after an insurgent went down, someone else made a run to take his weapon. This happened so often that the snipers kept their sights on the weapons, knowing that someone would soon try to pick it up.

All day the two sides traded fire, and soon the team got requests for support from marines on nearby rooftops. Reyes and Morgan went to their aid and learned that someone was taking well-aimed shots on their positions. The marines wanted Reyes and Morgan to stay and shoot from there, but Reyes could tell they had a better position from where they had been. Once they were back in position, Reyes told the marines to direct them to the building and window that they thought the fire was coming from. The next time it happened, Reyes and Morgan sent a few rounds into the windows and the gunfire stopped.

As darkness fell, the marines were concerned that the enemy had night vision devices. Reyes had the AN/PVS-10 mounted on his rifle and was excited to be hunting in the shadows. He had a perfect line of sight down the alleyway that the insurgents had been moving through all day. But there was very little light, making it impossible to identify targets at an extended distance, and except for a few shots, the night was uneventful. During the night, Reyes had a hard time sleeping. His adrenaline kept him awake and so did the nearby army units who blasted sounds of babies crying and heavy metal music through their gigantic megaphones. Their purpose was to counter the propaganda that flooded the city's prayer speakers every few hours.

Early the next morning Reyes was on his rifle getting ready for another fun-filled day of shooting. The team searched the alleyways and rooftops, but found no one in sight. Someone in the team noticed that men were using the walls to travel behind.

When Reyes focused in on the walls, he saw that the insurgents were moving low under them. Some of the walls were short, and when the men crawled below them, he saw parts of their weapons and bodies. Kowalski spotted something and guided Reyes to a gap in a wall. Kowalski caught a man poking his head out from the opening. Reyes saw him as well, and they both watched him for what seemed like minutes.

"I'm gonna shoot," said Reyes, and he sighted in. He aimed right where the man had been showing himself and waited for him to turn his head again while lightly squeezing the trigger. When his crosshairs covered the man's face he squeezed the trigger just a little farther. The rifle settled in time for him to see brain matter spraying in all directions, but he had missed the initial impact of his bullet.

"Who wants grape juice?" he said to his partner, who was patting him on the back for the good shot.

Before long, Bravo Company's commander asked Reyes for a two-man sniper team farther down the line. Although Morgan was making shots in his sector, Reyes and Kowalski stayed in place while Morgan and Gravel left the rooftop. As the day slipped into night, Reyes found it harder to fire on the more elusive gunmen, but he knew his team had succeeded in preventing RPGs from hitting their area.

On the second night, Reyes and Kowalski finally climbed from the roof to get some rest. Behind their hut, the two snipers ate and slept. When sunlight appeared on the third morning, they made their way back onto the shed. It was while doing their morning search of the area that they discovered wires running across the alley to a schoolhouse in the distance. The wires hadn't been there the day before, and Kowalski called for support from a nearby M1 Abrams tank. The tank rolled into the alley and crossed the wire causing a small explosion, which didn't affect the vehicle at all. Then, the tank moved back to the base of the snipers' building and shot a round into the school. The explosion wrecked the building, causing the walls and parts of the roof to tumble down.

Once Reyes really noticed the area, he began to realize just how destroyed that side of town was. Chipped concrete from bullet impacts punctured almost every building in sight; walls lay partly in rubble from rockets, mortars, bombs, and 40 mm grenades. The infantrymen had called mortars during the night, and it showed from the tops of buildings in the distance. The place seemed to be uninhabitable, but they could still see movement from the enemy.

During this time, the snipers of 1/5 kept the insurgents on the move and once the insurgents left their area, they walked into the hunting grounds of other snipers from the surrounding units.

Reyes and Kowalski had been taking turns on the sniper rifle for the last few days. Kowalski was on the gun and Reyes was behind the spotting scope when they both saw a man inside the schoolhouse, moving around on the second story. Half of the building had been destroyed by the tank, but there were still parts intact. While giving Kowalski the distance, Reyes saw an RPG on the insurgent's back while he crept low in the shadows trying to find a shooting position. Kowalski keyed in and had a side profile of the man; his target was the head. After he fired, Reyes watched through his spotting scope as the vapor trail from the bullet swirled down and disappeared. It was a strange sight to see the man's head explode, and he was beside himself when he saw it. He was in awe because it was the first time he actually got a good view of something like that. Reyes was overjoyed for his partner and congratulated him on his second kill—plus it was a phenomenal shot. They were both caught up in the moment and temporarily forgot where they were. Rolling onto their sides, they gave each other high fives, before realizing that they were exposed and taking cover again.

Through all of the chaos, Reyes began to better understand his role in support of the company. He knew it was an important one because his team was not only killing the enemy, they were also saving lives of the infantrymen below them. After all, if a few of the RPGs had found their marks, the company might have had more casualties. It was also apparent to Reyes that he and his partner might never be found by the enemy, but the grunts below them were taking fire all day long.

Predictably, the enemy mortar fire was progressively more precise. When night fell again, the team climbed off the roof and that evening, a few mortars actually landed on their building. Reyes and Kowalski had the presence of mind to dive for cover and bunch together when they heard the whistling of the rounds falling.

All of the action had taken a toll on their bodies, and exhaustion set in. When they were on the roof they didn't eat much and now they felt the hunger in their stomachs. Their eyes were weary from constantly observing, and their bodies ached from lying down. Reyes understood why he went through such strict training. He had spent many hours in conditions worse than the one he now found himself in, and even though his body felt fatigued, he knew that he could endure much more.

That night when the mortars stopped, the two snipers

slept behind the hut. They didn't have to worry about security, because the marines around them had set up a firewatch. Although the machine gunners were still spraying targets all night and making it hard to sleep, both Reyes and Kowalski did get the rest their bodies needed.

When the sun rose the next morning, the two snipers took to their position again. Reyes was on the rifle and Kowalski was behind the spotting scope when they went into their normal routine of searching the immediate area. The streets and rooftops were empty, and most of the scene hadn't changed except for what Kowalski found next. On the roof of a house just 200 yards north of their position, Kowalski saw two pipes sitting side by side. When he concentrated on those items, he noticed that there were two rockets sticking out of the tips of the pipes. They were aimed at the marines below them. The team immediately called the company and told them what they had found. The lieutenant from the weapons platoon observed the rooftop as well and agreed with the snipers. The company tried to detonate them by using indirect fire but their mortars weren't precise enough to hit the roof that the rockets were on. Then, Reyes got the call to shoot the rockets; however, he wanted Kowalski to shoot, because he was the one who had spotted them. It took two bullets to destroy them. The first round hit a rocket, but didn't do anything. The second bullet hit the same rocket again and detonated it. As it flew away, the pipe that held it tipped over onto the one sitting beside it, which caused the second rocket to ignite. They both impacted the road and exploded, but they didn't injure anyone. Just after this happened, Reyes noticed an ambulance driving down the road toward them. Ambulances were allowed to pick up the dead and wounded insurgents, so

Reyes assumed that the vehicle was driving to a body that was 75 meters away on the other side of the road. A dead man and his AK had been lying there since before the snipers took to the roof. The infantrymen had killed him.

The marines had been told to watch the ambulances, because they weren't supposed to pick up the weapons, only the bodies. And they were known for transporting fighters and weapons throughout the city. It was no surprise that when it arrived at the body, all the marines on the roof eyed the vehicle. When it stopped, two men jumped from the cab and picked the body up, throwing it into the back. Reyes and Kowalski had just crawled from the roof to talk to the lieutenant about the rockets, but while doing so, Reyes was also watching the men from the ambulance with his M16. He was waiting to see if the men would grab the rifle. Sure enough, one of the men reached for the AK and then swung the rifle toward the marines but didn't have time to shoot it. Reyes was able to fill the man's torso with five shots before he fell to the ground. When he fell, Reyes examined the body through his scope to make sure he was dead.

Because they had spent the last few days shooting from that roof, and because there were no more insurgents moving through the alley, the two snipers decided to move positions. They packed their gear and headed east onto another rooftop where they could observe down another alley. Grunts were on nearby buildings. Right away Reyes noticed a makeshift barrier made up of cinder blocks and loose debris stretching halfway across the alley. He used that, and several other areas where insurgents could potentially enter the alley, as target reference points. The areas were mostly driveways and openings in the walls that ran along the alley. Meanwhile, Kowalski decided to use the mortars for support. He talked to the weapons platoon mortar section, calling in pre-designated targets and giving them the grid coordinates to certain areas including the barrier in the alley.

After settling in their new position, Reyes asked the machine gunners on a roof nearby for ammunition because he had yet to be resupplied. Once back in position he decided to chip away at the barrier. He hadn't expected anyone to be behind it and when he shot the wall, loosening some of the rubble, he was surprised to see three gunmen lean over the top of it. Before this, Reyes had noticed a pattern when engaging the enemy. The insurgents traveled and fought in groups of three. Typically one man had an RPG and the other two had rifles and machine guns, so it wasn't unusual when Reyes saw that two men were holding AKs, and one had an RPG. The man with the RPG was the immediate threat, and Reyes aimed in on him. Kowalski took hold of the radio, and in seconds he was calling in a fire mission with the 60 mm mortars. Reyes kept his crosshairs on the lower chest of the man with the RPG, who was now rising above the rubble. The man couldn't see the snipers and was trying to find where Reyes's shot had come from. When the man stood a little higher, Reyes shot. At the same time Kowalski had finished sending the information for the fire mission, and he heard the mortars being shot out. Reyes's bullet hit the man dead center and the RPG slipped from his shoulder when he went down. The other two ducked below the barrier, while trying to pull their friend to a nearby wall, but it was too late. The men disappeared into a dust cloud from the mortar splashing into the alley. It had first-round effects on the three men and there was no chance of survival. Kowalski quickly told the mortar men to "fire for effect" and soon the hiss and thump of the landing mortars shook the area. The alley and surrounding buildings filled with dust from the impact, and when it was all clear, the area where the men had been was in ruins. He and Kowalski were astonished, and they agreed to use the mortars more often.

Soon, Reyes traded positions with Kowalski. Reyes wasn't greedy on the gun, and even though it felt good getting kills, to him it felt better when he spotted for his friend. Even after the mortar incident, the enemy still moved through the area. Kowalski was observing down the alley when another insurgent poked his head out from behind a wall. It was obvious that he was going to run across the alley. The Iraqi glanced around one more time, and then took off sprinting with an RPG on his shoulder. Kowalski put a lead on the man and shot, hitting him in the leg. The gunman tumbled to the ground while the weapon landed behind him. Reyes was watching this unfold through the spotting scope. The man was in pain and blood gushed from his thigh. Reyes reminded Kowalski to keep him alive, hoping that others would come out and drag him away. Their patience paid off, and not long after, another insurgent ran out. But instead of helping his friend, he picked up the RPG and aimed it in the direction of the team. Kowalski was busy squeezing the trigger at the exact same moment. The man stood in place long enough for the grenade to speed from the launcher, but just as it did, Kowalski's bullet landed directly in his chest knocking him onto his back. The RPG raced aimlessly into the air and exploded in the distance while Kowalski shot twice more and finished off both men.

The snipers spent the rest of the time searching for targets in that alley and in surrounding areas, but the insurgents stopped moving through there. Reyes and Kowalski didn't spot anyone else from that rooftop, so when night came, they moved back to their original position. They didn't want to take a risk by returning to the hut, so they moved one building back and stayed on that building's roof while still being able to see most of the area that they had observed before.

The next morning, from the building behind their original position, Reyes and Kowalski scanned the area. It was hard to believe that insurgents were still coming around. Now, though, they were making themselves harder targets and when the snipers did catch gunmen on the streets, it was only seconds before they disappeared. This caused Reyes to make a habit of searching everything over and over again, trying to find anything out of the ordinary. While looking in the partly demolished building of the schoolhouse, Reyes noticed a man lying in the rubble facing them. He wanted to make sure that he wasn't imagining the person and he asked Kowalski to look as well. It was a man, and soon he was shooting at the infantrymen in the building in front of them. His muzzle flash helped to give him away. He was in a decent position and was concealed in shade, but with their optics, the snipers could see him. Reyes fixed his dope, making it just a little higher, because he was farther back than when he had shot from that area last. Because he only had sight of the man's chest and head, Reyes needed to wait for him to move so that he could make a precision shot. After a few moments, the insurgent repositioned himself, so Reyes let his crosshairs sit on the man's chest, and took a shot. Kowalski spotted the round and said the man had leaned back right after Reyes fired, causing the bullet to skip off the ground in front of him and bounce up into the lower part of his neck. The man was down and he wasn't moving. Reyes knew that others would be around, so he kept his sights on the dead man. Like clockwork, minutes later another man crawled out to get the AK while his friend bled out from his neck. Reyes wasted no time killing him. Before long, Reyes and Kowalski traded positions again. Not long after Kowalski took over the rifle, he saw two more gunmen on the roof of the schoolhouse. When he dropped the first one, the wounded man's partner tried to drag him to safety, but Kowalski easily shot him as well. In a matter of an hour the sniper team was able to get four kills. When the operation began, Reyes and Kowalski were excited about their kills, but now that they had been doing so much of it, the thrill was gone.

After the first three days, Reyes and Kowalski mentally prepared themselves to sweep through most of the city and stay inside of it. But nobody seemed to know when they were going to attack farther. Reyes wondered why they didn't go through the whole city, but as usual, politics were involved, which hindered the marines' ability to end the fight. Not long afterward, the rules of engagement changed. The new rules prohibited the marines from killing anyone with a weapon. They now had to positively identify that the men they were about to shoot were planning to use hostile intent toward the marines.

By the time the operation ended, in early March, Reyes fully came to understand his importance and role as a sniper. One day he heard that one of the leaders in the battalion had been killed; an enemy sniper had shot him in the neck. The marines flooded the house from which the enemy sniper was shooting and killed him. It was always obvious, but Reyes realized that the enemy snipers were killing marines just like he was killing insurgents. He understood that what happened to that enemy sniper could also happen to him and his team. He couldn't help but dwell on the fact that it was true that they killed a lot of the enemy, but in reality, he knew that they had saved more lives than they took.

8

Recon Sniper

Name: Sergeant A., Jack

Billet: Assistant Team Leader/Platoon Sniper, Team Leader/Platoon Sniper

Area of Operation: Kuwait to Baghdad, Operation Iraqi Freedom I, 2003; City of Najaf, An Najaf Province, Operation Iraqi Freedom II, 2004

On September 11, 2001, former marine Jack A., stood in his kitchen, shocked at what was unfolding before his eyes. Minutes earlier he had been getting ready for work when his wife told him that he needed to see what was happening on the television. He was surprised to see the northern tower of the World Trade Center smoldering, and he was trying to piece the story together when suddenly a jumbo jet flew directly into the south tower. Both he and his wife watched in silence as the plane disappeared into the side of the building and exploded, causing a phenomenal fireball. They were even more shocked when minutes later, the two buildings collapsed. In the end, the death toll was staggering. For Jack, it was unthinkable that anyone could attack America this way. Days later, when Al Qaeda claimed that they were responsible and the United States announced a war on terror, Jack knew that he had to go back into the marines.

He originally joined the marines in September of 1989. At seventeen years old he needed his mother's signature to enlist. As a young man, Jack wanted nothing more than to experience life in the infantry, and that is exactly what he did. But for his first eighteen months, he was a security forces marine with the duty of guarding aircraft in Bermuda. After his tour there, he was sent to an infantry platoon with the Third Battalion, Second Marines stationed at Camp Lejeune, North Carolina.

Life in the infantry is sometimes monotonous and it took only three weeks before Jack knew that it wasn't for him. Luckily, the battalion scout/sniper platoon, formerly known as STA (meaning Surveillance and Target Acquisition) was holding a screening. He didn't know much about hunting, let alone sniping, but he wanted more than the infantry. The screening was difficult, and the five months of being a PIG were even worse. But he was motivated, and it wasn't long until Jack was given a chance to attend the Second Marine Division scout/sniper school at Stone Bay, Camp Lejeune, North Carolina. The class started out with twenty-three marines, and only seven passed, including Jack. When he returned to his platoon he worked his way up and became a team leader for his third deployment.

His first enlistment ended in 1992, and Jack missed a few of the conflicts that occurred during that time. When the Gulf War began, his unit never left their ship, and later they were overlooked for operations in South America. Soon Jack was discharged, but he often went to different reserve units just to stay up on training. In 1997 he finally called it quits, until September 11, 2001.

It took some time to process the paperwork after his 9/11

re-enlistment, and in the meantime, he stayed at his home in Las Vegas. Months went by until he was standing tall at Camp Pendleton, California. He received orders to an infantry platoon from the Second Battalion, Fifth Marines, but first, he needed to check into First Marine Division at Camp Margarita, located on Camp Pendleton.

Jack had spent so many years out of the military that his rank was reduced from sergeant to lance corporal. As he waited to check into his unit, other marines stared at him. At the time it was unusual to see a thirty-one-year-old lance corporal with two rows of ribbons and two hash marks. Everyone just assumed that he had been demoted, and when someone finally asked what he did, Jack replied, "I punched an officer."

After checking in, Jack was able to leave the base but as he got into his truck, he contemplated the situation. The command wanted to send him back to a line platoon, but he remembered what that was like, and didn't want to go. He had heard that First Reconnaissance Battalion was at the same camp as the one he was on, and remembered that before leaving Las Vegas, he had performed the recon screening and passed.

Being thirty-one years old and having the experience and knowledge of military life, Jack formed a plan and walked over to First Reconnaissance Battalion headquarters only a few hundred meters away. He marched straight up to the battalion sergeant major's door and asked to speak with him.

"How do I get over here to Recon?" asked Jack, as he handed the senior marine his paperwork. The sergeant major took a look at his service record book and at his appearance and announced, "Come back here Friday and we'll get you in, but if you screw up, I'm sending you to 2/5."

"Thank you, Sergeant Major," said Jack, who then turned around and walked out.

The very next week Jack checked into First Recon Battalion and was sent to Alpha Company, Second Platoon. The platoon was on its way to the desert of Twenty-nine Palms for training, and Jack was going with them. It was a wake-up call for him. He hadn't put on a heavy pack in years, and to top it off, his teammates had it in for him. They didn't like how he made it to the battalion, and they were determined to make him prove his worth during the desert training. He carried his weapon and pack, as well as the five-gallon water jug, extra radio batteries, and the hide kit. It was a long few weeks, but in the end, Jack showed that he could hang.

Over the next year Jack had to relearn many tactics. The last time he operated, it was in a two-man sniper team, as opposed to the six-man recon team, but it wasn't hard for him to adjust. Before long he became the assistant team leader. He also passed the Basic Reconnaissance Course and took on the role of team sniper.

A year and two months passed before Jack was told that his unit was going to Iraq. There had been speculation that it was going to happen, so he wasn't totally surprised. In fact, he was excited because he'd been waiting for something like this for the last decade.

In January of 2003, First Recon Battalion loaded on ship to float to the Middle East. The boat ride was forty-three days, and during this time the recon marines trained hard. They readied their Humvees by welding extra racks on the top, practiced battlefield trauma, shot their weapons, and went over their operating procedures. By the time they reached Kuwait they were ready for war.

The marines waited and trained in Kuwait for a short while. Jack made sure to zero his sniper rifle and taught one of his teammates to spot. Soon the marines received their ammo and explosives, and Jack also received ammunition for the sniper rifle. He even took one round and deemed it "The One." He polished that single bullet every day and kept it in a secure place because it was going to be the bullet that he got his first kill with.

Everyone was anxious to start combat operations. As far as they all knew, it was going to be a ferocious fight, but they were ready. Jack also mentally prepared himself for what was to come. Finally on March 17, orders came down for everyone to load their vehicles because they were heading to the Iraqi border. But there weren't enough Humvees to carry all of the teams. Unfortunately, Jack's team was stuck riding in a five-ton truck. Although the truck was crammed full of marines and their packs, nobody was too upset, because they enjoyed the security of all of the firepower consolidated in the back. At the border the marines waited for another few days until they were unleashed.

It had taken Jack over ten years to reach this point. He was one of the oldest operators in the platoon, and he felt that maybe the younger guys weren't as prepared as he was. But as he looked around, he could tell that the other marines had also been waiting for this. It was their time as well, and he was sure they would prevail in combat.

When it came time to cross the border, everyone was on full alert. Driving into Iraq, Jack noticed that the scenery looked much like some of the places he'd trained. He sat at the back of the truck with his binoculars, searching constantly. His main priority was to spot the enemy before they spotted him. It was an intense feeling waiting to meet the enemy on the battlefield, but for the first few days there was no action—until they reached An Nasiriyah.

Just before First Recon Battalion arrived in Nasiriyah, it was said that there was stiff resistance in the city. As far as Jack knew, the major fighting was happening at two bridges crossing the Euphrates River. He heard that a few amtracks were destroyed and that a battalion formed a perimeter and was in a heavy firefight. Recon's mission was to move up to the Euphrates River and become the support-by-fire element for the marines crossing the bridges.

While driving into the area, Jack quickly realized how dangerous the situation was. Helicopters fired rockets onto the other side of the river, while ground troops traded bullets. The noise was thunderous. *This is what combat is supposed to be like,* thought Jack, as he dismounted the vehicle. He jumped from the five-ton, while assuring that the sniper rifle was securely on his back. It was in a drag bag so he could have his hands free to carry his M4.

The entire battalion was moving through the palm groves toward the river. The vegetation on the banks gave them concealment as they patrolled. Jack could see that the other side of the river had places for the Iraqis to hide, but it wouldn't be hard to search for them through his optics. When they were close enough to the river, the marines were told to find an individual position and dig a hole just big enough to lie in and shoot from. The gunfire from Jack's unit started when he began to dig. He hurried, and when he was finished, he loaded his sniper rifle and made sure to put the polished round on the top. Then he searched for people across the river.

This was a dreamlike moment for him. He was used to finding

targets while training but now, finally, he would be looking for real targets. Although he wanted to shoot, he took his time and relaxed. With no laser range finder, he would have to use the methods that he had been taught to find distances. He even had a calculator for exact formulas. Meanwhile his teammates were already shooting at Iraqis across the river.

The M40A1 is capable of effects on targets past 1,000 yards, and Jack reasoned that his teammates were able to take care of anyone closer than 500 yards. He made reference points to objects across the river and started to look for shooters. His attention turned to a man who was standing just past 700 yards. He had an AK and stood watching the area. It was obvious that the Iraqi didn't think he was in the range of small arms. He was only moments away from learning that he was wrong.

Jack was shooting for center mass; he squeezed the trigger to send "The One" into the man's chest. But instead of recoil, there was only a "click." Surprised, he ejected the round to check whether the primer was dented or not. It was. Immediately, he knew that he had spent too much time polishing "The One." He worked the bolt to chamber another round, and when he focused on his target, the man was gone.

Disappointed, he started to search again. The Iraqis had realized they were outmatched, and they began to disappear. Jack had the discipline not to engage the closer targets, but couldn't help himself when he found a man at 500 yards. It was an Iraqi who was also searching for targets—but his sights were on the marines. Using the 7.62 by 51 mm NATO match-grade ammunition, Jack tagged the man, who was standing still. He instantly collapsed, with no chance of surviving the chest shot. Minutes later, an ambulance recovered the body.

It was his first kill, but Jack didn't dwell on the moment. There were plenty more targets, and he soon found another one. He was searching near a reference point, when he caught a man with a rifle running in the distance. A moving target isn't always an easy shot, but Jack knew it would be relatively easy, because the Iraqi was moving exactly right to left though his scope. After repositioning his rifle, Jack put a lead on the Iraqi, and while keeping the rifle as steady as possible, he pulled on the trigger. The AK in the gunman's hand pumped back and forth as he ran. When the bullet hit him it looked as though he were sliding for second base. He took a headfirst dive and tumbled out of sight.

The other marines around Jack were in skirmisher trenches, each taking shots. The enemy was trying to keep up with the gunfire but they were overwhelmed. As the entire battalion was shooting, other marines were pushing across the bridge. Suddenly, from behind the marines, more gunfire opened up. They were taking fire from both sides. Jack rolled to his side to get a better view behind him but wasn't able to see. The bullets were landing closer now, and Jack moved to the radio operator's position to hear the traffic over the net.

"Do not let anyone go into the tree line!" Gunny yelled over the radio.

Just as Jack realized what was said, three marines ran toward the trees just twenty-five meters away. It was a corporal who took two junior marines to go and engage the enemy. As they made their way toward that area, enemy mortars began to fall inside the palm grove, and explosions went off close by. The three marines who were separated immediately came back. They were shaken but their lives were spared.

Two hours passed before the area began to calm down, but it was evident that a major engagement had taken place. The marines from Second Platoon pulled back from their positions and consolidated with the company. It was Jack's first experience of war, and it had lived up to what he had thought it would be.

The next morning the battalion drove through Nasiriyah. The gunfights had cooled down, and only a few stray bullets flew toward them.

Riding in the five-ton was uncomfortable for most, but Jack didn't mind except for when they called, "Gas, gas, gas!" and everyone scrambled to put on their heavy MOPP suit and gas mask. Then it became a little strenuous. It didn't help that it was amazingly hot, and driving through the desert made it all the more miserable.

On the back of the vehicle, Jack went back to observing. He would have the convoy stop regularly, so he could scan the forward area. Some of the other marines thought he was a little weird, but in a scout/sniper platoon, Jack remembered spending hours and hours behind his optics with the intention of finding one thing out of place. It was that one thing that could be the difference between life or death. After passing through Nasiriyah, the battalion stopped for a resupply. Jack was looking toward the left of his vehicle. In the distance there was a wall, with houses behind it. Something caught his attention. Small round holes that looked unusual compared to the background stood out from over the top of a wall. When he looked closer, they looked like the Russian-made BM-21 multiple rocket launcher tubes mounted to the vehicle. He immediately radioed higher. A patrol was sent to check it out, and Jack had been right.

The battalion traveled day and night. The towns they passed

through seemed empty and desolate, but then again, they were advancing quickly through them. Jack got word that they were going to be used as a flanking element in a town called Al Gharraf. An infantry battalion, reenforced by tanks, artillery, and light armored vehicles, were engaged in the town and wanted recon for support.

The battalion was going to try to flank the enemy fighters. When the recon marines arrived at the city, they moved off the main road. Jack noticed that they were following a donkey trail on the side of a hill. It was awkward to see a thirty-five-vehicle convoy traveling though people's yards. When they were close to the top of the hill, Jack could hear explosions. The convoy was only on the hill for a few minutes before they started to receive fire. The enemy was at a distance, but their bullets were still landing close by. Jack and his team, as well as the other marines, dismounted their vehicles and began to travel on foot. He was caught off guard at the odd sound of an incoming mortar that landed only twenty meters away.

"Wow, that's what a mortar does, huh?" is all that Jack could say, while the concussion and blast passed over him. More began to land. It was weird for Jack to see mortars dropping around him, but he was more in awe than fright. After he took cover, Jack pulled his rifle from the drag bag in hopes of finding the enemy, but he was unsuccessful.

Meanwhile, the city was under intense fire. The marines were in a defensive position on one side of the city, shooting all they had. The Iraqis were moving throughout buildings and on the roads, trying to shoot at the marines. The two sides had been exchanging fire for hours. Smoke billowed from within the city, a result of bombs, missiles, and artillery. Recon battalion wanted to join the fight, but the only way they could get permission to do so was if they traveled directly through the city to link up with the other unit.

Jack was still sitting down when he got the news.

"We're doing what?" was his reply when he was told that they were actually going to speed through the city.

The pucker factor for Jack jumped a few notches when they traveled back down the hill. He kept his head low as they made a left turn to get onto the main street running through the city. Sweat was pouring from his body, and he wiped it from his eyes while bullets struck the side of his truck. The sound of bullets hitting metal is never good. The enemy was firing on them from windows and rooftops. RPGs flew by and exploded on the other side of the road. But the convoy returned fire. It sounded as though everyone was shooting. The smell of gunpowder filled the air, and Jack looked at the driver of his truck. He was leaning down as bullets hit the hood. Jack turned and began to shoot as well. The vehicles were traveling so fast that it was impossible to pinpoint the enemy. One of the grenadiers was letting loose with his grenades. Jack tried to shoot through any window he could, but when he stood up to get a better shot, the truck hit a bump causing him to lose his grip. He almost fell out of the back of the truck.

Once he gathered his composure, he looked around. Power lines were lying in the middle of the street, cars were on fire, and smoke was rising from buildings. It was a sight straight out of Hollywood. After about ten minutes of driving, Jack looked forward, and through the smoke he could see the barrels of the tanks, light armored vehicles, and the infantrymen. It was a relief to see them. Jack thanked God after they moved through friendly lines. It was miraculous that they made it through what they deemed "the Gauntlet," and only one person was injured.

That night the battalion dug in and got some rest. Jack thought about how easy it would be to let the fog of war overwhelm a person. In the midst of combat it was a challenge not to let emotions and adrenaline take over. The key for him, however, was to let training and decisiveness be the answer.

The next day the battalion was tasked with taking an airfield. Jack and his team were still in the back of the five-ton as they made their way toward that area. One day before they made it to the airfield, Jack found that they had been rerouted. Apparently, in a town farther back, a Humvee had flipped over. The three marines that were in the vehicle died, but only two of their bodies had been recovered. Reports began to circulate that the other body had been left behind and was being desecrated in the town. First Recon Battalion was going to be in support of the main unit as they went door to door trying to recover his body. In the city, the battalion held position on a main road. Jack set his rifle up on the cab of his truck. The sun was blazing overhead while he searched for anyone trying to shoot toward the marines. He began by looking directly around the infantrymen who were patrolling the streets. Then he moved forward of them. His spotter was searching, too, when in the distance, he caught sight of a man in a doorway holding an AK and looking toward the marines. Jack and his spotter had to get the range to the Iraqi quickly and request permission to take the shot. It was approved. Jack realized the shot was going to be a hard one. The distance to the man was 1,140 yards. The man was still in place, so Jack aimed in and took a deep breath while closing his eyes. The center of his crosshairs was well above the man's head when Jack squeezed the trigger. The jerk of the rifle caused Jack temporarily to lose sight of the man. He hurried to get back on sight to see if the shot had hit him, but the man was gone.

"Did I just hit him?" asked Jack.

"Yeah, he went down," answered his spotter.

"Describe it for me, because I couldn't see it," said Jack.

His spotter had seen that the bullet dropped the man right where he stood. Other marines in the back of the truck had seen it as well. It was a great shot. Hours passed and no other shots were fired. In the end, it was reported that a couple of Iraqi doctors had found the marine's body and buried him.

The next day the battalion made their way back to the airfield and cleared it with only a minor incident. On their way to Baghdad they came upon another town but a few hundred meters outside of it, they were ambushed. Jack pulled his rifle from the drag bag while the shooting increased. He started to hunt when he was called up to the lead vehicle. It was pulled off to the side of the road, and as he ran up, he was told that he needed to find the bad guys who were holding the convoy up. Jack found a position to shoot from while the first sergeant stood over his shoulder. Mortars began to fall around them as the first sergeant ordered Jack to shoot.

"Did you see him? Take the shot! Take the shot!" he yelled, as Jack looked for anything. But he couldn't find any targets at first. Eventually he did find a few and the first sergeant was amused when Jack killed three of the enemy.

Days later the battalion was entering Baghdad. Jack was astonished at the number of people gathered and waiting for them. Thousands of Iraqis crowded the vehicles as they drove into the city. He was worried about someone's throwing grenades into the back of their truck, but the crowd was cheering for the marines. It was a feeling of accomplishment for Jack to be a part of this.

In Baghdad, Jack mostly took part in overwatch missions for the marines around him. The battalion stayed in Baghdad for two days before moving into a nearby base. They stayed at the base for a few weeks before driving to Kuwait in order to fly back to the United States. On the plane, Jack contemplated his first experience of war. He had thought that the enemy would put up more resistance. He was surprised at how fast the time had gone by and all they had done during that time.

Eleven months passed before Jack was slated to redeploy for Operation Iraqi Freedom II. His time spent at home seemed short. The training his unit underwent in order to deploy was intense. The recon marines were in support of the Eleventh Marine Expeditionary Unit (MEU). Jack was promoted to team leader as well as sergeant, and his role as team leader and team sniper caused more stress than normal. He went through the Special Operations Training Group (SOTG) training with his platoon, and immediately afterward, he attended the Urban Sniper Course also held by SOTG. Finally, after six months of training with the MEU, Jack and his platoon were ready to deploy.

It took thirty-six days to float to Iraq. Jack had an idea of what combat was going to be like and the anticipation wasn't as extreme as it had been on his first trip over. After landing in Kuwait, the marines disembarked, and with their vehicles, they traveled for days to the city of Najaf in Iraq.

They reached the area of operations in early July and covered the lively cities of Najaf, Nasiriyah, and Fallujah. The heat was unbearable to some, but Jack didn't mind most of the time.

From the first day they reached their destination, Jack and his marines were responsible for vehicle patrols throughout the cities. They also helped with escorting coalition convoys trekking from base to base.

A few things had changed in the year that he had been gone. Traveling through the cities and on the roads was more risky now, and the marines were taking a chance every time they left the base. Roadside bombs were becoming the main enemy. Also during the invasion, U.S. troops had known who the enemy fighters were. Everyone with a gun was considered hostile then, but now the rules of engagement stated otherwise. Plus, the enemy fighters were now called "insurgents" and had no identifying uniforms. The mood of the locals had changed as well. It wasn't the same welcome they had the first time.

One of the main areas they patrolled was the city of Najaf. The city is home to over half a million people and is the capital of the Najaf province. Within the city, Jack learned there were boundaries for his patrols. It was astonishing to him that they couldn't enter certain neighborhoods. But during this time the Mahdi Army controlled those areas. The Mahdi Army is a group of Shiite militants created by the Iraqi cleric Muqtada al-Sadr. Initially the group wasn't hostile, but by the end of April 2004 they engaged in battles with coalition forces.

On patrol, Jack and his marines traveled in a pack of six vehicles. Their desert-colored Humvees became home when they were away from base. He kept his sniper rifle in a drag bag attached to the side rack of his vehicle, so when it came time for action, all he would have to do was to slide the rifle out and get to work. Their mission was relatively simple at times, and they typically set out on recon patrols. They passed through areas to gather intelligence and then reported back to higher. Jack already trusted his platoon commander's leadership, and he quickly realized and appreciated his initiative as well. Once, when they were traveling through a neighborhood, a group of men, obviously hostile and aggressive, stared the marines down as they passed by. Suddenly the captain stopped the convoy in the middle of the street and asked one of the men why they were angry at them. The men were upset with their community living conditions, but the captain explained that if they were to take control of their area, and not allow militants to run the area, their conditions would be just fine.

After three weeks in country it seemed as though his tour would be dull; however, after one incident, Jack was squeezing triggers again.

He was on patrol when he heard the news over the radio. Militants had shot down an American helicopter in Najaf. A quick reaction force was sent to secure the site where the UH-1H crash had landed, and they were ambushed. A firefight ensued that resulted in the death of one marine.

This would prove to be a fatal mistake by the militants of Muqtada al-Sadr, because in the next few days, over 3,000 coalition forces backed by U.S. airpower and mechanized vehicles would attack the group's strongholds within Najaf.

On August 5, 2004, the battalion landing team of the Eleventh MEU and other coalition forces entered the city searching for militants. Recon platoon was attached to a line company to sweep through the world's largest cemetery located in the city. It was reported that 2,000 fighters from the Mahdi Army would be waiting.

It was well past sunrise as the marines made it to the cem-

etery. Rows of headstones and tombs spread as far as the eye
could see. Jack carried the sniper rifle on his back as his team
took to the far right flank. He was already drenched in sweat
while they moved into the area. It was to be a daunting task.
The militants knew the area well, and it would be difficult to
corner them. They had also spent weeks setting up defensive
positions and booby traps. It didn't take long before Jack heard
the familiar sound of bullets snapping nearby. He knew that
someone was shooting, and he wanted to return fire. But when
he scanned, he wasn't able to see anyone. The cemetery looked
endless. Thankfully, the marines on the ground had help.
Above them, attack helicopters pushed forward and fired their
ordnance. The rockets sent from the helicopters hissed overhead and not only destroyed insurgents but also motivated the
marines. Within hours it was a vicious fight. Jack kept constant
communications with his team. He didn't want anyone to get
separated in this maze of concrete.

Soon mortars landed near Jack while enemy gunfire surged.
The rush of combat was intensifying. Jack briefly spotted fighters in the distance, but he knew that his bullets would only suppress the enemy, because they were firing short bursts before
taking cover. It was nerve-wracking and frustrating, trying to
move through the cemetery. In order to go forward, the marines
had to take their attention off the enemy to climb over and move
around obstacles. The space was severely limited. Jack desperately wanted to use the sniper rifle but he needed to stay on line
with the rest of the platoon.

It was impossible to clear all of the gravesites, and many
were locked from the inside, but Jack and his team tried to
search as many as they could. When the team came across wires

that obviously led to IEDs, Jack thought back to the night before when he watched AC-130 Spectre gunships rake the cemetery with their firepower. He realized that they must have blown most of the explosives that the insurgents had set in place.

The marines made it to their line of advance and set up a defense. Their superior airpower had killed many of the fighters, and now they were on the opposite side of the cemetery. Jack inspected the houses that were across the street just 100 meters away. He positioned his sniper rifle between two headstones and waited. Later, a resupply truck came, and the marines were surprised to receive fresh grapes. Jack was lying on the concrete thinking about how odd the experience was. It was 120 degrees outside, and he was devouring cold, juicy grapes while people were shooting at him.

The area across the street was mostly quiet with the exception of an occasional gunshot. While searching, Jack found a hole in a wall 156 yards away. He oriented his team members to the opening, and asked them what they thought it could be. It was too dark to completely identify what was on the other side of the hole, but Jack thought it was a mortar tube set to aim down the road. He called the platoon commander on the radio and told him what he thought it was. He also requested permission to shoot and was cleared to do so. It was his first time in his second deployment using the sniper rifle, and he was excited. He put two well-aimed shots into the hole and was satisfied that he had hit whatever was on the other side.

To the left of Jack's team was a first sergeant from the battalion. Jack asked him to take his marines over to investigate the scene. The older marine simply said that it wasn't his show. Jack reminded him that he was one of the most senior men on the line, but the first sergeant just shook his head no. Jack was disgusted at his lack of desire to take control of the situation, but he could easily recognize the drill instructor mentality. He immediately ran down the line to his platoon commander to ask the same question, and he was told to take a seven-man patrol to check it out. Jack gave the vehicles in support an idea of what the foot patrol was doing. It was an electrifying feeling for him to take point man, but he didn't want anyone else to do the dirty work.

They moved up to the first house and stacked up against the wall. Jack looked to his left at the other team leader just before they breached the gate, which led them to a courtyard. The gate was unlocked and they rushed into the opening. In front of them were rockets with wires lying about. Jack turned to his right and was startled as he realized that he was staring down the open end of a 74 mm recoilless rifle. The rifle is capable of being, and is usually used as, an antitank weapon. Luckily for them, it was unmanned. The courtyard was empty, and they moved into the house.

It was an exciting duty, clearing houses and each time was different. The possibility of booby traps and close-quarter battles was always present. But the marines specialized in that environment, and they smoothly cleared each room. The house seemed empty, but Jack came across one man. He surrendered with his hands up; however, Jack's adrenaline was still flowing, and he aimed at the man's chest almost squeezing the trigger. He knew that the man was an enemy fighter because he had a gunshot wound, but he wasn't armed. At the last second, Jack lowered his weapon although he felt like killing the man. It was disgusting that the cowardly Iraqi could shoot the marines but then surrender once he was wounded.

When the area was cleared, Jack grabbed the recoilless rifle and walked out with it proudly. It was great to know that the weapon couldn't be used against anyone else. Soon one of the gunnery sergeants took the wounded man and the captured weapon back to base, while the rest of the marines moved up into the housing area.

The marines took to the buildings and later in the day, as everyone was resting, a single bullet tore through one of the windows. Jack crawled into the room to examine the entrance of the bullet. Everyone wanted to find the enemy sniper, and eventually most of the marines were searching for him. Jack estimated the direction of the shot and moved into another room to begin seeking him out. He placed himself in the mind-set of the shooter and found likely sniping positions. It wasn't hard to surgically plant a single round into the likely enemy sniper positions. But after Jack would do so, he made sure to leave his shooting position and move to another room or window. Three hours of this went by before the marines were called out of the building. The operation had come to an end. It was stunning to the men that they could go through all of this and end up not finishing the job.

Back at the base camp, Jack finished debriefing his experience. It was routine. He sat next to the recoilless rifle that he had helped to capture and pondered whether he knew any of the marines who had been killed during the mission. He was in thought when a photographer for the *New York Times* approached.

"Did you hear the story about this?" asked the photographer.

Jack just smirked and said, "No, tell me."

The photographer told the story of how a gunny and his men had captured the gun and an insurgent.

Jack was disappointed that the gunny would lie for glory, especially when he had left the combat zone, and marines were giving their lives out there for one another. Normally, he would have brushed it off, but just for principle, Jack told the man the truth and how it really happened.

On the twenty-fourth of August the marines finally got permission to go back into the city. The militants had been delivering rockets and mortars and were regularly shooting at the marines. It was only a matter of time before coalition forces reacted. Jack prepared his team again for what was to come. The day before they were to go into the city, artillery and fighter jets prepared the targets. Precision guided bombs destroyed the militants' strongholds and hideouts.

Early the next morning Jack and his team traveled with the infantrymen into the city. They were on their way to raid a hotel building that was a suspected hideout. City lights were still on and dogs howled as the marines moved in. Jack had his NVGs (night vision goggles) locked into his helmet, and they were covering his eyes so that he could see. Everything was quiet except for their vehicles.

One block away from the building, the marines stopped. Jack slung the sniper rifle on his back and organized his team. They were attached to the squad that was breaching the door and entering the building first. When the raid force made it up to the building everyone stacked on the outside wall. Jack was in the lead of his team but was in the rear of the infantrymen. After the squad moved up to the door to make entry, Jack heard what sounded like a scuffle and looked toward the front of the stack but saw nothing unusual. Moments later, the marines were in the building. On his way in, Jack was surprised to see a bloody Iraqi lying just inside the front door. An RPG was on the ground beside him. He would later find out that the point man had killed him.

The point man had been preparing to throw a grenade into the room before entering. He had put his M16 against the building and reached for a grenade, but just as he did, the front door swung open and a man holding an RPG stood two feet away. The two killers stared at each other for a moment and then reacted. The young marine instinctively reached for his knife as the Iraqi aimed his weapon, but the marine was on him in a second, stabbing him in the face and neck.

Inside the building, Jack could hear the grunt lieutenant yelling for a recon team to clear the basement. Jack was tasked with clearing the roof and holding security with his sniper rifle. The other recon team found the officer and the stairs leading to the basement. Everything seemed quiet amidst the chaos, and Jack heard someone throw a grenade down to the basement. It clanged against a wall and bounced a few more times before exploding. The blast injured a few men who were waiting to ambush the marines. Moans and screams could be heard throughout the first floor. Jack was waiting at the base of an elevator shaft with his team. He could see up to the fifth floor and could tell where the levels were, because rebar stuck out of the walls and pointed up at each level. As Jack looked up he could hear the other team descending into the basement.

"Hey, they're moving!" someone said from the basement.

Jack recognized the marine's voice. It was the other team's SAW gunner.

"Shoot 'em!" was the reply.

Jack chuckled when the SAW gunner laid down a twenty-round burst of fire. The gunshots reverberated throughout the building.

The basement was clear, and Jack was about to head for the roof when he heard a faint yell and the sound of someone falling. He turned around and asked the marine behind him if he heard the same thing. Jack tried to search the stairs, but everything was too dark, so he pulled out his flashlight to examine the area. When he looked into the elevator shaft, he was surprised to find a marine hanging from the rebar. He had fallen five stories and miraculously bypassed all the rebar. But his legs caught the bar before he hit the basement floor.

Jack tried to pull him up, but his sniper rifle was in his way. The marine was moaning as Jack took his rifle off. He couldn't help but think that a piece of bar was sticking through his chest. Jack told him to hold on, because it was going to hurt when they lifted him out. Another marine helped to pull him out, and he was screaming in pain. They searched his body for blood and for any life-threatening wounds and he was immediately evacuated.

Minutes later Jack was on the roof. He and his team stayed there until the next morning, and then they moved forward a couple of buildings. He and his team took over a three-story house and stayed there for three days. The roof was good for sniping, and Jack took advantage of being ahead of the grunts. The battalion snipers were in the hotel, so he would be able to find targets farther than they could. By midafternoon on the second day, an unbelievable amount of mortars began to rain down. Everyone stayed low, but in between the impacts Jack could see men with weapons running in the distance. He tried to keep an eye on them, but the explosions were distracting. Close to ninety mortars fell in the volley, and Jack prayed that none would land directly on his rooftop. When the barrage was over, he looked over the rooftop toward the men. He could see that they were launching RPGs toward the building he was in, but the rockets weren't exploding. They simply bounced off the ground and skidded to a halt. It was amazing that no one was injured by the rockets and mortars.

Jack struck gold when he found a man who was using a telescope. He was standing behind a building with the optics looking toward the marines. He had to be the one calling in the mortars. Jack quickly positioned his rifle to where he could shoot. He aimed for the piece of equipment and fired. But the target was small. His bullet landed close enough to cause the man to move, but it wasn't precise enough to hit him. A minute or two passed before the man came back, and Jack caught sight of his head. He aimed in and steadied his rifle, but the man moved just as he shot. It was a disappointing feeling that he wasn't able to get the kill and the man never returned.

Suddenly, another round of mortars began to splash down, but this time the mortars landed in a tighter group than the last. For a moment, Jack was stunned. The noise and concussion were overwhelming. When he came to his senses, he looked to his side at his spotter. Blood was flowing from his mouth and his shoulder. Confused, Jack asked him if he was all right, while he looked over his body. One of the rounds had landed on the side of the house while the spotter had had his head over the side of the building. Downstairs one of the marines was injured as well. In the end it was discovered that the mortars were friendly.

The mortar men had been given the wrong grid and fired upon the house.

Four hours later, as dusk settled in, Jack found another gunman. He was walking to the curb of the street and setting in an IED. He must have thought that the haze of darkness was covering him. Jack took aim as he set the IED down. The masked man didn't know that a set of crosshairs was leading him as he turned to run away. The first bullet that Jack fired sent him to the ground, and in a matter of seconds, Jack pumped two more rounds into his body to finish him off. *No mercy for these cowards,* thought Jack, as he remembered his partner getting injured hours earlier. Minutes later, a man came out to drag the body away. He was an easy target, and Jack put one round in his chest.

The marines were pulled off the roof after the third day. Later, Jack took part in a raid on a parking structure that was full of car bombs and other explosives. The major part of combat operations came to an end, and the recon marines went back to patrols.

Over the next six months Jack and his team would conduct over 200 combat patrols in Iraq. In the end, he knew that taking lives was not what he imagined it to be. It was just a job for him. He fully realized how important life was during a routine patrol one night. They had set up a checkpoint to search vehicles for weapons, explosives, and insurgents. A short time afterward, a van sped toward their checkpoint. It was common for suicide car bombers to drive into coalition vehicles, and everyone had that in mind. A couple of marines fired at the engine to disable the van, but it didn't stop. In the next few seconds Jack and the other marines had to make a decision whether or not to engage the van. They knew of fellow marines who had been annihilated by bombs like these, but they also knew that the locals sometimes unknowingly sped through checkpoints. The decision was to stop the van. It was too dangerous to let it get any closer, and they opened fire. Unfortunately, only civilians were in the vehicle. The instant choice that was made is just one that presents itself in the realm of combat. That night Jack realized that every life was sacred. He would later find out that his first son was born around the exact same time as the incident.

9

November in Fallujah

Name: Sergeant S., Memo
Billet: Scout/Sniper Team Leader
Area of Operations: City of Fallujah, Al Anbar Province,
 Operation Iraqi Freedom II, September 2004–March 2005

By November of 2004, the war-torn city of Fallujah proved to be a thorn in the side of U.S. forces. The peace accord made after Operation Vigilant Resolve, which took place the April prior, had unraveled. The terms of the agreement were not enforced by Iraqi officials, who promised to police the city for rebel activities. Instead insurgents ran much of Fallujah, and the marines who encompassed the city as their Area of Operations recognized that the region was dangerously out of control. But October was the turning point; U.S. forces began air strikes within the city to eliminate specific targets and to prepare for Operation Phantom Fury.

The purpose of the operation was to regain control of the city, and to do so before Iraq's January elections. Finally, on

November 8, after weeks of bombardment, ground troops began the push into Fallujah.

On the night of November 7, along the northwestern fringes of the city, the Third Battalion, Fifth Marines waited for the order to attack. They were part of over 8,000 troops storming the city, and their mission was to help secure one of the most dangerous areas—the Jolan district.

Sergeant Memo, the team leader of a two-man sniper team assigned to the battalion headquarters element, wondered why the attack was scheduled at sunrise. Marines always had the advantage at night. But when he learned that not every marine had thermals or night vision, it made sense to wait until daylight, in order to prevent friendly fire.

Memo and his partner, Sergeant Pasciuti, talked about their role. It was to move into and clear an apartment complex with the infantry. When the building was secure they planned to set up on the fourth floor and hunt for insurgents. They also wanted to get into position quickly, because they were carrying plenty of equipment. Pasciuti packed the 50-cal (SASR) and an M16 with the M203, while Memo used the M40A3, an M16, and a shotgun. Both had pistols as well. It was unusual to see an individual in a sniper team carrying a shotgun, and people questioned Memo's reason for using one. He knew it would come in handy for blasting through locks and clearing rooms.

That evening, Memo found a satellite phone and called his wife, knowing that it might be his last time hearing her voice. From the news she knew about the assault but he told her his job in Iraq was to help out on a rifle range and that he was safe. It was believable, because a year earlier, he did work on a range. It was the recruit rifle range on Camp Pendleton, California, and he had been a marksmanship instructor there for three years. He felt bad lying to his wife, but it gave him comfort knowing that she wasn't worrying about him.

Memo had been a marine since 1997. A native of El Paso, Texas, he joined the infantry only because it was the fastest way to become a sniper. As a kid, he always mimicked the snipers from the movies when fighting in BB gun wars with his friends. Growing up, he yearned for the time when he would be sniping for real. He also wanted to carry on the tradition of serving in the military, because his father had been in the infantry during Vietnam.

Before sunrise on the morning of the assault, the battalion staged outside of the city. When the command came down to strike, Memo and Pasciuti climbed into an armored Humvee on their way to the battlefield. This would be their baptism into combat.

The sound of helicopters and explosions were the first things Memo noticed as they moved closer to the city. His mind had begun to play out scenarios that he might find himself in during the fighting when suddenly the shooting started.

From the city, small-arms fire opened up on the vehicles. Groups of insurgents fired machine guns and lobbed mortars. The gunners in the turrets returned fire, and men in the back of the trucks shot from the sides. Memo looked over the top of armor toward the city but couldn't see the enemy. This made him wonder what everyone else was shooting at. The gunfire lasted minutes before the convoy stopped in front of the apartments. The breaching element was the first to move toward the complex, and when a hail of bullets from the insurgents snapped around them, Memo thought it sounded like pulling targets in the pits at the rifle range.

Planning to use a different entry point into the apartments than the other marines, Memo and his partner broke away and headed for the front entrance. As they rounded the corner, Memo quickly realized the mistake. There was no entrance on that side, and now enemy bullets passed close by and pounded the wall next to them. He remembered from a map study that the only thing separating the apartments from the city was a set of railroad tracks from which the insurgents shot. Looking at his partner, Memo told him to turn around and Pasciuti wasn't about to argue. When they went around the corner, Memo saw the last man of a fire team enter the building, followed by a burst of gunfire. Memo put the buttstock of the shotgun in his shoulder, expecting the worst as he entered the room.

Something caught his eye as he moved through the doorway. It was a man lying in a pool of blood near the far wall. The man's body was only partly exposed because his legs were behind an improvised barricade, and an AK was near his head. A young SAW gunner looked toward Memo and asked if he was in trouble for killing the man.

"You're good, Bubba. Just keep moving," Memo replied. But Memo was momentarily transfixed on the man who was lying on the floor, because it was his first time seeing a dead person up close. Moments later he and Pasciuti were clearing rooms on their way up to the fourth floor. Outside, the rest of the battalion was entering houses and buildings. The fight was on.

The apartments were quickly deemed clear and the two snipers took up positions on the fourth floor. Once in a room, Memo recalled what he was taught from the urban sniper course. The first thing he needed to do was set up a shooting position. He found a baby's cradle and placed it ten feet back from a window facing the city. After turning it onto its side, he laid a door on top, making a stable shooting platform. Pasciuti used the side of a refrigerator to observe from.

Memo stripped off his flak jacket and helmet and crawled behind the gun. Through the scope, he happily scanned the nearby houses for insurgents. He was finally hunting for real.

Having spent three years on San Diego's Marine Corps Recruit Depot rifle and pistol team, Memo was a highly skilled rifleman. On the team he had the opportunity to travel the United States and even to England to participate in shooting matches. In the beginning, he was nervous, but as his experience grew, so did his skill. One of the more proficient subjects he prided himself on was being able to call wind, and during sniper school he had done it so well that his partner shot a perfect score on qualification day. By the time Memo left the shooting team he had placed first in a few events and was one of the most seasoned shooters.

Back on the cradle, Memo was frustrated. He knew that he was good at finding targets but the machine gunners seemed to be better than he was. Every time he found someone to shoot, the machine gunners beat him to the kill. This happened more than a few times, before it dawned on him that he could shoot farther than everyone else. At the same time Pasciuti asked what to do with the SASR. It made sense to use both weapons, but because the SASR was so loud, Memo didn't want to be in the same room as it when it went off, so he helped Pasciuti set up next door.

In his room, Memo started to search again, but the housing area that he was watching was complicated. The buildings seemed to run together, and it was hard to tell where one began and one ended. Fortunately, the doors and gates to the courtyards were different colors, and he used them as reference points. While finding the distances to the doors, he stumbled across his first target.

Initially, it didn't look like the insurgent was doing anything wrong. He was facing Memo but didn't have any weapons. When he turned around, however, Memo could see a bundle of green RPGs protruding from the top of his backpack. He checked the distance to the man, and it was at 505 yards. After adjusting his dope, and making sure that his shot would clear the window-sill, Memo aimed in. It was his first live target through a scope. Fixing his crosshairs center mass, he started a slow squeeze on the trigger, but the man turned into a building and out of sight before the shot was fired.

Even more frustrated, Memo looked elsewhere but was unable to find anyone. Twenty minutes passed and everyone seemed to be firing but him. He wondered how, in all-out com-bat, he was the only one incapable of finding anyone to shoot. But minutes later, he found a target. It was an insurgent who ran into an alley and stopped next to a wall. Memo used his laser range finder to locate the distance to the wall, and translated it onto his scope. The man was wearing all black garb and was handling an AK before he started running toward the complex. Memo took aim on his lower stomach knowing that the bullet could land higher. He didn't want to miss another opportunity, and he applied slow but steady pressure on the trigger.

After the shot was fired, Memo tried to fight the recoil in hopes of staying on target, but it was pointless. When he regained focus, the man was standing still. In an instant, Memo began to doubt the shot. He knew, however, that the zero on his scope was good, because he had spent two days confirming it. He watched the man for a moment and noticed that he was staggering forward. Memo quickly aimed at the same spot and fired. The bullet, which was traveling at 2,600 feet per second, connected with the man's head as he fell forward. Brain matter spattered throughout the alley and wall behind him. It was a lucky shot. Memo contemplated telling his partner but was embarrassed, thinking that he was the only sniper not getting "one shot, one kill" results.

After looking over his first kill, he began to get greedy. He wanted to up his kill count and hungrily scanned for more fighters. After a short time, though, the insurgents began to hide and stay behind cover. Memo wanted to check up on his partner, so he went over to his room. Pasciuti was behind the SASR and was hunting as well. Memo was using his binos to spot for his partner when he noticed a man with his head sticking over the top of a red gate. The man stood in place for a few seconds, pulled out an AK, and shot before disappearing. Memo kept an eye on the gate and the man did the same thing again. Memo told Pasciuti to focus on the center of the gate, and he would let him know over the radio the exact moment to shoot.

Memo ran to his room and found the red gate. The range was 400 yards even. He informed Pasciuti, and they both waited for the man to return. Within minutes, he was back. Memo could see the top of his head as he was moving around the courtyard. Then he settled behind the gate. Memo told Pasciuti to shoot. The discharge from the SASR was deafening. Memo was watching the gate as the first shot rang out. The man's head and upper body tumbled backward but out of sight. The second shot flung open one side of the gate. Memo let his partner know that it looked like a kill, but he couldn't confirm, because the body wasn't within his view.

The longer the marines stayed in the area, the scarcer the targets became, and in an hour of searching, Memo hardly found any. Soon a navy SEAL sniper showed up at Memo's position. Memo gave him an update on the area, and the SEAL disappeared into a room nearby. When the SEAL began firing, Memo went over to his room and asked him what he was shooting at, because he couldn't find any targets. The SEAL was using a .300 Winchester Magnum, which meant he could shoot farther than Memo by about 400 yards, and he was firing on targets at that distance. Memo hid his anger until he went back to his room. He was irritated that the SEAL was invading his hunting grounds. But he came to his senses and realized that they were both on the same team. Soon Memo went over to the SEAL's room and challenged him to a competition; they would see who could shoot the most targets. To confirm the shot, they would have to go to the other person's room and look through that person's scope at the body. For the rest of the day, Memo and the SEAL traded fire until nightfall. Occasionally, Memo would be amazed at the will of the insurgents. He shot more than a few who were able to run away after they'd been hit.

That night the battalion staff held a meeting and concluded that the companies would enter the city the next day. Memo and Pasciuti were disappointed after finding out that they would be staying back at the apartment complex with the headquarters element while the rest of the sniper teams went into the city.

The next day, the battalion blew a path through the railroad tracks rather than travel through an underpass that was suspected of being rigged with explosives. As the battalion pushed into the city, the marines at the apartments received several mortars and rockets. Memo and Pasciuti traveled west of the apartments to observe the area.

When the sniper team returned to the complex after sundown, Memo was ordered to attend the battalion staff meeting. He was warned that the battalion executive officer was angry and wanted to talk to him. After the meeting, the officer pulled Memo aside.

"I don't care what you have to do. I want you to kill the people mortaring us!" he said. The challenge was appealing to Memo and Pasciuti, and they were excited to have a direct mission.

Based on the information they were given from intel, the enemy mortar teams weren't skilled enough for long-range mortars. They would have to be within eyesight of their target. On the first day, the team left the complex before sunrise. They found an observation position in a building west of the apartments and searched all day for the enemy mortar team. Memo was disappointed when he had to report that they hadn't found anything. This was especially frustrating, because the apartments had been fired upon again.

The second day was no different from the first, and again the apartments were mortared. Memo attended the staff meeting where the officer called him out in front of everyone. He asked Memo what good his team was, because they were supposed to be experts at finding enemy targets, and they couldn't find the mortar men. That night Memo took it personally and planned on finding the men.

The morning of the third day, Memo and Pasciuti found a rooftop west of the apartments. When they started searching, they could see palm groves next to the Euphrates River farther west of them. They could also see buildings to the south. As the sun began to rise, the team was searching for target reference points when they noticed a farmer who was working in a field close by. Minutes later the farmer strolled toward their building. When he was within a hundred meters, he put his hands in the air, because Memo aimed in on him with his M16. The farmer moved a little closer but never looked at the snipers. Instead he walked up to a bush next to their house and began to talk to it.

"The men who shoot at you, from field," he said to the bush while pointing to the edge of the palm groves. "If they know, I die," he said, indicating that if the insurgents found out that he had told the marines, he would be killed.

Memo and Pasciuti weren't sure if they should trust the farmer, because it was unusual to be given that sort of information. They decided to change houses just in case they were being set up for an ambush.

They found another building, but also made sure to keep an eye on the area that the farmer had designated. Memo and Pasciuti spent the entire day searching but came up empty-handed. Toward the end of the day, they were down to their last battery for the radio, and the sun was still overhead. Memo was scanning with his binos when suddenly he spotted a flash of light in the palm groves. He didn't think much about it, but decided to look at the area through a spotting scope. As he focused, he saw the back end of a white pickup truck. The light that he had seen was a reflection off the back window. The pickup was in reverse when Memo spotted it, but soon it stopped.

Two men got out of the passenger's side and walked to the rear of the truck. When they dropped the tailgate, one of the men pulled a tarp from the bed, and they both climbed into the truck. Memo saw one of the men grab a tube and position it upright. It immediately dawned on him that this was the mortar team.

"I found them," he told Pasciuti, while reaching for the laser range finder. But Pasciuti didn't believe him until Memo gave him the spotting scope.

Memo lazed the truck three times so he could get the average distance to the vehicle. It turned out to be 950 yards. Memo knew that it was going to be a long shot, and he prepared the rifle. Pasciuti was stunned and excited when he saw that it was the mortar men, and he grabbed the radio to inform the battalion.

Memo adjusted the elevation knob on his scope and looked at the vegetation around the truck to see what the wind was doing. He estimated that it was moving six to eight miles per hour from left to right. Pasciuti confirmed and then radioed the battalion for permission to engage. The battalion denied the snipers because the direction of the shot might have caused a round to hit the friendly troops on the other side of the river. But Memo knew that his shot wouldn't affect anyone but the enemy mortar men, and he decided to engage anyway.

Two men in the back of the truck were easily distinguishable. One man had on a dirty-looking light brown shirt with black slacks. He also had his back turned to the team and was bent at the knees working on the tube. The other man was wearing a crisp white shirt and was standing closest to the cab. Memo set his crosshairs on the center of the light brown shirt. He took a deep breath, causing the crosshairs to dip below the truck and then rise as he exhaled, settling on the man once more. It's common to let the recoil surprise you while squeezing the trigger, which Memo did. Moments after the shot was fired, both Memo and Pasciuti spotted the impact. The bullet landed below the truck, but was directly in line with the target. Memo didn't wait for the men to move. He corrected his sights and aimed well above the same target's head and fired his second shot. The man with the light brown shirt slumped forward onto the tube when the bullet struck him. Memo naturally chambered another round and aimed above the man with the crisp white shirt. He was looking down at his partner when Memo fired. The third bullet tore through the white shirt and into the man's upper torso, sending him stumbling backward. Falling against the cab of the truck, the man reached for his chest.

The marines from the apartments heard the shooting and called the sniper team over the radio. Pasciuti tried to get Memo's attention, but he was focused intently on the last target. When the second man went down, the driver got out of the truck and walked to the side of the bed. He looked surprised. Memo had a side view of him and thought he was going to run for the tree line. Instead, he darted for the driver's seat. He wouldn't get far, however, because just as he lifted his foot to get into the cab, Memo fired. The man fell to the ground but managed to scramble into the cab. Memo wondered if the man was hit or just frightened, and soon the truck began to move forward. Memo aimed where he thought he could possibly get a head shot and fired. Moments afterward, the truck rolled to a stop.

By now the battalion was yelling for the team over the radio. Pasciuti told them that they had engaged three men with four shots, but the battalion wanted the team to abort the mission and report to the complex. Memo was ecstatic and Pasciuti congratulated him. They both packed their gear, and in minutes they were patrolling swiftly back to headquarters. They were moving next to a road that had houses on either side. When they were within 200 meters, Memo grabbed the handset from Pasciuti and requested permission to enter friendly lines. Just as he was through talking, a marine manning a machine gun opened fire toward them. The snipers leaned against a wall and were furious that they were being shot at. Suddenly, an RPG passed by them and exploded near the apartments.

The snipers realized that they were sandwiched between the guard force and an RPG team. Pasciuti was the first to react. He was shooting behind Memo, when Memo turned and transitioned to his M16 and began to lay down fire toward three men with RPGs standing next to a truck. Pasciuti told Memo that the guard force at the apartments wanted the snipers to move, because they were in the line of fire. Memo kept shooting until two of the gunmen appeared to be wounded. When the snipers moved down an alley and out of the way, they heard the marines from the apartments unload.

After the snipers made it back to base, Memo was proud to tell the executive officer that the mortar team had been eliminated. A patrol was sent to examine the truck. The man wearing the dirty brown shirt had been hit in the neck, the man wearing the crisp white shirt had been hit in the chest, and the driver was struck underneath the armpit. All three men had bled to death and in the back of the truck the marines also recovered ten mortar rounds and a base plate to the mortar tube but the tube itself was missing. The apartments didn't receive mortars for about six more weeks.

One week later, the sniper team was in a building due east of the apartments. They were hoping to counter-ambush insurgents who had been firing on supply trucks returning from the front lines to the apartments. They also kept an eye out for insurgent reinforcements. It was said that the enemy would be traveling through the open desert to get into the city. Because of that, no vehicles were supposed to be entering the city.

Memo was on watch while Pasciuti was sleeping close by. As a rule, most sniper teams never left the base without at least one claymore for security, and this team was no exception. Memo was sitting against a wall in the shadows and was looking out a window on the eastern side of the building.

Memo hoped to find unsuspecting gunmen as he scoured the windows and rooftops nearby. When he passed over the edge of the city with his optics, he noticed a dust trail and a vehicle. It was a truck. It was moving toward the city but still too far away for him to tell the exact distance. Memo radioed the battalion and gave them a description of the truck and the direction it was traveling. He asked if they would be sending air support to deal with it, but the battalion had no air assets available. They told Memo that he would have to engage it. Memo kicked his partner to wake him as he reached for the SASR. It took a minute to position the heavy sniper rifle. When it was in place, Memo had a good view of the truck, and could see men inside, but it was traveling too fast to shoot, so the snipers waited.

Soon the truck reduced its speed to pass over small ditches, which, luckily for the snipers, also doubled as speed bumps. The vehicle was moving from left to right through Memo's sights, and the men inside were holding weapons. Pasciuti found the range to the truck. It was 600 yards, and with that, Memo began to fire. The Raufoss round, which is what Memo was using, has armor-piercing, explosive, and incendiary effects on its target.

When Memo's first bullet (a 7.62 mm tungsten carbide pene-
trater inside the 12.7 mm bullet, traveling at over 4,000 feet
per second), hit the front of the truck, it ripped a hole into the
metal panel and sent sparks into the air. The truck had rolled
almost to a complete stop when Memo aimed near its center
and sent another round slicing into it. The truck coasted to a
halt, and black smoke seeped from it. As the men tried to get
out, the truck caught fire and was quickly consumed. Memo got
off the gun and called battalion to tell them that the vehicle was
disabled.

"Hey, Memo, the guys are stuck inside," Pasciuti said.

Memo thought for a second and told him to do them a favor
by putting them out of their misery. Pasciuti emptied the rest of
the magazine into the burning truck. When the cab was investi-
gated, machine guns and other small arms were recovered.

Two weeks passed before major combat operations in the
city were finished. Now, the main threat was coming from the
small pockets of resistance. U.S. forces learned the major difference in the two types of enemy fighters found in Fallujah. They
were labeled "martyrs" and "guerrillas." The martyrs waited in
barricaded rooms hoping to kill as many marines as they could
before they were killed. The guerrillas, on the other hand, used
tactics and their objective was to live to fight another day.

It was during this time that Memo and Pasciuti had been
helping with back-clearing operations. The objective was to find
and eliminate weapons caches that had been overlooked and
to kill insurgents that made it behind the advancing marines.
Usually for these missions Memo and Pasciuti split up and both
took other marines for security while they helped to provide
covering fire for the infantry.

One morning, Memo was involved with another back-clearing mission. It was hours after sunrise and Memo prepared for a long day. He was riding in the back of a seven-ton as part of a convoy. His sniper rifle was between his legs, and he was carrying the shotgun. He didn't bring his M16, because he had the security element with him. On their way into the city, sections of flattened buildings and wreckage lined the sides of the roads. Memo guessed from the damage that it would take a long time to rebuild the city.

As they entered their designated area, the seven-ton drove toward the center of the neighborhood. The plan called for the marines from the company to head for a different area to start their sweep. The snipers would take up positions on the center buildings to have 360-degree coverage.

At their destination, Memo saw two houses. He took his security element to the one on the right, while a four-man team seized the house to the left. The buildings were two stories high and seemed normal, but as Memo moved to the front entrance, he sensed that something was out of place. The front door was made up of wrought-iron bars with a glass panel behind it, but the glass was broken out and scattered on the ground in front. Memo glanced inside and saw a couch jammed against the door. He knew that a person on the inside could hear the glass being broken if it was stepped on. It was an early detection tactic that he'd also used. His mind raced, thinking of an alternate entrance, and he turned around en route to the back door. As he moved closer, he found an MRE (meals ready to eat) sleeve, which indicated to him that marines might be in the house. He radioed higher and asked if any other units were in the area and waited against a wall. The other marines lingered behind him.

Over the radio, he was told that no other units were around. Memo anxiously had turned to make entry when explosions, preceded by AK fire, resounded from the house next door. On impulse, Memo ran through the courtyard, sprinting for the other building. He could hear marines yelling and screaming.

The house was roaring with gunfire as he cautiously entered the door. A light haze filled the small hallway where he was standing, and he noticed something hit the wall next to him and roll toward his feet. His heart stopped when he realized it was a grenade. Scrambling backward, trying to escape the blast, he bumped into the marines behind him, but he was only able to turn around before the right side of his body was hit with shrapnel. The concussion hurt his ears, and it was worse than the throbbing coming from his legs and arm. Momentarily shocked, Memo realized that others were still trapped in the house, and he rushed back inside.

Past the hallway and to the left was a set of stairs leading to the second floor; to his right was the room and a wall. Four marines, who had soaked up most of the grenade, were injured at the bottom of the stairs. They were still trading bullets with insurgents who were no more than ten feet away at the top of the stairway. Memo wasted no time opening fire with his shotgun. He glanced at the leg of one of the marines whose cammies were soaked in blood. The marine was injured badly.

Memo yelled for support as he frantically pumped his shotgun to shoot and reload. Others rushed into the house and pulled the injured marines out of the building while Memo and another marine kept the insurgents at bay. Soon the insurgents disappeared from Memo's view, but they had a direct shot into the hallway leading to the door. They succeeded in keeping further marines from entering the house, thus trapping Memo and the other marine inside. A few insurgents dashed in and out of the doorway firing aimlessly while dodging Memo's bullets. Before long Memo was backed up against a wall that was ten feet from the bottom of the stairs. In between the firing, he heard the men on the second floor repeatedly yelling, *"Allah Akbar!"*

The two marines were alone in the house and didn't know how many insurgents were upstairs. Memo wished that he'd brought his M16. The shotgun was great for close range, but after five yards the "lock buster" ammunition dispersed and didn't have enough damaging effects on a target. But the enemy's bullets easily ripped into the wall just a few feet away from Memo. During a lull in the fire the other marine raced for the stairs and tossed a grenade up while Memo covered him. The M67 fragmentation grenade has a three-to-five-second fuse. Memo wondered if the marine remembered to milk it or hold the grenade, allowing the time fuse to wind down, before throwing it so that the enemy wouldn't be able to use it against them, but he knew the answer as it bounced back down the stairs.

The next few seconds happened in slow motion. A million things passed through Memo's mind. He wanted to run out of the room, but the doorway was being pounded by the enemy. As the grenade spun toward them, Memo pulled the other marine by the back of his flak jacket, trying to distance him from the blast. But in an instant they were both hit.

Before the blast Memo managed to lower his head and brace himself, but at once he felt shrapnel hit his face and legs. He realized that something warm was oozing from his ears, and the ringing in his head was unbearable. He opened his eyes to find the marine next to him lying on the ground. The marine was able to get to his feet but said that his leg felt broken. The two needed to get out of the house, but the insurgents still had the doorway covered and were saturating the hallway with bullets.

A window on the other side of the room looked like a good exit, and Memo contemplated jumping through it. The other marine wanted to race for the door, but Memo told him he was crazy and assured him that they would be killed on the way out. They had to do something fast. Memo was thinking of a way to get out of the house when suddenly, the other marine ran to the stairs and threw another grenade. This time the explosion killed one of the gunmen. Memo watched his body slump in the stairway and was stunned when the other marine turned and ran out of the house. Memo couldn't believe that he had left him. The marine barely made it through the hallway when the machine gun opened up again.

Alone in the house, the outlook was grim. Memo didn't have grenades, and his shotgun was useless. A looming feeling of death crept into his head. For some reason he thought about his wife. He was afraid that she was going to be mad when she found out he had died in combat, because he had told her that he wouldn't be involved in the fighting. He regretted lying to her.

Soon the gunfire stopped, but Memo wasn't going to fall for the deception. He knew that if he dared run through the hallway, he'd be cut down. In the disturbing silence that followed, he recognized that the enemy was probably forming a plan. Memo kept his eyes and weapon fixed on the second story. He guessed that the gunmen thought that both marines had run out because someone started down the stairs.

If I'm gonna die, I'm going out in a blaze of glory, he thought, as he concentrated the sights of his shotgun on a pair of white sneakers. Memo had the upper hand, because the enemy had to make it partway down the stairs to see him but he could see their feet first. Memo fired at the man but wasn't able to injure him. Instead the insurgent ran back up the stairs. Thinking of a way out, Memo again looked toward the window and was on the verge of running for it. Fortunately, he hesitated, because the men upstairs dropped grenades right outside of it, blowing shards of glass into his room.

Memo realized that he desperately needed to change weapons before another person came down the stairs. His sniper rifle was strapped to his pack and was useless in close-quarters battle. His last option was his pistol, and he reached for it, figuring that it would give him a better chance. After putting the shotgun between his legs, he aimed in with two hands, but it didn't feel natural. He was used to competition pistol shooting on the rifle team, which allowed only one hand. Memo took the weapon in his right hand while leaning against the wall with his left. His decision was to let the insurgents take a few more steps so he could get a better shot on their legs. He wouldn't have to wait long to find out if this idea would work, because soon another insurgent came walking down.

When Memo could see the man's knees, he shot and hit him in the ankle, which made him trip and tumble down the stairs. The wounded insurgent came to a rest facing Memo. He could see fear in the Arab man's eyes as he pointed the pistol at his face and fired two shots into his head. Blood splattered from the back of his skull. It was a gruesome kill, but Memo was unfazed—not out of cold blood but out of survival.

He heard more men upstairs and formed a plan. He decided to stay and shoot until they killed him or he was able to run out of the building. Moments later two grenades landed by the stairs. Memo was able to turn away from the explosions, but he questioned how many more grenades he could take.

After the blasts, dust filled the air, and another man charged down the stairs. Memo opened fire on his legs and wasn't sure that he hit the man, until he fell and landed with his back to Memo. In a flash Memo decided that he was going to paralyze the man and shot for his spine. But his aim wasn't surgical enough to cause the damage he wanted, and the bullets ripped into the insurgent's buttocks and back. The man was screaming hysterically, and Memo couldn't stand hearing him. He fired one shot into the back of his head, killing him. As he did so, another man came running down the stairs and caught Memo off guard. The insurgent stopped halfway down and while crouching, he fired an AK from the hip, spraying toward Memo. Memo swung his pistol toward the man and unloaded the rest of his magazine into his chest. From ten feet away it was hard not to notice pain in the man's face as he was hit with 9 mm bullets. The insurgent dropped his rifle while collapsing down the steps. Memo made the fastest magazine change of his life and refocused on the stairs. He wasn't going to be caught off guard again. Leaning against the wall, he could feel a severe ache in his chest, but adrenaline and fear dulled most of the pain. Luckily the SAPI plates stopped three bullets from entering his upper body.

The insurgent that he had shot was still alive and was screaming, *"Allah Akbar,"* at the bottom of the stairs. He was lying in the blood of the two dead men beside him. Memo screamed at the man, *"Shut up!"* Then Memo decided to keep him alive so that his screams might prevent others from coming down. But after a minute of listening to him, Memo changed his mind and shot him in the chest. A short while later, another insurgent tried to make it down the stairs, but Memo killed him easily. He wondered how many more men there were and was afraid that he might run out of ammunition.

It was unbelievable that the insurgents tried to attack, especially with the bodies of their dead companions lying at the base of the steps. But Memo killed two more before he figured a way to get out of the house. He remembered that he had a claymore on an outside pouch of his pack. His plan was to throw the claymore up the stairs and detonate it. Hopefully the explosion would face the bad guys and buy him enough time to make it out. He also hoped that the marines outside didn't shoot him.

He kept his aim with the pistol while sliding his pack off enough to pull out the explosive. When he put his pack on, he prepared the claymore. It took him a second to think over his plan but in a flash, he was running for the stairs. He had to move quickly because he was vulnerable. He holstered his pistol, because he needed both hands. At the bottom of the steps, he didn't bother to look up as he flung the claymore onto the second floor. The detonator was in his left hand, and he was smashing it before the claymore landed.

The explosion was powerful enough to destroy the upper portion of the stairs and a part of the ceiling. Memo was knocked unconscious when the rubble collapsed on top of him. He wasn't out for long, and when he came to, his mind was groggy. He couldn't remember what had happened and was confused to find himself lying under chunks of concrete. The room was filled with dust, and he could taste it on his lips. Quickly, he picked himself out of rubble, but he could tell that his hip was injured. He looked up to see that part of the stairs and ceiling were missing and realized that it had fallen on him when the claymore exploded. On the second level he could see four insurgents; they were bloodied and shocked from the blast. Memo checked the ground around him to see if he had dropped anything, and then rushed out of the house.

Outside, Memo ran toward the nearest Humvee. The other marines who had been shot or hit in the house were being helped, but reinforcements hadn't arrived yet. A marine met Memo and helped him to cover. Memo was dirty, bloody, and sweating but alive. The marine explained that they had called for backup to get Memo out. Also, they didn't know if he was dead or alive so they had denied an air attack on the building.

Memo let him know that there were still bad guys inside, and he noticed that the machine gun on the seven-ton wasn't being manned. He told the marine that they needed to fire on the insurgents to keep them trapped inside. Memo climbed into the seven-ton and asked the driver to pull up to the house. In the turret, Memo readied the machine gun. He didn't want anyone to get away. When the seven-ton stopped, he fired through the second-story windows of the house. He was able to get off two extended bursts before the weapon jammed. He knew how to clear the weapon, but when he went to fire again, it was useless. He asked the driver how to get the gun working, but the marine replied that he was "just a truck driver." Memo took the marine's M16 and unloaded five magazines into the house.

As he was shooting, four trucks full of marines arrived. Memo climbed out of the seven-ton and explained to them the situation. The wounded were being evacuated and Memo was directed to leave as well, but when he got into the truck he took one of the wounded marine's M16 and loaded his pockets with grenades.

Memo jumped from the truck and told the nearest marine to follow him. He ran to the house just across from the one full of insurgents, while the other marines gathered outside of the courtyard to assault the house. On the second story, Memo noticed that the marine with him was the executive officer. When they looked toward the other house, a few insurgents were running for the courtyard walls. Memo couldn't see exactly where they were but knew that they were pressed up against the wall about fifteen yards away. He and the officer stood up and threw grenades, but when they did, their position was compromised, and the insurgents threw grenades back. Memo tried milking one so that it would blow up over their heads, but it exploded too close for comfort. There was no more milking after that. Memo looked down at the marines beginning to form a stack on the wall, getting ready to go into the courtyard. Memo yelled down at them not to go in, and when he stood up, bullets sprayed the wall below him.

Moments later a tank could be heard driving down the road toward them. The marines on the ground pulled away from the wall, and the men from the courtyard ran inside as the tank drove into the driveway facing the insurgents' house. Memo threw a grenade as they ran, but the tank fired as well, knocking him to the ground. Minutes later everyone was ordered to clear the area, because fighter jets were inbound. The fixed-wing assets dropped five bombs—one on the insurgents' house and one for each of the four houses surrounding it. The marines didn't want anyone to escape.

When the insurgents' house was inspected, eighteen bodies were pulled from the rubble. Six were at the bottom of the stairs. The experience gave Memo a greater appreciation for life. He had eighteen pieces of shrapnel pulled from his leg, six from his right arm, and four from his face. He also had a stress fracture in his right hip from the stairs and ceiling falling on him, and a class-three concussion. Three bullets were found in the body armor on his chest. These had caused a broken sternum. But for him, the worst part was that he wasn't able to operate for three weeks.

10

Bad Comm

Name: Sergeant Longoria, J.
Billet: Scout/Sniper Team Leader
Area of Operations: City of Ar Ramadi, Al Anbar Province,
   Operation Iraqi Freedom II, February 2004–September 2004

The upper-level, blackened windows of concrete buildings in Ramadi went unnoticed by oblivious Iraqis in the summer of 2004. On the streets below, civilians performed daily activities while gunmen and insurgents moved cautiously amid the city, knowing that marine snipers, eager for the opportunity to kill, struck from lairs such as these. In the city, 1,500 meters from forward operating base Combat Outpost, an eight-man sniper team kept on watch from one such building. Their mission was to prevent insurgents from planting IEDs along the road below them.

Inside, Sergeant Longoria, a team leader, asked an ever-so-frequent and puzzling question, "What's wrong with the radio?"

"It's been going down all day," replied Corporal Finch, his

radio operator. They were using the AN/PRC-119B. The old blocky radio was heavier than the newer 119F and less reliable. Finch didn't appreciate having to use the radio, but it was the only one available to them at the time.

"W-we need to get it w-working," stuttered Longoria. He was sitting next to his best friend and the other team leader, Sergeant Lopez. Lopez was from California and Longoria was from Texas, but they had plenty in common besides the fact that they looked more like street thugs than marines, with shaved heads and tattoos. They met seven years before, after boot camp at the Infantry Training Battalion, and since then, they had been in the same platoon. Their duty station was with the Second Battalion, Fourth Marines and after four years in the infantry, they elected to try the sniper indoc. On their first try they both underestimated the challenge and failed, which meant they would have to wait two more years. When their second chance came they both passed. For Lopez it was a little more satisfying because he wanted to be a sniper as a young marine, but Longoria wasn't so sure. When he talked to a recruiter about joining the marines, he simply said that he wanted to "run around in the woods and shoot guns." But after years in the infantry Longoria saw the independence and responsibility of the battalion's snipers and their ability to operate as two- and four-man teams. It was then that he knew he wanted to be a part of them.

Once in the platoon, Longoria underwent training as a PIG. It was hard at first because he was used to being in charge and most of the HOGs were his peers. He was also a sergeant having to thrash for junior marines, however, he realized that experience as a sniper was senior to rank. And like most in the infantry, he learned from the beginning not to get upset by the little things and he paid his dues as a PIG until it was his time to lead.

In the room, Longoria's team rested. His assistant team leader was Corporal Corona from northern California. A former guard at San Quentin State Prison, Corona was the oldest, shortest, and meanest member of the team. Corporal Finch, the radio operator, was Longoria's go-to marine. He appreciated Finch's work ethic and that he didn't complain when something needed to be done. Corporal Stotts was the point man of the team and very intelligent. Longoria was glad that he was a well-rounded operator. The two teams were set on one goal, hunting insurgents. But killing insurgents was nothing new; they had been in country for six months, and by now it was a regular occurrence.

A mix of vehicles traveled the road outside, but orange-and-white-colored taxis were the majority. Like most snipers in Iraq, Longoria and his team played a dangerous game of cat and mouse with the enemy. The snipers commonly acted as the hunters but insurgents knew that they abided by strict rules of engagement. The snipers had to confirm and report enemy actions before they engaged anyone. As a result, insurgents often held the upper hand. They could disguise their activities, and by striking when they wanted, action-hungry marines became bored and complacent while waiting. But snipers are masters in the art of patience, and two months earlier Longoria used an unlikely disguise of his own to kill insurgents emplacing IEDs.

It was April and the snipers were assigned to IED duty. A road designated Route No Name, which was a detour from the main road called Route Michigan, also doubled as a shortcut for supply convoys traveling through the city hoping to avoid heavy traffic and ambushes. But as convoys used the road more frequently, attacks also increased, and soon Longoria and his team were assigned to watch over the area.

Route No Name connected to Route Michigan a quarter mile west of their base. Because of such a short distance the team patrolled on foot to the vicinity. The section of road they watched was in the open and they found limited positions to set up. One of the more frequent buildings that they used was called the AG Center, short for agricultural center. On the first mission Longoria noticed dusty books scattered in rooms as they moved through the building onto the roof. It seemed to be more like an old library.

By now the snipers had a routine once they found a position. One person was left by the stairs for rear security while the others observed. From the AG Center they could see 360 degrees around them and over 200 meters of the road. A soccer field ran along No Name, and one thing that seemed out of place was a giant, ten-foot-by-ten-foot bush at the edge of the field and only inches off the road.

After three weeks, the snipers were still unable to find insurgents. But convoys were still succumbing to IEDs and because of a limited selection of hide sites the snipers suspected that someone knew their positions.

On the night of May 15, Longoria decided to change tactics. When they moved onto the roof of the AG Center, he was determined to find another place to observe from. Waiting until it was pitch black, they sneaked through the area, moving through abandoned houses and fields before coming across the giant lone bush next to the road.

It's too obvious, Longoria thought, as he walked up on it.

Everything he was taught went against hiding in it. Snipers never used the most blatant positions and never set up without an escape route.

But if everyone thought that it was too obvious, then everyone would think that nobody would be in it, he concluded.

The next day, back at base, Longoria explained his plan to the team. He and the new teammate, Sergeant Endito, a Native American sniper from New Mexico, would wear their ghillie suits and lay in the bush. The other teammates would be on the AG Center rooftop, covering them if something happened. Nobody was to say a word about the mission because Longoria knew that the higher command wouldn't approve.

Longoria's teammates looked at him like he was nuts. The thought of using a ghillie suit in the city was ridiculous. Also, the bush was in the wide open and if somebody noticed them, one grenade could kill them both. But Longoria knew that if they were out of sight, they had a good chance of catching bad guys.

The next night the team set out for the mission. They made it to the AG Center at midnight. When 0200 rolled around, Endito and Longoria dressed in their ghillie suits and set out for the bush, leaving their helmets and flak jackets on the roof. Longoria was using the M40A3 with the AN/PVS-10 day/night scope. He let Endito take point because he had an M16.

Crawling into the bush, they hadn't anticipated the thorns. Two-inch-long barbs dug into their arms and legs as they shimmied under small branches. Although painful, Longoria was more amused at his partner. Endito was upset with the fact that he was wearing a ghillie suit in the city, lying in the most obvious place, and now he had to deal with the thorns. Longoria could antagonize him because Endito was a good friend. They were both accepted into the sniper platoon together and were now two of the senior marines. Longoria respected Endito; he was a good shot and graduated "high shooter" of his class. Although Longoria hadn't officially graduated sniper school, he attended the course three times and was one of the most experienced operators in the platoon. And because of his knowledge, he was elected team leader over some HOGs.

Nearby, Corona and Finch stayed out of sight but still kept watch. In the bush Longoria and Endito set aside their weapons and took turns resting. Before sunrise a series of prayers boomed throughout the city. As the morning wore on, Longoria asked Corona if he could see them, but they blended perfectly into the bush and the plan was working.

By 0730, the normal stream of traffic sped by on the road. The bush was so close to the road that it swayed after vehicles went by. Covered by vegetation and fully camouflaged in ghillie suits, Longoria and Endito were unseen by passing cars. They both gazed in different directions watching for anything suspicious. Strips of burlap on the ghillie suits acted as insulation and Longoria was trying not to doze off when Endito shook his shoulder.

"Hey, a taxi just stopped and tossed something out the window," he said.

But it happened so fast that he couldn't tell what the object was.

"If they come back, let me know," said Longoria.

Fifteen minutes later the taxi returned. Pulling to the side of the road, the vehicle stopped facing the snipers only 150 meters away. In the bush, Longoria and Endito turned their attention in that direction. The driver was the first to get out. He walked to the front of the car and opened the hood. It was possible that the vehicle was having engine problems but Longoria knew that it could be a diversion, and he reached for his sniper rifle. Slowly and quietly he positioned the weapon. He was trying not to catch his clothing on thorns and cause the bush to shake. Resting his face on the buttstock, Longoria honed in on the man under the hood and immediately realized how close they were. The man's body filled most of the scope and his head looked like a basketball. Moments later the rear passenger door opened up and another man stepped out. He nervously stood to the rear of the car looking in all directions. Longoria watched him, when suddenly the rear passenger door swung open again but nobody got out. Rather, a man leaned out under the door, revealing only his upper body. In his hands were a pipe and some wires. When he started piecing the objects together, it was all that Longoria needed for evidence.

"I'm taking 'em out," he said to Endito, but Endito wanted him to hold on until he radioed higher for permission to engage. It was the normal procedure.

As Endito grabbed the radio, Longoria sighted in on the man dangling from the backseat. With a left-side, upper-torso body shot, he located the man's ribs and armpit, hoping to put one in his heart. He knew better than wait for permission to engage because by the time they received it, the men would be long gone.

Sensing that Longoria was about to shoot, Endito anxiously whispered for him to "Wait, wait, wait!" But it was all that he could say before the boom of the rifle went off. The blast caused dust to fill the bush, but Longoria caught a glimpse of his target who after being hit, flopped on the ground outside of the car. Forced into action, Endito kneeled in the bush and opened fire with his M16. A heavy metal rocker, this was his dream. He was shooting at the driver, who managed to drop the hood and run for the cab. In the dust cloud, Longoria searched out the other man. He was by the rear passenger door and was helping the wounded insurgent into the car. For a brief moment Longoria found his silhouette and fired. With the driver in the car, Endito opened up on the man as well.

Unfortunately all three insurgents made in into the taxi and it sped backward. Endito was still shooting as they drove off.

"We need to get out of here," said Longoria. They were vulnerable and needed to move. Endito radioed for a quick react force. When vehicles arrived at the bush, they formed a hasty perimeter and allowed the snipers to pull out of the area. A huge pipe laden with explosives was found next to the road. It was an IED. After Explosive Ordnance Disposal teams detonated the bomb, the team moved back to base.

Later the snipers learned that two of the men died. Throughout the city, marines held observation posts. Minutes after Longoria and Endito wreaked havoc on the taxi, marines manning the observation post near the hospital reported that a cab dropped off two dead men but the driver left the scene. The command wasn't pleased with the team's tactics, but they couldn't argue with the end result. No convoy was hit with bombs on Route No Name as long as 2/4 was in town. But this wasn't Longoria's first engagement with the enemy in Ramadi.

His first firefight took place at Combat Outpost.

When the Second Battalion, Fourth Marines arrived in the city, the first couple of weeks were peaceful. The army unit they replaced explained that in Ramadi there was no action. Longoria was told that the enemy attacks were few and far between, plus when they did attack it was only random shootings and the gunmen would slip away before they could be caught. The main hazard was being hit with an IED. And so for three weeks, insurgents occasionally shot at and eluded the marines, but early April was the turning point.

Longoria and his team were sleeping when the shooting started. Hours earlier they had returned to base from a three-day IED mission and were exhausted. Lying in bed, Longoria quickly put his boots on and grabbed his weapon when he heard the gunshots. Outside, a squad prepared to leave base and Longoria asked one of the marines what the situation was.

"A squad is pinned down in the city, and insurgents are planning to take over our compound!" yelled the marine.

Longoria ran to the command post to get more information. Machine guns rattled in the background while the thought of being overran stuck in his mind. He was told that two squads and a sniper team were being ambushed in the city and the compound was next on the list for the insurgents. Also, he needed to get his team and take up positions with the guards on post. He raced back to his room and told the others the situation. At first they were upset at being awakened. They didn't fully understand the seriousness of it all. Longoria didn't have time to explain that marines were being killed in the city and the compound was the next target.

Longoria directed his team to spread out among different positions while he and Finch went to a post facing the city. It was fifteen feet above ground and just big enough to lie in. Doubled-up sandbags lined the inside walls and a small hole at the floor of the post was used for shooting. Before long the snipers received instructions on who to target. It was reported that the shooting began when a squad on foot patrol in the marketplace came under intense enemy fire from rooftops. The battalion told the snipers to search into the city and engage anyone on the tops of buildings sending signals about marine positions or with weapons. At first Longoria only saw civilians. He was looking for anyone using hand and arm signals or carrying weapons. While scanning, he came across his first target.

The man was standing 600 yards away. He was looking over the edge of a building while swinging his arms back and forth appearing to signal others to come or go. His body wasn't entirely showing; his legs were behind a wall. Longoria directed Finch onto the man. Finch gave Longoria the distance and he fine-tuned the scope, then took aim. Longoria had a method for shooting: he always aimed near the base of the throat. This way if the bullet was high it would impact the head, and if low, the bullet would hit the upper torso. Finch had the enemy at the bottom of his scope when Longoria shot. The man dropped, but out of view, and throughout the day Longoria hit seven men but was unable to confirm their death because they all fell out of sight.

When nightfall came they pulled out of their positions and received an intel update. That morning, insurgents planned a three-day jihad or holy war against the marines in Ramadi. But instead of being fearful, the marines were eager to encounter the insurgents because now they would fight face-to-face.

Early the next morning Longoria and his team returned to the posts. As the sun floated in the eastern sky, they knew it was going to be hot. Heat waves from the city's rooftops swayed upward through the team's optics. But it would also be a good day to spot vapor trail and Finch knew he would be able to see it perfectly behind a forty-power adjustable Leupold scope. Over the radio marines were told to be on the lookout for men dressed in all black with red headbands. Soon a squad on foot patrol was in a firefight 200 meters outside of the base. Longoria smelled gunpowder from the battle and searched that area for targets. It wasn't long before he noticed a white car turn a corner and stop next to a building.

A thin row of bushes stood between the car and the compound, and after stopping, five men congregated around the trunk. The insurgents believed the bushes would shield them from the compound, but they didn't know that through their scopes, Longoria and Finch could see right through the thin bushes.

"They're pulling weapons from the trunk," said Finch.

Longoria radioed the activity to higher and they were cleared to engage. With the car gone, the men started to move. Longoria aimed for his first target, setting the crosshairs on the insurgent's neck. After shooting, Finch watched the spiraling trace of vapor trail behind the speeding bullet. The round easily punched through the soft tissue of the man's throat and his legs instantly gave out. He fell in front of the other insurgents. Without delay they scattered, but were clueless about the direction from which the shots came and two made the grave mistake of running toward the bush. It was humorous to see them moving toward him and Longoria fired again, hitting another man in the upper chest. Finch watched him drop to his knees and come to a rest lying facedown. Another man was running toward him and Longoria took another shot. He wasn't able to tell the exact impact area but the man also surrendered to his bullet. Finch was cheering Longoria on, but Longoria was trying to find the two men that slipped away. When the shooting was finished, Finch could tell that Longoria was elated because he stuttered more than normal.

After the shootings Finch informed higher of the situation. A platoon was sent to inspect the bodies. They found the back of one insurgent's head blown out. The other two had holes in the neck and upper back. But to Longoria the feeling of killing the men wasn't as satisfying as knowing that he prevented the men from firing on other marines.

When the three days of jihad were over, 2/4 lost sixteen marines. The thought of dying in combat was always present for Longoria but as he attended the funeral for his fellow marines, he truly recognized that in Ramadi, his life could be over at any moment.

As the summer in Ramadi rolled on, the IED missions seemed endless.

It was late afternoon when Finch broke Longoria's intense gaze.

"The radio's working."

Longoria wanted to switch, but Finch didn't mind observing. He liked the idea of catching insurgents in the act and he helped to save a convoy from a vehicle-borne IED weeks before. It was afternoon and by chance they were drawn to a truck as it drove by their position. After making a U-turn and parking, the driver opened the hood and jumped into another car. Corona radioed battalion and they were able to stop a convoy just a few hundred meters away from the truck. Minutes later Iraqi police showed up. Behind binoculars, Finch watched six Iraqis approach the vehicle. As they circled the truck one of the men pulled on the driver's door handle and all of the men disappeared in a fireball. The blast shook the area and nothing was found of the Iraqi policemen.

At dusk, Finch switched observing with Corona. He noticed a taxi stop next to the Iraqi National Guard post just a few hundred meters away. The man driving approached the Iraqi compound and returned to his car; Corona asked Finch if they should call that in to higher. They decided not to because the man wasn't parked long enough to do anything and if he did, the Iraqis would have lit him up from the post.

At 2200, the snipers packed their gear and waited for extract. The MAP, or Mobile Assault Platoon, was usually the squad who extracted the snipers, and they didn't want to become sitting ducks by keeping their vehicles in the road while waiting for the snipers to exit the building. The team automatically knew that when the Humvees approached, they would meet them on the road. Longoria jumped into the second vehicle on the passenger's side. Across from him, Lopez posted on the cab for security with Finch right next to him.

The city was quiet while the marines headed toward base. Longoria appreciated the breeze as they drove. It was satisfying to know that he had completed another mission and now he could relax when he got back to base. Three hundred meters from Combat Outpost, Finch tried calling the guards for permission to reenter friendly lines. But as he was about to speak, the radio died again. Longoria was contemplating what movie he was going to watch that night when Finch spoke.

"Sergeant Longoria, I need your red lens flashlight to look at the radio," Finch said, agitated at having to deal with it once more.

Longoria remembered that it was in his left cargo pocket. He was holding the sniper rifle by the upper barrel with his right hand while leaning forward to dig for his flashlight. Suddenly, while Longoria was bent over, a brilliant flash lit up the night and changed his life forever.

The vehicle shook, and at first he was mystified by the light. He didn't hear or feel anything, but immediately following the blast his right arm was limp. Looking up at his teammates he came to the realization that they had been hit with an IED.

Finch was hunched over, breathless as the Humvee rolled to a stop. He also saw a flash and was then slammed against the vehicle armor. Although it had never happened to him before, he thought that this is what it must feel like to be hit by a car. He couldn't hear anything except a loud ringing and when he sat up, blood gushed from his head and face. The only thing he could think was to keep his helmet on.

Lopez was on the cab when the explosion rocked the Humvee. He heard Finch say something about the radio and turned to see for himself. Just as he faced forward, the blast went off, violently snapping his head backward, and it felt like being kicked in the face.

"Longoria, I'm hit," said Lopez.

"Me, too," he heard.

Longoria was sitting on the side of the vehicle nearest to the blast. After the explosion he recognized that he was injured and a single thought ran through his head, "How am I going to look after this?" he questioned. He didn't want to be one of the people that others stared at in disgust. His body was in shock and he couldn't feel any pain. He knew that they needed to exit the vehicle just in case they began to take fire and he yelled for everyone to get out, but the ambush that they waited for never happened.

The stunned marines leaped from the vehicle, as others gathered around and asked if anyone was injured. Longoria smelled flesh and powder from the bomb. Unintentionally, he had been holding his arm up the entire time. In all the commotion he didn't bother to check his wounds, but standing in the darkness he saw the damage.

From the middle of his right forearm to his fingers, his arm was split in half. The blast melted his skin and bone was protruding through. As the shock wore off he began to feel the agonizing pain. He couldn't see his middle finger, index finger, and thumb and then realized that they had slipped down into his sleeve and were rubbing against his elbow. Once Lopez saw that Longoria was injured, he reacted to his brother's pain. Although shrapnel was embedded in his face, he immediately jumped into the driver's seat while others helped Longoria into the back. Without waiting for the other vehicles, Lopez sped toward base hoping to save his best friend's life.

Longoria was beginning to feel light-headed. Blood gushed from his arm but another marine helped to apply pressure to prevent further blood loss. His arm throbbed and he tried not to panic, but at base he saw the damage under full light, and that's when he lost his cool. Lopez was also losing blood, and he passed out in the driver's seat after arriving at base.

In the medical tent, Longoria was stripped down. Lying naked on a table they applied a catheter and started morphine, and minutes later he drifted out of consciousness.

The next morning he woke up in a hospital. When it dawned on him where he was, he began to look around. The man in the bed to his left was missing his leg and the man on his right was missing his arm. Right then he knew that he wasn't in good company. It was an indication that his injuries were just as bad. He tried to sit up but was dizzy from the morphine and threw up on the floor next to his bed. Minutes later a man in a wheelchair came rolling into the room. Longoria watched as the man moved toward him. His eyes were purple and swollen, and he had bandages wrapped around his head.

"Hey, man, how you doin'? That was pretty screwed up what happened last night, huh?"

But Longoria didn't recognize him and asked who he was.

"It's me, Finch!" he said.

At once Longoria was comforted in the fact that he was with one of his own.

A few weeks later, Longoria was evacuated to the States. In the end he lost the use of his right hand. All the tendons, nerves, and bone from his mid forearm to his knuckles were blown out. The bone was replaced with a metal plate. Finch and Lopez took shrapnel and bone fragments from Longoria's arm to the face. Finch also had shrapnel in his brain. But both Finch and Longoria knew that if it wasn't for the bad radio, they wouldn't be alive. The explosion happened at the exact moment they were bending down below the armor of the Humvee.

11

Hunting in Husaybah

Name: Sergeant May, L.

Billet: Chief Scout/Sniper

Area of Operations: City of Husaybah, Al Anbar Province,
Operation Iraqi Freedom II, August 2004–February 2005

In 2004, as the sweltering Iraqi summer drew to a close, the calloused warriors from Lima Company, Third Battalion, Seventh Marines were preparing to rotate stateside. Their stay in the border town of Husaybah (pronounced "Who-Say-Ba") was originally thought to be nothing more than security and stabilization operations, but as their tour progressed, the marines did more fighting than stabilizing. Much to their relief, in late August, Baker Company from the First Battalion, Seventh Marines arrived to replace them.

Baker Company and an eight-man sniper team took over a small combat outpost northwest of Husaybah. The outpost had recently been named Camp Gannon, after Lima Company's commander, Captain Richard Gannon II, who died in a fire-fight while rescuing one of his wounded marines.

Camp Gannon sat between the city and the Syrian border, and actually, the west and northwest edges of the camp were only yards from Syria. Inside its walls were watchtowers, buildings, and tents. Four reinforced observation positions sat on every corner, and on the east end was the abandoned Iraqi National Guard compound, occupied by one squad of marines. The rest of the company lived on the west end. A strip of unpaved road supplied with razor wire and concrete barriers connected the two separate living spaces. South and southeast of camp, only 100 yards away from the marines perimeter, was the city limits to one of Iraq's most violent and dangerous cities, Husaybah.

Shaped like a square on the northwestern edge of Al Anbar province, Husaybah rests a few hundred yards from Syria. It was home to no more than 35,000 residents, but a majority of whom were local gunmen, gangs, and an overwhelming number of foreign fighters who easily slipped across the border and stopped in the city on their way farther into Iraq. Another threat to the marines was the local Sunni tribes who sympathized with the insurgency and often provided men for the cause. These separate groups didn't particularly mix, but the one thing that united them was the idea of killing U.S. servicemen.

The eight-man sniper team attached to the company was led by a twenty-eight-year-old HOG named Sergeant May. May enlisted into the marines from Jonesboro, Louisiana, in 1995. His motivation to join the military came partly from relatives who had been in World War II, but it was his cousin who was an Army Special Forces medic who made him really take the step.

He joined the corps as an infantryman and was sent to the

Second Battalion, Fourth Marines. On his first deployment he noticed the STA (Surveillance and Target Acquisition) Platoon. Their independence and small teams opened his eyes to another facet of the infantry, and he knew that he wanted to become a sniper. Plus, the idea of using a sniper rifle in combat was appealing.

Though he failed his first indoc because of land navigation, he promised to pass the next time, and did. Once in the platoon, he operated as a PIG for one year before graduating scout/sniper school on his first attempt. After sniper school, he deployed for his second time and was on his way to the Middle East for Operation Sudden Storm/Desert Fox. For May and his team the operation was nothing more than patrolling the border of Iraq from Kuwait and using sniper hides to report on specific areas. Although May hoped to use his rifle during this time, he was never given the chance.

In 1998, his time in the marines was up, and he moved back to Louisiana to work as a prison guard until September 11, 2001. Having been a sniper during peacetime, May always wondered if he could have done his job in combat, and he wanted the opportunity to find out. Following the terrorist attacks, he knew that America would retaliate, and he rejoined the marines. After a long process of paperwork, he was back in the corps. Unfortunately, he broke his foot, which delayed his operational status. At the time, Operation Iraqi Freedom had already begun.

When he was finally able to operate, he was assigned to First Battalion, Seventh Marines in Twentynine Palms, California, but it was early 2003 and the battalion was already in Iraq. After pleading with his command to let him fly over, he was granted permission and in April, he was in the war. He arrived at the battalion when they took control of An Najaf but unfortunately for him, major combat operations were finished and it looked as if there was no combat left. At first he was in an infantry platoon, but as a school-trained sniper he wanted to use his specialty. He fought to get into the battalion's scout/ sniper platoon and after a screening he was operating again. As a HOG, May was senior to most of the marines in the platoon and when he returned home, he became the chief scout/sniper. Roughly a year later his battalion was scheduled to deploy to Iraq once more.

In Husaybah, as the chief scout/sniper, Sergeant May's job was to employ his teams in order to assist the company as much as possible. He and Sergeant Butler, the only other HOG and team leader, didn't know what to expect at first, but with the trust they held in their marines, they were ready for anything.

In May's team was Corporal Avila, a former mortar man who earned the nickname "The Terminator" because of his strength and intelligence. May's spotter was Corporal Padron, who had been in the platoon the year before in Iraq. Although he failed sniper school, Padron had May's utmost confidence. Lance Corporal Kochergin was a former infantryman who just arrived to the platoon. A very professional marine, Kochergin didn't think twice about carrying the SAW. Later, May knew he had made the right choice by giving him that weapon, because he proved to be an animal with it.

Sergeant Butler also had a strong team in Corporal Crog, Lance Corporal Garcia, and Corporal Adams.

During the turnover brief, the information that May received about the city was eye-opening. The area was likened to the wild, wild west. He was told about the ferocious battles that the marines fought against insurgents, local gunmen, and Al Qaeda operatives in Husaybah. There was no Iraqi military force in the city because the Iraqi police and Iraqi national guardsmen had been massacred, and any remaining had fled. May was also told to expect IEDs, mines, car bombs, enemy snipers, constant indirect and small-arms fire, ambushes, and anything else that could kill or maim them. The news was uneasy yet exciting, and before long, Baker Company and the sniper teams were on their own.

One afternoon, three days after arriving at Husaybah, May was given the chance to use his sniper rifle. The incident started when a sergeant in charge of the camp guard found May and told him that they needed him and his rifle on observation post six. In his tent, May snatched his rifle and made his way to the southern post, while his spotter followed. Running through the camp, he was glad to finally be using the skill that he had trained in for seven years. When they arrived at the post, they were surprised to find it full of officers. Nevertheless, they were pointed to two men digging holes south of the camp on a road near the 440 district. The 440 district was a group of identical government homes that added up to 440, hence the name. After setting into a shooting position, May saw the men and confirmed their activity.

"I see them. What do you want me to do?" he asked.

One officer radioed the company commander, and he approved the shot, giving May the green light to engage. Adjusting his scope to 625 yards, May experienced buck fever. Not only was it his first shot in a combat situation, but the pressure was on, because behind him stood the company's executive officer. Also, the entire camp waited for the outcome because this was the first engagement.

In his sights, May focused on the chest of the man digging. His shooting position was flawless, and he took his time finding his natural point of aim. When he felt sure of the shot he squeezed the trigger. The bullet knocked the man to the ground and threw the tool from his hands while his arms flailed toward the sky. Stunned, the man next to him ran for his life. May put a quick lead on him and fired, but missed. The man ran out of view.

Shortly afterward, a squad was sent to recover the body. Surprisingly, the man was actually a fourteen-year-old, and he was still alive, but May had severed his arm with the shot. The teenager was given care by U.S. forces and during interrogation, he explained that insurgents paid him to dig holes for them. For May, the exhilaration of his first shot quickly passed, washed away by the anticipation of the rest of his deployment. He had only been in Husaybah three days, and he had shot a fourteen-year-old.

Soon the sniper teams began missions on areas of interest. These areas typically were roads that were constantly exposed to mines and IEDs. One of the roads was the main street running through town, called Market Street, which was never used by the marines, because they would surely be hit if they traveled it. The others were four roads that outlined the edges of the city and were the ones frequently traveled by U.S. forces.

A week after arriving, the sniper teams were tasked with watching the southwesternmost intersection of the city, because it had recently been rigged with an IED. May and Butler decided that in the city their teams would operate as an eight-man element. The concept was useful because they often needed to use houses that were occupied. If a house was occupied, one team gathered the family members in one room and kept guard on them, while the others hunted. The idea was the same if the building was unoccupied, except one team stayed on the bottom level for security.

In an abandoned house 100 yards from the intersection, the team waited for activity. Inside, four marines held security on the bottom level while May and Butler set up the hide. May found enough items to make a suitable platform to shoot from. Early the next morning, May was on watch when a man with a shovel walked into his view on the road. Through the darkened window, he tracked the man with his scope. His heart sped up because the opportunity for a kill was close at hand. The man didn't know that he was under observation, or he wouldn't have started to dig on the road. Whispering, Padron radioed the situation to higher. The team needed to be quiet so as not to give their position away. From 100 yards May could have shot him with a pistol, let alone his rifle.

The man was facing away from the house, and May had a direct view on his back. Aiming for his spine, May shot, instantly dropping the man. Amazingly, he was able to crawl a few yards before dying. Afterward, the team called for a vehicle patrol to pick them up, believing that their position was compromised from the blast, and because moving after a shot is elementary sniping. The Humvees arrived and the extract was smooth. May thought the rest of his missions would be this great, but he was mistaken.

Later in the deployment, May would understand that in an urban environment, it's not necessary to move positions, because the origin of his shots would almost always go unnoticed. Another thing he would come to understand is that the gunfire drew insurgents into the open.

As the snipers settled into the city, the action slowly esca-
lated. The roadside bombs increased, especially on the east side
of the city. The bombings were happening on the eastern side of
Market Street and the northern area of the East End Road. The
"East End Road" is a north-to-south-running road on the east
side of Husaybah. The road runs directly into Market Street,
and where the two roads connect is known as the "Intersection
of Death." Around the intersection was a mix of cafés, houses,
and shops. The marines were aware of the intersection because
as the name suggested, many marines and vehicles had been
destroyed there.

The sniper teams were assigned to cover the intersection to
prevent the bombings. They had been to the area before with
no luck and knew that it was only a matter of time before they
caught somebody.

When they began missions on the Intersection of Death,
they occupied houses north of it. Using an ideal shooting position, they had a straight shot to the intersection and cafés, only
a few hundred yards away. On one particular mission, May and
Butler were able to get a kill apiece.

The teams moved into position late in the night and at noon,
they spotted two men wandering from the café, just after the
city prayers. The two men were wearing black jumpsuits with
tennis shoes and carrying AKs.

"Let's wait to see what they're going to do," said May.

Butler was in the next room with his spotter, and the two
teams were communicating with handheld radios.

The two men stood outside of the café talking, as May's spotter called the situation back to the company. The company gave
the snipers permission to engage. From the different rooms, the

snipers chose their targets. The plan was to fire simultaneously on Adams's mark. He was in the hallway between both rooms counting down. On the count of one, they shot and killed both men. A car pulled up moments later and recovered the bodies. The snipers found out later that they had killed them, because the bodies were dropped off at the hospital.

When the company asked if the teams needed extract, May declined, because he wanted to see if any more fighters would rally. If so, there would be more kills. Later in the day, the teams spotted a man near the intersection. He was just west of it, close to the bridge next to the intersection. The man walked up from the riverbed, known as a wadi, that is full only during times of heavy rain. Because the man was digging in a known area of interest, the ROEs (rules of engagement) made him a target. May killed him. That evening, the team moved out of the area unnoticed.

As the weeks progressed, so did the attacks on the marines. The base received fire almost every day, and when the squads mounted vehicle patrols, the potshots turned into five- to ten-minute engagements. Also one day, the company had two marines shot in the head, on different sides of the city. May's team was dispatched, and they spent a week trying to find the enemy sniper. May found it tough to operate with the restrictions put on his team. He wanted to use vehicles to snipe from, but the battalion deemed it too dangerous, and the team wasn't able to kill the enemy sniper.

By mid-November, May and his team were pushing farther into the city. On one mission they were in an unoccupied house watching East End Road. Along the east side of the road ran a soccer stadium. The snipers took up buildings south of that.

From their house they had a good view north and south of East End Road. It had been three months since the team had done any missions on that road, and the men planting bombs felt comfortable enough to move during the day. May was using a vent to observe and shoot from. It was an awkward shooting position, because he had to stick his rifle into the vent before shooting.

The next morning, two men with weapons walked in front of the soccer stadium only 100 yards away. May decided to take a headshot. He alerted the team, and they all were able to see the outcome. May quietly set his rifle in the vent and moved his crosshairs onto the man. The platform was stable, and when he shot, the man's head flew back sending brains into the air. Butler, in another room, also made a great shot. He took aim on the other man who was running north. Butler was able to hit the man in the hip even though his target was running at a dead sprint, making him stumble to the ground. Even so, the man was able to crawl to the side of a building and out of sight.

When the shots were fired, it seemed that everyone from the houses poured out into the street to see what was happening. The marines tucked into the house, because if they were spotted, the situation could have gotten bad. Despite their caution, a man was walking by the house and was able to see May. The team immediately called extract and a CAAT (combined anti-armor team) team pulled up to their house. Usually the team only moved under darkness, but they knew that it was better to move out of that area. While driving off, May stared at the angry Iraqis throwing rocks at them.

By January, Camp Gannon was under regular fire. Mortars, rockets, and small-arms fire hammered the camp daily.

In Husaybah, a detachment from Second Force Reconnaissance was with Baker Company. It was near the detachment's time to move out of the area, and one evening they asked May for assistance. The force recon marines wanted to drive down Market Street, which to May seemed dangerous. He knew that these marines wanted one last firefight because no one, besides Amphibious Assault Vehicles, had driven completely down this road. The road ran straight through the heart of the city, and the enemy activity in that area was off the charts. The company estimated that the street was rigged with explosives twenty-four hours a day.

The detachment wanted May and his team to get into a position to cover them from the east side of the city while they moved down the road. This should have been pretty much an easy overwatch mission for May and his team. After the marines made it through the city, the snipers would extract and head for base.

On the evening of the mission, May briefed his plan to the elements involved. The sniper team was going to take up an old hide that they had used before, in an abandoned hotel. It offered a great view down Market Street. The CAAT team, using four vehicles, was to drop them off. Usually the CAAT team carried dismounts, but because of limited space due to the eight-man sniper team, they couldn't take any. Around 0130, the teams loaded into the Humvees and drove into Husaybah.

With all the gear that snipers carry, it's easy to forget items for missions, and as they left base, May knew that he was missing something. A gut feeling told him that something was wrong. He couldn't place it at first, but then he realized that he had left his HOG's tooth on his bedpost. Although he wasn't a superstitious man, he felt forewarned that something was going to happen.

He was thinking about the intelligence report from battalion that stated enemy fighters had an aversion to dying in the cold. It meant that they were not willing to fight if it was raining or cold outside. This was a comforting thought because it was drizzling and definitely cold.

The marines knew their way through Husaybah, but even if they hadn't, it was hard to get lost. The streets ran either north to south or east to west. This made the city packed with hundreds of small city blocks, like a checkerboard. If they did get lost, they remembered that whichever direction they traveled, they would eventually come to one of the city's main roads, whether it was the west road, south road, east road, or Market Street.

Under a soft layer of mist, the city was dark and damp, except for the occasional streetlight shining through the haze. On the narrow city streets, the marines passed courtyards and walls while driving east two blocks south of Market Street. Everyone was at alert on the small street, with NVGs strapped to their helmets. Sitting behind the passenger seat, May had his gear handy to exit the vehicle quickly. He wanted to be inserted east of the town's cemetery and then patrol into position on foot.

Near their drop-off point, the driver noticed something moving on the street south of them. At 0200, normally the streets were empty, especially in that type of weather. May looked to the right, down the next street when, without warning, an RPG hit the wall next to his vehicle. Machine-gun fire and AKs followed the explosion. The marines had driven right into a hornet's nest. They were unaware that insurgents had been reporting on their every move since they had left their base. Insurgents had checkpoints of their own in the city, and when the marines passed by, the enemy informed their attack force on the marines' location. By chance, the marine patrol had driven right into a well-planned ambush.

In the turrets, the machine gunners opened up firing toward the muzzle flashes coming from rooftops all around them. The Humvees sped up, and May saw through his door window that every time they passed through an intersection, enemy machine gunners were waiting to fire on them. Hearing the bullets hit his vehicle, May was angry that he couldn't fire his weapon.

Luckily, the marines weren't pinned in and they pushed through the ambush. Once on East End Road, they turned south to move back to base. The CAAT patrol leader radioed for the vehicles to follow close behind, and miraculously, no one was hurt.

Driving south on East End Road, the patrol was still under fire, but much less now. The lead vehicle was surprised to find a semitruck parked across the road, forcing the patrol to turn around. The patrol leader decided to turn back into the city. As the team leader for the snipers, May needed to know what the situation was. He was stunned to learn that they were moving back through the city.

"Are you crazy? Why are we turning back?" May yelled at the driver. "We just came out of that unscathed and you wanna go back through it!" But May didn't know that there was no other choice.

Driving back into the city, the marines anxiously waited to make contact. This time they were two blocks south of the last road, and when the vehicles passed through the general area, they received heavy fire again. The gunmen were on rooftops shooting the vehicles as they passed. As the marines sped up, the driver of the lead vehicle saw the road they were on was coming to an end. He turned north, and one block later, tried turning west, but misjudged the angle and crashed into a courtyard wall, getting stuck. Over the radio the driver yelled that he couldn't back up. In the darkness, May and the others couldn't see what was happening, but the vehicle commander told him the situation.

"I'll get my guys and we'll dismount," said May.

Outside, the desert night would have normally made May cold, but he didn't notice because his adrenaline was through the roof. He had stepped from his vehicle into a brawl, and was immediately aware of the RPGs destroying the area. The enemy fire was extremely close and their machine guns strafed the walls around him. Muzzle flashes lit up from the buildings down both sides of the street, but May realized that because it was so dark in the streets, the shooting wasn't accurate. Although the weather was nasty, it helped the marines because of limited visibility. May fired from the street while his teammates piled out of their Humvees and moved toward him. He directed them to set up a perimeter around the downed vehicle which was also taking fire.

Upon surrounding the vehicle, the marines went into action. Each held different sectors and began to fire. They had a slight advantage because of their NVGs but it was still hard to find targets in the dark. With his M4, May quickly scanned the roofs for outlines before shooting. He moved from marine to marine, orienting them on targets. Once, while he was telling someone to move forward, an RPG hit the wall a few yards in front of them, sending chucks of concrete everywhere. May was glad that he hadn't told him to go any sooner.

Minutes later, the second vehicle pulled the first one out of the wall. May directed his men to mount up, and soon they were driving again, still under fire. Vehicle one, the one that had gotten stuck, drove off toward base, alone. The three other vehicles were reversing to get room to make the turn. As the patrol started west again, toward base, May was relieved. He realized how easy getting shot could have been, and still nobody was injured. Speeding down the road, the patrol leader questioned the location of vehicle one, because they didn't have communications with it. They didn't know that vehicle one's antenna had been blown off and that they were already back at camp.

What happened next was stunning. The vehicles stopped and turned around. May couldn't believe what was happening. The patrol leader, unaware of vehicle one's location, made the call to turn back into the city to find the lost Humvee. Now as they drove back toward the fire, May was speechless. He wondered how many more things could go wrong. It was funny that he was actually participating in the worst-case scenario. He thought about telling the drivers to let his team out so that they could walk back to base, but knew that was unrealistic.

As soon as they moved back into the area, the fire erupted again. May hunched to the center of his vehicle, leaning away from the door. Their Humvee was the middle of the three. He stared through the windshield at the lead vehicle's machine gunner in the turret. It was Lance Corporal Cisneros, who was unloading on enemy positions as they drove. His 50-cal thundered. He was doing enough damage for all of the marines in the patrol, but just as they were nearing an intersection, May watched something zip from the darkness and into the lead Humvee. It was an RPG. The rocket smashed into the turret, sending flames and sparks into the air. Cisneros died instantly and shrapnel riddled all of the marines inside. The top of the cab caught fire and with everyone incapacitated, the Humvee rolled to a stop in the intersection, right into the enemy's kill zone.

The driver in May's vehicle was in shock, and May screamed for him to push through the crossroads or they would be hit by machine guns. The enemy was already spraying the downed Humvee and as expected, when May's vehicle sped through, it received fire. It was clear that they needed to get the marines out of the burning Humvee or they would be killed, if they were not dead already. After stopping, May jumped from his vehicle and yelled for the gunner to lay down fire up the road, to the north. The last Humvee also made it through the intersection, and everyone dismounted except the gunner.

Instantly, the marines were outnumbered and were taking heavy fire. May was next to a wall shooting at houses across the street when he noticed a vehicle commander standing next to him.

"We need to get your corpsman ready! There's gonna be casualties!" shouted May. The marine was in the process of throwing two grenades over the wall next to them, to kill anyone on the other side.

"We don't have a corpsman. He was in vehicle one!" the marine answered.

Murphy's Law was officially in full effect. May shook his head in disbelief. He looked back to the burning Humvee only thirty yards away, and two marines, the driver and A-driver, or assistant driver, were shuffling across the road. He could tell that they were both injured. Since May was the closest to the scene, they ran toward him. The A-driver, barely holding on to his pistol, was bleeding from his arm and leg.

"I can't fire this! What do you want me to do with it?" said the A-driver in pain. May told him to put it in a pocket, because he might need it later. He knew that the fight was going to get worse. As soon as the other gunmen in the city realized that they had disabled a vehicle, they would converge on the marines' position to try and finish them off. May led the two drivers to a causality collection point between a wall and a Humvee.

If we could hang on for a few minutes, the quick react force will be here soon, thought May. He started to apply pressure bandages on the A-driver, while the driver told him where his injuries were. May was able to see a small piece of shrapnel in his back, and he told him to get into the fight, because they needed every weapon available to make it out of there.

Although scared, May told himself to stay calm. He briefly looked around and grasped the entire situation. RPGs and bullets pounded the vehicles, walls, and road near him, and in a flash, he accepted the fact that he might not live through the fight. His wife and daughter passed through his mind. He understood the possibility of dying on that dirty street in the middle of nowhere, but he promised to fight until he was killed.

After applying the bandages, May was back in the firefight. He glided to the corner to see two marines opening the back passenger doors of the burning Humvee. It was Adams and Garcia from Butler's team. Butler and his spotter were in vehicle one, already at base. May was proud that they were doing the right things. The two calmly pulled their serialized gear and equipment from the burning vehicle, but both of them had been hit with shrapnel in the neck, back, arms, and legs. When they had their gear out, Adams had the presence of mind to climb back into the Humvee to pull Cisneros from his harness before the vehicle was fully engulfed in flames. When Avila saw his friends, he ran through a hail of bullets to help them. The insurgents, seeing the three isolated marines, let loose with all they had. Garcia reacted to the shooting and returned fire, along with May from the street corner. With lead landing all around them, Adams and Avila began dragging Cisneros across the road while Garcia laid down covering fire. By now the other marines were aware of the situation and two went to May's aid. They huddled near the street corner before stepping into the street, providing enough suppressive fire for the three marines to make it to safety.

May realized that his marines were injured, and although he hoped that Cisneros might have lived, once he saw him, he knew that there was no chance. The marine was missing body parts and badly burned. At the street corner Adams held in place while May carried Cisneros' body to the nearest Humvee, shielding him from the other marines in order not to lower the morale.

The insurgents closed in and RPGs were getting closer. In the mayhem, the situation looked bleak. The marines were trapped in the city with one destroyed vehicle, one KIA, four wounded, and everyone was running low on ammo. However, because the marine patrol had passed through the area twice already, May thought that the insurgents would soon be low on ammo, too.

At the casualty collection point, Garcia needed medical aid badly. The fog of war took him over for a minute, and he hesitated to get back into the fight. But after a few choice words from Sergeant May, Garcia took his weapon and joined the battle. He moved to the street corner and worked the M203 sending 40 mm grenades onto enemy positions. May admired Garcia's determination because he had a huge gash on his right arm and it was hard for him to load the grenades.

The fight had been going on for some time, and May was beginning to wonder where the QRF was. He reached for the vehicle's radio and informed the company of the situation. He gave them an assessment on the casualties and was told that the react force had been sent. With a larger force on the way, May and the patrol leader told the marines to mount up, but not everyone could fit into the vehicles. Avila, Padron, and Adams had to run beside the vehicles as they drove toward base. The last Humvee was left in the street, but thanks to Adams and Garcia, all essential equipment was removed before the vehicle was a burned crisp.

With six marines in his hardback Humvee, May had people lying across him. The marines outside didn't have to run for long, because soon they met up with the react force and were escorted back to base. At base the wounded were evacuated while May and the others loaded into amtracks only to go back into the city to secure the site. This time there was no action.

Adams and Garcia's injuries were severe enough to send them back to the States. It was reported that fifteen enemy fighters were killed in the engagement. May felt lucky to make it out without a scratch.

In the weeks after the attack, the camp began to receive an enormous amount of indirect fire. Mortars and rockets began impacting three times a day. The battalion was close to rotating home, and they wanted to relieve as much pressure as possible from the unit taking their place in the next few months. As a result, May and his team were tasked with finding and eliminating the mortar men.

Using counter-battery radar, the company had an idea of where the firing originated. They estimated that is was in the very eastern suburbs of the city, known as the H and K triangle. The area got its name because on a map, two roads and an open area dissect a congested housing area, forming a small triangle located a few miles east of Market Street. From intelligence, the marines learned that the mortar men were using mobile mortar teams. The men drove into the H and K area in trucks, fired their ordnance, and drove off east toward the nearest town.

May hoped to catch the men and get some payback, and little did he know that he would be the one doing the ambushing this time.

On the night of the mission, May and Butler led their sniper teams into the community from the south after being inserted in the open desert. The company was concerned that they were too far from base for a QRF to reach them in a reasonable time, so the patrol that inserted them stayed minutes away.

In the area, the teams took up separate buildings. May and his four-man team found a two-story abandoned house north of the northern road. Butler's team wasn't so lucky. The house they were in had a family. They gathered the civilians together in one room. Their house was north of the southern road, but south of May's team and one block over. This way the two teams covered both roads and weren't too far from each other. That morning the area was quiet, but in his hide, May had a bad feeling about the mission, and because of it, he nagged his team all day about noise discipline.

Late in the afternoon, about the time that Camp Gannon was to receive mortars, May heard over the radio that Butler thought his team was compromised. It happened when the son of the man whose house they were in pulled up in a car and knocked on the front door. Butler signaled the old man to tell his son to go away and stood behind the door while the two talked. When the son left, the old man acted strange and desperately wanted to leave with his family. Butler found out that the son knew they were there, and he had told his father he was coming back to kill the marines.

After hearing the situation, May warned Butler to hunker down because something didn't sit right with him. At the same time, one of May's team members noticed a group of older men congregating across the street. In minutes they were gone.

"Sergeant May, there's a truck with something in the back, over here," said one of May's teammates. May looked through the window and saw the truck. It was the typical Iraqi vehicle—an old white Nissan that had seen better days. A tarp covered something that resembled a tube in the bed. It was also less than 100 yards away. Instantly the whole team was ready to kill, and everyone positioned their weapons. Munoz, another sniper who came from Al Qa'im, was on the SASR. Kochergin was behind the SAW, Padron had the M203 grenade launcher with 40 mms handy, and May was on the M40A3.

May told his team to wait for everyone to get out of the truck before they started firing. Moments later a car and van, both loaded with men, stopped next to the truck. May thought they were waiting for the sun to go down before shooting, but instead the three vehicles started south down a road, toward Butler's house.

When the vehicles were out of sight, May grabbed the radio to warn Butler, but as he picked up the handset, gunfire exploded. The cars were able to surround Butler's position, and what they thought was a mortar tube mounted in the truck was actually a recoilless rifle. The powerful rifle sent rockets through the building, knocking holes through the walls. Men from the van and car were also shooting while Butler and his men returned fire.

Two of May's marines went onto the roof to see if they could support with the SASR but were unable to see anything. From May's position, he saw the explosions and dust drifting toward the sky but couldn't directly see the house. Over the radio, the marines were calling for the QRF but suddenly, the shooting was over just as fast as it had started.

For May, the next few minutes were surreal. He called to ask if Butler had any casualties, and he didn't. At that time the car drove out of an alley about fifty yards away. The gunmen in the car had their weapons out the windows, screaming, *"Allah Akbar!"* celebrating their great victory. Behind the car was the truck followed by the van. The occupants in the van, and four men standing in the bed of the truck handling the recoilless rifle, cheered as they drove away from Butler's house. In line, all three vehicles turned east, toward May's building. His marines drew a bead, and everyone took aim on different vehicles while waiting for the order to shoot. When the men were directly in front of the house, May told his team to fire with everything they had.

On the SAW, Kochergin tore into the lead car. With deadly accuracy, he ruthlessly wasted the driver and sprayed everyone inside, disabling the car and trapping the two other vehicles behind it. With the entire team firing, in seconds all three vehicles were stopped forty yards away. From the roof, the SASR tore through the vehicle's thin metal and ripped through gunmen who hoped to use the doors as shields. At such short distance May fired his M4, shooting anyone he could see. The men were so close that he estimated that he could hit them with hand grenades, and he even threw a few. With his M203, Padron lobbed grenades onto each vehicle, and soon they were all on fire. In their death traps, the gunmen went from cheering to screaming. They had been hit so fast they had no time to react. As they fled the vehicles, May saw that some were on fire. Others weren't, but they were all injured. In the open, Kochergin clipped anyone moving, but what stood out to May was the SASR. Munoz was plugging the men who were on fire and every time he hit someone, the bullet took a chunk of their bodies off until some of the men were burning in pieces.

When no one was moving, May called a cease fire and ended their killing spree. Butler reported seeing fifteen to twenty men who had shot at their house, running to a mosque 150 yards away. Avila, the former mortar man, called in a fire mission with 81 mm mortars on the group. Less than a minute later, the incoming mortars splashed down on the targets. May's team was dangerously close, and he could feel the concussion.

When the shooting was done, the marines heard *"Allah Akbar!"* again. But this time, it wasn't in celebration. The men were groaning in pain. As psychological warfare would have it, May and Butler's team screamed and laughed their own mocking version of *"Allah Akbar"* to taunt their enemy before they died.

Shortly afterward, May had air support on station. The helicopters circled overhead while May tried to get the pilot to shoot a Hellfire missile at the truck with the recoilless rifle mounted on it, wanting to fully disable it. However, once the pilot saw the wreckage, he told May there was no way that the weapon could be used again, and he didn't want to waste a missile on it.

By sundown the two teams were extracted with amtracks. The enemy body count was roughly fifteen Iraqis in the vehicles and ten to fifteen men with the mortars.

Later that month, the battalion's relief arrived. Before May left the country his camp was hit with a suicide vehicle-borne improvised explosive device. Through all of the attacks and firefights, May was thankful that he wasn't injured.

12

Operator's Journey

Name: Sergeant Q., CJ

Billet: Scout/Sniper Team Leader—Chief Scout/Sniper

Area of Operations: City of An Nasiriyah, Dhi Qar Province, Operation
  Iraqi Freedom I, 2003; City of Husaybah, Al Anbar Province
  Operation Iraqi Freedom III, February–September 2005

Sitting behind a desk at Camp Geiger, North Carolina, was
not Sergeant CJ's passion. He enjoyed being the chief instructor at Second Marine Division scout/sniper school because the
job itself was satisfying. So was having a direct effect on teach-
ing marines to become snipers. But hearing the experiences of
marines returning from Iraq and keeping in contact with others
still in country, CJ was unintentionally persuaded to return to
the dangerous region for a third time. It seemed that no matter
what he did, he couldn't help but be drawn to his true desire—
operating. It was something he had been doing since 1987, and
it was now 2004.

At eighteen, CJ had realized his goal of twelve years and

become a marine. He was physically prepared for the challenging boot camp, and at the time he was anxious to be in the infantry. However, his first duty station was in Washington State, guarding a nuclear base, and that's where he got his first taste of sniping.

Growing up in Rantoul, Illinois, CJ was taught to shoot at an early age by his grandfather, who was in World War II. So, naturally he was the primary choice as the designated marksman on his unit's Special Reaction Team. As a young marine, he was familiar with shooting and knew more about it than most. Yet, during the four-week designated marksman shooting course, he was blown away by one of the instructor's expertise in ballistics, shooting, and tactics. The instructor was a HOG and often spoke about sniping, and the method of becoming one. Being a marksman was fine, but CJ wanted to become a sniper. He learned that it was a tough path to take, and that only a few marines actually succeeded in doing so. As a result, when he made it to the fleet, he had a new goal.

One year passed and CJ was shipped to Charlie Company, First Battalion, Sixth Marines. There he fit in well and was one of the more disciplined and self-motivated marines, just what it takes to excel in the infantry. But his success worked against him, and when he showed interest in trying out for the scout/ sniper platoon, his company recognized that he was too much of an asset to lose. And while CJ desperately yearned to become a sniper, the opportunity quickly diminished on his first enlistment, because of Operation Desert Storm.

During the Gulf War, CJ was disappointed with his first combat experience, but driving into Iraq was one of the most frightening events of his life. When Saddam Hussein threatened the "mother of all wars," Corporal CJ, a fire team leader, seriously questioned if he would live through it all. His perception of battle had been spawned from veterans who fought in Vietnam, Korea, and the world wars. CJ figured that his time in combat would be no different and suspected that this was his generation's great conflict. The night that U.S. forces crossed the border from Saudi Arabia, he and his squad occupied the eleventh AAV (Amphibious Assault Vehicle) entering Iraq. Crammed in back of the speeding vehicle, the marines sat in darkness. CJ tried to keep alert but was light-headed and nauseous because the two overhead cargo hatches were shut and trapped the stench of diesel and exhaust fumes in the back. The worst part of it all was the helplessness CJ felt as artillery shells exploded outside and shook his vehicle. There was no way to defend against that. When it finally came time to meet the enemy, CJ expected the fight of his life, but instead, he cleared only a few trenches. Sadly, after four days, the war was over without his ever experiencing the type of combat that he had trained so hard for.

Returning from Iraq, he was discharged from the marines. Being a task-oriented, goal-driven person, he stuck to his plan and moved home to Illinois to pursue law enforcement. But in time, he found that the military had shaped his life in such a way that law enforcement didn't meet the disciplined standard that he had anticipated. After eight months he knew that the job wasn't for him.

CJ hoped to rejoin the marines, but because of downsizing, the marines wouldn't accept anyone with prior service. At the recruiting office, CJ heard the bad news. On his way out of the building, he stopped to talk to his friend who was an army recruiter. When his friend learned that the marines wouldn't accept CJ, he took the opportunity and persuaded CJ to join the army.

In 1997, after a five-and-a-half-year enlistment, CJ left the army and tried his hand at law enforcement once again. He moved back to Illinois and joined the local police, and soon transferred to the sheriff's department. There he was able to join the SWAT team and also become a K-9 handler. It was also where he met his wife. Soon, however, he remembered why he had quit the police force.

He was used to doing his job, doing it right, and with 100 percent commitment. The department didn't operate that way. It seemed that his command wanted him to do his job only when necessary, to appease people, and to get by. He also had a hard time comprehending that he couldn't arrest certain people because they were affiliated with someone "important." For CJ that wasn't good enough. For him it was all or nothing.

In 2001, four years after leaving the army, he was back in a marine recruiter's office. Being a police officer was disappointing. At first, the marine in charge hesitated to work with CJ because of his age. He was thirty-one years old. But after easily passing the physical fitness test, CJ was on his way to the infantry.

The "Betio Bastards" of the Third Battalion, Second Marines was his new unit. At once CJ noticed the battalion's snipers and made friends with most of them. His time in the army allowed him to share ideas on tactics, but some of the marines weren't welcoming. A few felt threatened that he might take their position in the platoon. But as they spent more time around him, it became clear that that was not his intentions. In the line company, the old-man jokes started from the younger guys. But his experience surpassed that of most marines. Regardless, CJ easily transitioned into the military and soon his battalion deployed to Okinawa, Japan.

A year passed before the battalion was in Twentynine Palms, California, for desert training. CJ was attached to the Headquarters Company and was the assistant to the battalion gunner. He helped to train the marines in the battalion on several weapon systems and optics. But as much fun as it was sharing his knowledge, he really wanted to be in the scout/sniper platoon. It had been a desire for over ten years. The officer in charge of him eventually recognized that this was one of his career goals and let him go, despite the fact that he was losing a good marine. At the same time the members of the sniper platoon knew that CJ wanted to join them, and they planned to put him through an indoc without his knowing it.

Their objective was to see how well he could hang. They questioned his age and stocky build, but after two weeks in the desert, they didn't question his ability. For CJ the two weeks were tough, but he passed the evaluation and was in the platoon.

A short time later he started scout/sniper school. During the course, CJ paid close attention to the news and saw the possibility of another war with Iraq. Reports that his battalion was deploying to that area excited him, because he knew that he would be a Hunter of Gunmen by then and would be carrying a sniper rifle.

Indeed, weeks after graduating sniper school, the Third Battalion, Second Marines were on their way to the Middle East. In Kuwait, CJ was ready for action. He secretly hoped that war was nothing like Desert Storm because he wanted to fight. This time he was a sniper team leader and his partner was Jeremy, a good friend who had attended sniper school with him. An intellectual type, CJ was skeptical of Jeremy at first, because they were opposites. But after spending more time together, CJ didn't want anyone else as a partner. The other two teammates were new to the platoon and were PIGs.

Once in Kuwait, CJ lived at a small tent camp called Camp Shoup, about thirty miles from the Iraqi border. For the anxious marines, the wait for combat was draining. They trained so much that they couldn't wait to start real operations. As the vehicles and equipment massed, CJ knew that the attack was coming soon but months passed until they were finally given the command to move into Iraq.

CJ's battalion was part of the Second Marine Expeditionary Brigade called Task Force Tarawa, and on March 21, 2003, the task force was summoned to action. This time CJ was in a seven-ton truck, driving into Iraq. He was part of an endless convoy of green-and-tan vehicles. The ride was long and tedious, and he couldn't remember a time as miserable. Sitting on a box of water, his face and clothes were caked with dust. It was ironic that they spent hours and hours cleaning weapons and gear, but in vain, because after the first day everything was layered in dirt.

Two days passed and CJ questioned whether he would see battle. News of other battalions fighting circulated, but he still hadn't fired a shot. Then he learned that he might get a chance, because his unit was tasked with seizing the Eleventh Iraqi Engineer compound in the southern city of An Nasiriyah.

Before the battalion arrived, marines were in a fierce fight. No one expected the amount of resistance in the city. It started when a U.S. Army transportation unit unknowingly drove into the city and was ambushed by well-prepared Iraqi forces. Unlike the majority of Iraqi units, these fighters were willing to make a stand. In the ensuing attack, U.S. soldiers were killed, and many of the U.S. Army vehicles were destroyed. With the Iraqis jubilant from the small victory, the marines arrived to Nasiriyah and found themselves fighting to take strongholds on two bridges leading into the city. When CJ's battalion reached the city, the fighting was full scale. He couldn't wait for his turn to shoot, but it didn't come until the next day.

That night he and his team received the mission of conducting reconnaissance on the Eleventh Iraqi Engineer compound. They were told that high-value targets would be there and to take them out if given the opportunity. After sundown, CJ and his team were able to watch the complex from a room in a nearby schoolhouse. From his position, CJ could see that the area was lightly guarded, and before sunrise, the snipers found their target. It was an Iraqi colonel in charge of the area. CJ held the man in his sights, waiting for permission to engage. But when they radioed the battalion, they were ordered to stand down. The battalion wanted to capture the man for intelligence. Following orders, CJ kept the crosshairs on him but didn't fire. The colonel eventually drove away, never knowing how close to death he had been.

The next day, as the marines seized the compound, the sniper team provided overwatch. The attack was fast and without shots fired, until suddenly a truck sped into the compound. CJ watched through his scope as marines unloaded on the vehicle and killed all of the occupants except one. When the man stumbled out, he saw that it was the Iraqi colonel.

Hours later, CJ and his team consolidated in the compound

on top of a building named the Citadel. Other sniper teams were also on top. Everyone was careful of giant holes in the roof left from air raids. Keeping security, CJ's team and another team aimed west, down a main road. The last team took the southwest. In the distance to the northeast were the bridges where the other unit was fighting. LAVs (Light Armored Vehicles) were parked between the snipers and the bridges, holding flank security. With intermittent fighting in that area, the LAVs often fired across the river.

The surroundings were quite a change from the desert that they'd been driving through. Lush green plants and palm trees grew next to the river, while lines of houses and buildings crowded the road that CJ observed down. From his position, he could see 1,000 yards into the lively city. Civilians packed the sidewalks and cars jammed the street.

Two hours passed and CJ was off the gun tearing into an MRE (meals ready to eat) when suddenly a spotter yelled, "RPG, RPG!" CJ dropped everything and jumped toward his gun. As he did, the other sniper facing west shot twice. The spotter explained that men with AKs and RPGs had pulled up in a vehicle.

"Where they at?" asked CJ.

"Down the main road," said the spotter. A burst of energy shot through CJ while he tried to find a target. In the distance the crowd immediately disappeared, and CJ saw a few men sprinting across the street with weapons. Their truck was parked on the left side of the road, and they were traveling right. The men were either Iraqi Army or Saddam Hussein's "Men of Sacrifice" known as Fedayeen Saddam. CJ knew that they were Fedayeen because any time they came around, civilians vanished.

"What's the range?" CJ asked the spotter.

"Nine hundred," he replied, after ranging the building behind the men.

Quickly spinning the knobs on his scope, CJ took aim. He put a lead on one of the men wearing a black suit. The distance was far enough that after CJ fired, he was able to see the bullet splash against a wall behind the man.

"You're one foot high!" said his spotter. Disappointed, and in frustration, CJ asked again for the distance. Once more, the spotter ranged the wall behind the man and the distance was the same. As he sighted in, CJ realized that the man was closer to them than the wall. Though they perceived the man to be next to the wall, at that distance they couldn't tell if he was next to it or not. It was a matter of depth perception. CJ did the math in his head and aimed at the target's feet, knowing that the bullet would impact high. As fate would have it, the man stopped, giving CJ enough time to stabilize the sights under him. The bullet exploded from the barrel, and this time CJ found his mark. The gunman dropped like a ton of bricks and began crawling to the nearest building. Out of the corner of his eye, CJ noticed the sniper who was holding security to the southwest was hurrying to get into the fight. He held his rifle in one hand and a box of ammo in the other and was running on a two-foot-wide slab of concrete between the holes in the roof. CJ pictured him falling and killing himself, but the sniper had other plans. He made it across the path and found a position, raring to shoot. Later, he spotted a man carrying an RPG. The man was moving from east to west and hiding between buildings. The sniper realized that he was maneuvering on the LAVs. When the RPG gunner was within 100 yards of the vehicle, he made the fatal mistake of exposing himself, and the sniper shot him in the chest. Later CJ found out that his cousin was the vehicle commander of the LAV being targeted.

Meanwhile, CJ was covering the area where he had first shot. The sniper next to him was firing on men moving in the area. The targets were running for their lives, and CJ was able to shoot once more, before they were completely gone. He fired at a man trying to hide in a cluster of bushes. His outline was prominent and he appeared to fall after CJ shot, but CJ and his spotter weren't able to confirm a hit.

After An Nasiriyah the action died down. CJ was assigned to Personal Security Detail, raids and counter-ambushes, but much to his disappointment, there were no more gunfights.

When the major ground war was declared over, the Third Battalion, Second Marines departed for home. Back in North Carolina CJ requested orders to become an instructor at the Second Marine Division scout/sniper school. The choice was easy for the command and they accepted his offer. After his superiors saw his work, CJ was elected to become the chief instructor. He fully accepted the role and felt fortunate to be working with other instructors who had experience in combat as well. Together they were able to pass on the essential knowledge that it takes to be a successful sniper in battle.

As months and years passed, CJ sensed that he needed to go back to Iraq. It was evident that his brothers in arms fought a different kind of war than he knew. Hearing stories of entire sniper teams being wiped out and other unfortunate events motivated him to get back into the fight. He wanted to face off against the new enemy—insurgents. And by chance his old unit, 3/2, was preparing to deploy for Operation Iraqi Freedom III.

CJ was asked by a few senior officers and enlisted marines to rejoin the battalion. The gesture was a significant factor in his returning for another deployment. When he arrived back at his old platoon, he became the chief scout/sniper. Having been an instructor at sniper school, he worked with a majority of the marines from the platoon and knew that the senior operators were very capable. But some didn't like the idea of having CJ as the chief scout. As strict as he was, he wouldn't put up with the "cowboy" image that a few snipers gladly portrayed. However, everyone promptly set their differences aside, knowing that in a month and a half, they would be in the unforgiving Al Anbar province.

CJ's third tour in Iraq began in February of 2005. He arrived at the northwestern city of Al Qa'im and was based with the battalion at an old train station nearby. One company and an eight-man team took up Camp Gannon in Husaybah, which was miles away.

As the salty chief scout, CJ wasn't the timid young man that he had been when he first entered Iraq in 1991. Having been a police officer and a combat experienced operator in both the army and marines since then, he was more than prepared for his third Iraqi tour. For him and his partner, the action began by running missions with Force Reconnaissance. The two of them provided support for the specialized unit during their first month in country. CJ's purpose was to cover the marines while they raided houses and buildings to apprehend HVTs or high-value targets, and he also intended to disrupt and prevent ambushes. Though they loved being involved with the missions, CJ and his partner were called to the lawless city of Husaybah after one major bombing.

India Company and an eight-man sniper team relieved Baker Company from the First Battalion, Seventh Marines at Camp Gannon. From the first day that the marines set foot in the camp they were fired upon. They were greeted weekly with AK and machine-gun fire, as well as mortars and RPGs. Outside the perimeter, gunmen often shot from the nearby buildings, and occasionally groups of men gathered to launch assaults on the camp but were always repelled. Despite the steadfast discipline of the marines, the fanatical insurgents were determined to deliver an attack like no other.

One morning, in March 2005, insurgents were able to make it to the camp and detonate two suicide vehicle bombs. CJ was in Al Qa'im when it happened. The attack started with a barrage of well-aimed mortars and RPGs. A dust cloud from the indirect fire covered the camp, while small-arms fire and RPGs opened up on the towers, forcing the marines to take cover. At the same time, three vehicles drove toward the camp. A dump truck took the lead. Under the dust screen, it plowed into two smaller trucks acting as a barrier into the camp. The insurgent driver smashed through the barrier, but because of the dust, he took a wrong turn into the old abandoned customs checkpoint, and he detonated his vehicle in the open. The massive explosion rocked the area. The second vehicle, a fire truck, followed close behind the lead. The stunned marines opened fire, but the windows and doors were reinforced with armor and bulletproof glass. The fire truck made it into the perimeter and detonated in the same area as the dump truck. The noise was deafening and the explosion sent debris flying in every direction. Two snipers were near the blast. They were standing outside of their tent when the fire truck went off just twenty feet away. But a seven-foot-tall, five-foot-wide, dirt-filled wall called a HESCO barrier saved their lives, as it caught most of the fragments. However, chunks of concrete and metal rained down on the camp. The snipers were injured and needed to be medically evacuated. The third vehicle was disabled before it could cause any damage. The well-coordinated attack failed to kill marines, but woke them up to the type of violence that the enemy was willing to use. With the two snipers wounded, CJ and his partner volunteered to fill in for them at Camp Gannon.

Once in Husaybah, CJ learned just how chaotic the border town was. Attacks on the camp happened biweekly, and the very night he arrived, mortars, RPGs, and gunfire hammered the camp. CJ decided to use the SASR exclusively. He wanted the power to disable vehicles and penetrate objects that city environments present. Over time the snipers' routine was to take up observation positions and to counter-ambush the attackers. They also hunted for the men launching indirect fire on the camp, and success came early for CJ and his SASR.

It happened weeks after arriving. In the observation posts, the sniper teams maintained continuous surveillance on the city, and one day a sniper noticed something unusual. From the rooftop of a nearby building, an Iraqi let loose a flock of pigeons at the exact time of Camp Gannon's change of guards. A short time afterward, mortars and rockets targeted the camp, while exposed marines scrambled for cover. Thinking that it happened by coincidence, the sniper didn't engage but took note. When it happened again, he notified the other teams that the man was using the pigeons to signal an attack at such a vulnerable time, and the sniper was able to identify the signalman before he vanished.

The next day CJ and his team were in an abandoned building

known as "the Three Story." From there, the western edge of the city was in plain view. So was the building where the birds had been seen. Suddenly, three men appeared from the building. When one of CJ's teammates recognized one of the men as the signalman, CJ began to set up for a shot. The target was 300 yards away unloading cargo from a building into a car. In the darkened position, CJ had the rifle on a firm shooting position and was tracking the suspected insurgent with his scope. It was then that it happened. The pigeons were released again. As the man walked back into the building, CJ was given permission to engage. This was his first real target on his third tour, and he was ready to shoot. When the man came out of the building, his upper body was hidden behind a box that he carried. Only his head was available to target. Not wanting to waste an opportunity, CJ aimed in on his lower face. There would be no lead because the man walked directly toward him. CJ's thoughts were on the target and not the repercussion of the trigger squeeze and the vicious recoil that follows. Anticipating the blow back of the SASR causes some snipers to jerk the trigger, which throws the round off target.

After the weapon fired, the blast caused dust to shudder from the interior sandbags. CJ thought he had missed; all he saw was the spark from the round puncturing the wall behind the man. But his spotter was in shock. The bullet had torn through the man's head without losing speed and hit the wall. The man's head looked like an apple being smashed with a sledgehammer. When CJ heard what he had done, a jolt of adrenaline filled his body so much that his hand was shaking. That energy kept him on the rifle for hours in hopes of finding more bad guys, but none dared come around that day.

As the weeks passed, CJ fell accustomed to the routine attacks. Being the senior sniper, he was the primary liaison for the company commander, who often needed sniper support at all times. One night CJ woke up to someone shaking him.

"Hey, Sergeant! We need a team out here. There's a sniper taking shots at our posts."

"We'll be out in a second," CJ said, wiping the sleep from his eyes.

He woke up his partner, Karl, who was up for the challenge of finding an enemy sniper. CJ grabbed the SASR and headed for a post near the middle of the camp.

A sky full of stars sparkled in the black desert night as CJ found a position to rest his gun. It was explained that a sniper had been taking potshots at one of the posts every few hours, and it was impossible for them to find him among the nooks and crannies of numerous buildings. CJ and his partner began to search the area but couldn't find anything out of place. They got a break when the sniper fired again, and the bullet hit the guard post about twenty yards from them. The sniper made the mistake of giving away his primary direction. After hearing the origin of the shot, the two snipers had a clue to his vicinity and began carefully searching the buildings in that area.

At first they looked to see if anything was abnormal, then they scanned doorways and windows. One door in particular stuck out to CJ. It was on a corner building next to a streetlight about 200 yards away. He found that the door had a peculiar strip of shade, about six inches thick, running from the top of the door to the bottom. That would only happen if the door was cracked open. Of course, CJ wasn't able to see into the crack, but the room seemed to be a likely sniper position. He kept his sights on the doorway and waited.

A short while later, a dim flash lit up the room before a bullet cracked nearby. "Jackpot!" whispered CJ to himself. Calculating the placement of his return fire, CJ took into account that a small wall outside of the front door would force the shooter to be elevated, possibly on a chair or desk. Also because the muzzle flash wasn't extreme, he guessed that the enemy sniper was near the center or the back of the room. Because CJ wasn't directly in the path of the crack, he knew that he needed to shoot the center of the door to get a possible hit. Explaining this to his partner, CJ adjusted his gun. Taking aim, he wasn't worried about the flimsy metal door because the .50-caliber Raufoss round would slice through it with no problem.

The blast from the rifle shattered the early morning silence and sparks flickered from the door as the bullet punched through it. Seconds after the first shot, CJ fired another one for good measure. After the echo, everyone waited for counterfire, but two hours passed and nothing happened.

Unknown to the snipers, F-16s on routine patrol were called to assist the situation by the battalion. They circled above the city, and with thermal pods, they scanned the buildings that CJ was targeting. After CJ shot, the pilots confirmed that a warm liquid spilled out from underneath the door. It ran almost into the street. The pilots relayed the information to the battalion, who congratulated the two snipers. The next week, a platoon conducting a raid confirmed the blood at the entrance of the building.

Weeks later on July 26, CJ was in another major attack. He jumped out of bed after a massive amount of gunfire broke out from northeast of the camp. In the darkness, he scrambled for his radio while hearing MK19s and 50-cal machine guns trading fire with enemy machine guns and RPGs.

An observation position north of the city, manned by marines, was under fire. The attack wasn't directed at Camp Gannon, but still CJ wondered if he could help. He told his spotter to grab his gear, and when they opened the tent door, there was absolute darkness. With no night vision capabilities, CJ knew that the SASR was useless. Hurrying for his bed, he found his M40A3 and the Simrad night vision attachment. Just then, the camp trembled from an explosion, followed by gunfire from the east. Outside of the tent, CJ and his partner hesitated to run "the Gauntlet."

A 100-yard strip of unpaved road connecting two sides of the camp was known as the Gauntlet. It was extremely dangerous to move through when insurgents attacked from the east. With enemy fire from that direction, the road became the impact area for bullets that missed their marks. By now, CJ had made the run many times and knew his way through the maze. Nevertheless, no matter how many times he passed through it, the thought of being hit with a stray round was alarming.

Running with the sniper rifle in one hand and a radio in the other, his arms were getting tired. But the sound of bullets cracking nearby and landing yards away from him inspired him to run faster. Once at the Iraqi National Guard complex on the other side of camp, he and his partner took up position on a second-story, concrete building inside a machine-gun bunker. The team quickly built a shooting position facing east into the city. Afterward CJ fastened the night vision to his sniper rifle, while his partner began scanning for insurgents.

Over the radio he heard that groups of insurgents were closing in on the OP, trying to overrun them. From the snipers' view, they could see down the long access of a main road that ran east into the city. Sections of the road were illuminated, but still it was going to be hard to positively identify targets in such low light. CJ and his partner knew that the insurgents would have to move south across the road when they broke off their attack, and that's where they would be waiting.

Soon, the team found a group of insurgents traveling north across the road, trying to get into the fight. Six to eight men with AKs moved in the shadows 550 yards out, along the street. As they crossed the road, CJ focused his night vision and saw that two of the men were shooting at the OP. Their muzzle flash gave their exact position away. The marines at the OP opened up on them with an MK19 grenade launcher. The high-explosive rounds blew up close to the gunmen, and the flashes lit up the area. Through the scope, CJ was amazed at the amount of light that the Simrad was able to collect. The explosive flashes let CJ see the black profiles of insurgents against the wall, but they disappeared after the light was gone.

CJ steadied his sights on the wall while the area went dim. He knew that it was only a matter of time before marines at the OP shot another burst of grenades. Moments later CJ was given the opportunity to engage, when a volley of grenades impacted one street east of the men, lighting them up. Years of rapid target engagement training kicked in as CJ aimed at the closest target still near 550 yards away. His night vision granted a huge advantage as he directed the crosshairs over the target's upper body and firmly squeezed the trigger. The man fell. CJ's second target began to flee after his partner went down. Aiming in, CJ had only a limited view of him as the man quickly moved south. Leading the man anyway, he squeezed the trigger. It was evident, though, that he missed because the man kept running. With others still in the area CJ refocused, but the neighborhood went black.

Suddenly, the OP received a lengthy burst of machine-gun fire. CJ frantically searched for the shooter, while the marines at the OP answered with their own arsenal. They unloaded with machine guns, and CJ was surprised to hear an AT4 ripping through the air. The 84 mm, antitank rocket flew from the OP and tore into the second story of a building. What happened next was a treat for CJ.

The rocket exploded in an old bakery building. The room that suffered the impact was full of cooking oils. Once the rocket went off, the entire third story went up in flames, and instantly CJ was watching "green TV" through his scope. The fire brightened everything, and he could see men standing in the distance. His next target at 650 yards was a man dazed from having been next to the explosion. Regaining his composure, he turned and mistakenly ran west, toward CJ, who was aiming at his chest. With one shot, the man fell. CJ was able to see his next three targets around 715 yards. He aimed at one of the three men and shot, but the men were unfazed and kept moving. CJ and his partner were puzzled, but his spotter realized that a set of power lines were in the way. With the targets escaping, CJ fired two more shots but both were knocked off course by the power lines.

While the building was still ablaze, CJ was able find a target at 800 yards. He was lucky, because under normal circumstances it was impossible to positively identify targets at that range. The man was moving east when CJ aimed for his life. Seconds after the shot was fired, the man fell after making it fifteen yards away. Lying in the street, he never got up. As the flames subsided, so did the gunfire, and the city was peaceful again.

As CJ's wild tour in Husaybah came to an end, one incident made him realize how privileged a life he and his family lived. It happened after the assassination of a local Sunni sheik at the hands of Al Qaeda operatives. The killing was ordered after the sheik was found to be collaborating with the marines. As Al Qaeda insurgents flooded the city, civilians fled, and a mass of Iraqi Sunni tribal fighters known as "resistance fighters" met the terrorists, triggering an intense battle. The resistance fighters commonly worked side by side with the marines, who were well aware of the situation, but unable to assist due to the significant political nature of the fight. As the battle raged a hundred yards from Camp Gannon, it was difficult for CJ not to question the decision to stay out of the fight. The Marines purpose for being in the city was to protect it. CJ knew that eventually the men needed to stand on their own, but with the battle so close, the marines could have made a difference.

One group of resistance fighters fought until they ran out of ammunition and twenty escaped the terrorists, fleeing to a marine observation position. The marines took them in at the OP and brought them to Camp Gannon where CJ was able to get a glimpse of them. As the fighters walked into camp, CJ was surprised to see their average age. Some were older men but the vast majority of them looked to be his son's age. It hit him that fifteen- and fourteen-year-old kids were out fighting terrorists, while he was standing in a compound watching. Crushed, CJ couldn't believe that a well-trained, capable fighting force wasn't able to fight because of politics.

13

The Last Mission

Name: Sergeant Afong, M.

Billet: Scout/Sniper Team Leader

Area of Operations: City of Hit, Al Anbar Province,

Operation Iraqi Freedom II, August 2004–February 2005

In early February 2005, our unit was only a few short weeks away from returning to the States. We had served six and a half months in the forgotten wastelands of western Iraq, during which time our battalion had the unenviable task of patrolling endless amounts of roads and sweeping through unfriendly towns that had yet to be swayed by the American liberators. But our fun-filled tour was coming to an end with only one last obstacle, Operation River Blitz. As a whole, this was our unit's last mission. The reason for the operation was to oust insurgents that had been nesting in the sleepy towns along the Euphrates River from Ar Ramadi, which was close to Baghdad, to Al Qa'im on the Syrian border. Many of these insurgents fled Fallujah in November, and by now they enjoyed staying in towns that U.S. forces neglected to clamp down on. Operation River Blitz took place over a stretch of 200 miles and involved many different Iraqi National Guard and U.S. troops who each covered their separate sectors.

For this last operation our battalion was to conduct a search in the western city of Hit. Four sniper teams were needed for the mission. Three two-man teams were attached to the assault element pushing through the city, and their mission lasted a few days. Light Armored Reconnaissance or LAR company was in direct support of our battalion, and they wanted a sniper team with them in a fifteen-day blocking position. Of course, my team was on a mission when the assignments came down, so we were the obvious choice for the fifteen-day mission. My team and the company were to hold a blocking position on the east side of the Hit Bridge and to report on any potential ambushes and capture any insurgents trying to flee across the bridge while marines from the battalion pushed through the city.

My time in Iraq gave me a newfound respect for my latest unit, the First Battalion, Twenty-third Marines. Spending over four years on active duty, I was taught that "weekend warriors" were scum; but serving with these men proved otherwise. Because the typical age in the scout/sniper platoon was in the early thirties, the maturity level was a bit more than the average active-duty platoon. I was also surprised to learn that over half of the marines in the platoon had been on active duty, and many of them had already seen action. Marines like Sergeant Johnson, a Second Fleet Antiterrorist Security Team (FAST) company marine, and Sergeant Coats, an infantryman at the time, both saw action in Somalia. There were also a variety of law enforcement officers like Sergeant Hancock, the platoon's senior HOG, who had been in shootouts as a police officer in his home town. The seasoned Sergeant Allison, an operator in Afghanistan, along with Sergeant Rostro, another senior HOG, were both Texas Highway Patrol officers in their normal lives. My old partner, who graduated from Quantico, was a sheriff's deputy, and Sergeant Little, who also graduated from Quantico, was a cop in Washington, D.C. To me, the level of real-world experience in the platoon was impressive.

Corporal Stokley and I made up "Shadow Two." The platoon had been recently rearranged and my old partner moved to another team. This wasn't a problem for me because I liked Stokley. We'd spent enough time together over the last seven months and knew each other well. Although Stokley was aggressive, like my old partner who always wanted to kill first and ask questions last, I understood his mentality and took comfort in knowing that was the type of marine you wanted beside you in combat. I knew that he was more than willing to fight to the death if it came down to it.

Our sniper section lived in an old Iraqi Army barracks called FOB Hit just three miles outside of the city itself. Stokley and I couldn't wait to get this last mission over with because once finished, we would be leaving our forward operating base and transferring to Al Asad Air Base. Like many other FOBs, ours was constantly shelled, so much so that not one week went by without some type of indirect fire. For us, it wasn't unusual to wake up to explosions, or for one lucky marine, to be in the outhouse while a mortar landed yards away, piercing the booth instead of him. Al Asad on the other hand was rarely attacked because it was so far away from any town.

Packing for this mission was relatively easy as far as gear

was concerned because we took most of what we had. Weapons-wise, I carried the M40A3 with the Simrad night vision attach-ment, and an M16 and 9 mm. Stokley carried the M16 with an M203 grenade launcher and also a 9 mm. He and I would both be taking radios, optics, flares, claymores, grenades, and plenty of ammo.

As we prepared to leave the base, a marine with the platoon that we were attached to approached us and asked if we needed a SASR. Usually a Light Armored Reconnaissance company has at least one for their scouts. At first we didn't want it because it was extra weight, but since we were riding and not walking, we agreed to take it. Stokley and I smirked at each other when the young marine in charge of the weapon reluctantly gave it up. As he did, he made sure to tell us in his own jargon how to use the weapon—and in front of marines in his platoon. I wondered if the marine knew that we regularly use the weapon, and knew it was no when I asked him if he had ever shot it because he stopped talking.

Stokley and I boarded the vehicle along with six other marines. I dreaded the fact that it was going to be a cramped ride, especially with the sniper rifle between my legs, but I didn't dare lay it down since the bumpy ride might cause the scope to lose its zero. Plus the other marines would easily use the rifle as a foot rest in the dark hull of the vehicle. For Stokley and I there was no small talk because the engine of the LAV drowns out all other noise. Fortunately for me, over the years I specially trained myself to fall asleep in any clime and place, and it beat the other option of torturing myself by thinking about home and my girl-friend. I'd done so much of it already and it wasn't worth the misery. In the drowsy moments before drifting into tranquility, and with my head bobbing toward my chest, I thought back to a few months earlier while riding in another LAV.

Our team was on our way to getting inserted for a mission when the unit we were riding with received confirmation that three men in a white car had kidnapped two other men who worked on Al Asad Air Base. The car was traveling through a nearby town, and our patrol was ordered to intercept it. My team was just along for the ride. Once we entered the small town on the main road, we heard a loud thump on my side of the vehicle, behind me.

"Is someone knocking on the back door?" my partner asked.

Then over the radio, I heard the vehicle commander yell that we had just been hit by an IED. When I told everyone else what happened, there was a pause, and then we all cheered as if we had won something. But in a sense we had; nobody was hurt and the vehicle was hardly damaged. We all knew if we had been in a Humvee, which is what we normally rode in, the situation would have been a lot worse.

Back on the road, we all knew the ride to the blocking position was going to be long. We had to drive north to Haditha Dam, cross over the Euphrates, and then drive south to Hit. I hoped that we would stop at the dam to get some hot chow and so we could see the other teams because our platoon had been separated, and half the snipers went north to the dam to cover more areas.

When our convoy stopped in the desert somewhere, we exited the vehicles to eat and rest. Two buildings were in one direction, and in the other direction was nothing but sand and sparse vegetation. Stokley approached me and asked me to see something. The scope mounted on the SASR was terrible, there was no focus, and we wouldn't have been able to hit a camel at 100 yards through it. It took us only a few minutes to adjust, and we wanted to shoot the rifle to confirm the zero, but we left the area before we had the opportunity.

After bouncing around in the back of the vehicles, we finally stopped. It was after midnight and the drivers and gunners needed to get some rest before entering the city the next day. Since Stokley and I had been sleeping off and on for the last ten hours, I volunteered our team to help with fire watch.

Sitting high in a turret at 0200, it was hard not to notice the beauty above me. In a land so desolate and bare, the stars were amazing. Millions of them illuminated the night sky and they seemed to be so close you could reach out and grab them. Before sunrise we reloaded the vehicles and made our way to the east side of Hit.

Our loud vehicles stood out among the Iraqi cars and trucks, prompting stares from the locals as we rumbled through their community. Moving to the preplanned positions, we entered a palm grove and the heavy vehicles sank in the soft soil that became mud. Eventually ours became stuck and I climbed in the gunner's turret to witness the action. All the other marines had already exited the vehicles, and when I sat up to watch, some were pulling down dead palm trees and throwing them under the tires to get us out, but with no luck. Finally, after some time, another LAV pulled us free.

Overhead, the brilliant sun matched perfectly with the intense, blue morning sky. From riding in the dark, it took my eyes a minute to adjust to the bright colors when we stopped. Parked in the palm groves, the vehicles set up a security perimeter as Stokley and I unloaded our packs and rifles into the center of the formation. The platoon took turns holding security as the rest of us ate. When we finished eating, a squad was sent to scout the area. Stokley and I joined them at the rear of the patrol. We made our way through the palm groves, weaving on and off different trails, and eventually strayed onto a paved road. As we passed by houses, curious Iraqis flocked to get an eyeful of us small group of Americans. The men seemed angry, and the women stared from their windows and doorways but the fact that they were out was a good sign. Few locals on the streets during the day might be a clue that something bad was going to happen.

On patrol, we skirted the Euphrates River for a few hundred yards, passing houses and shacks. Inconspicuously, I kept in mind any potential places to hide and found one house to be ideal. It was a three-story house built almost on the river and it was in a good location because there was nothing obstructing the view across the river into the city. Also, neighbors wouldn't be able to see on the roof because palm trees surrounded the house, offering good concealment.

At the vehicles, I discussed with the platoon commander what our team's plan would be, and we set it in motion. He and his men were tasked with securing the right flank facing the city and they planned to set up nearby, while we took to the rooftop. The rest of the company held a position to our south, and the Iraqi National Guardsmen, along with a few marines, were constantly on the bridge. The platoon commander also delegated a four-man fire team to come with Stokley and me for security. They would make our job a lot easier.

As the six of us approached the house from the east, we realized that we might have to jump a large, white, rusted metal wall surrounding the property. But to our surprise the front gate was unlocked. We knocked on the front door but no one answered. We knocked again but still no answer, so we kicked the door in and immediately started to search for anyone inside. My adrenaline always flared when I cleared buildings, and as I entered the front door, my finger was on the trigger. Right away I could smell the scent of hajji spreading throughout the house.

Two large rooms were directly across from the front door as we entered. The one on the left had tables, chairs, and couches; the one on the right had only couches and a TV. The kitchen was down the hallway to the left and it led to the back door. The hallway to the right led to two rooms and a bathroom, complete with a shower and a toilet. The stairs leading to the second floor were on the right and on that level were four rooms, also completely furnished. One room even had old posters of Madonna and Debbie Gibson. There was also a door connecting to the second-story roof. I stayed low and walked out onto the porch and once I stepped outside, I knew we had scored a good observation position. On the roof we had a direct line of sight to the northeastern side of the city. A fence made of metal panels outlined the edge of the roof. The panels slanted in a way that made it impossible for anyone in the city to see us laying there, giving us the advantage of observing the area without being noticed. The third level of the house was a roof with a waist-high wall around it. From there we would be able to see the other roofs in the area. We could also see north, up the dirt road that sat next to the house. The third story was the best place to watch for anyone approaching our building.

Just as we were through clearing the house, an Iraqi man came to the front door and began to yell at us. We drew our guns on him, and he backed out into the road, while I called the platoon for an interpreter. The best they could provide us with was a marine who could read the Iraqi word handbook better than everyone else. Somehow we found out that the man didn't want us in the house because he was responsible for watching over it while the owner was in Baghdad. But he didn't understand that we were going to use it anyway. He finally got the point when I started to yell and push him away. We went back inside and locked the house down, then Stokley and I went to work.

We set up on the roof and began searching across the river for any targets or activity. The area was lively. The busiest section was a row of buildings at the northeastern side of the city, which was 450 yards from us. Traffic was nonstop as people walked the streets browsing the shops and markets. From those buildings, a main road ran south to the bridge and north to the palm groves. We could see over 800 meters north to south and 700 meters into the city. Rows of houses stood between the bridge and the northeastern buildings. The zone behind them, we named the "ruins." The ruins were an intricate patch of partially demolished and destroyed buildings located on a hill. The buildings had obviously been damaged and seemed uninhabitable.

Directly across from us was a road that ran parallel to the river for about 600 meters from north to south. It was the same road that ran past the market area. We could see three alleys that led to the road, and north of those alleys were more palm groves.

We began to find distances to every possible area. I had brought my trusty Leica laser range finder. It was simple to use. While looking through the optics, I placed the red box on an area and hit a button, and it gave me a distance to the target in yards. This was cheating for us, but the other way to find ranges was time-consuming.

Within the first hour of our being on the roof, the platoon commander came to our house. He was supposed to find a place where the men in his vehicles could see across the river, and because the house we were in had a large enough yard to fit at least one vehicle, he decided to make it their operating base as well. Stokley and I were happy. This meant that the platoon would be below us holding security.

The platoon spent hours setting up security. Trip flares and booby traps had been set in every approachable lane leading to the house. These men knew how to organize a good perimeter because they had had plenty of practice. A few months earlier the platoon had been used in Fallujah as a blocking force as well. They were on the opposite side of the Euphrates River looking directly into the city and were tasked with capturing or killing any escaping insurgents. Later in the week, one of the marines told me a story of when he was there.

His platoon had been stopping Iraqis as they crossed the river in boats and on a nearby bridge while the city was being assaulted by U.S. forces. Days after the offensive began, they spotted a man swimming across the river. They suspected him of being an insurgent, and the marine's squad approached the Iraqi as he was getting out of the water. They couldn't tell that he was clutching a grenade until he stood up. One of the marines lunged forward and wrestled it from his hands causing it to explode in the water a few meters away. They shot the insurgent and killed him. Hours later they caught another Iraqi who was trying to do the same thing, but he was detained before he could cause any damage. Upon interrogation the insurgent explained that he and many others had been told to swim across the river and kill as many marines as they could with hand grenades. It was a suicide mission. After that, the platoon killed anyone trying to cross the river.

Since we would be staying at that location for fifteen days, Stokley and I had to plan how we would take turns on watch. We decided that he and I would switch observing every four hours. The platoon volunteered to send a different person to spot for us whenever we switched. This way, one of us would always be on the gun, and we would have a spotter at all times. We had to remember to give a brief introduction about how to use some of the equipment to each new spotter.

The marines and Iraqis manning the bridge to the south of us made easy targets for the enemy. On that first day, they received two mortars, but they both landed in the river. Locals eventually came to our position to interact with some of the marines downstairs. Some brought food and cigarettes, but they mostly just wanted to talk. I later found out that the owner of the house and the people of that community belonged to a clan. The man who explained this said that the men in the clan added up to about 200. I wondered how we would fare against 200 angry Iraqis trying to take their house back.

The next morning, Stokley and I were on the roof watching together. We had the 50-caliber sniper rifle positioned on the far right of the roof and the M40A3 was five feet to the left of that. I wasn't going to shoot the 50 because we hadn't zeroed the thing, and I didn't want to waste my time trying to adjust each shot. But if Stokley wanted to shoot it that was up to him. I would spot for him if he did.

The main road that ran on the other side of the river had many alleys connecting to it, and one of the most prominent ones was directly across from us. The alley was slanted at an angle from right to left allowing us to see only about ten feet into it. If we wanted to see all the way down it, we would had to have been farther north. In front of the alley was an open field that looked as though a house once stood there. Stokley and I were both on the roof just before noon, and I was looking toward the city. Stokley noticed something from the alley and scanned the area through his binos. He excitedly told me where he was looking. When I focused on the area, I saw three men standing in the field in front of the alley. They all had head wraps on their faces. As I adjusted my position, I immediately noticed the gun that one of them was holding. It appeared to be a variant of the H and K MP5.

"How did they get such an expensive weapon?" I wondered. One of the others was holding a tube on the ground, angled toward the bridge. The last guy dropped something into the tube. Seconds later, dust from the ground kicked up, and I immediately knew that it was a mortar being shot.

"They're dropping mortars," I said to Stokley, who already knew the situation. My heart raced, and I knew I was going to shoot. I moved my sights and focused on the man who had just dropped the mortar. The thought of him firing another mortar came to mind, and he became the biggest threat. My scope's black crosshairs made perfect lines against this man's white shirt, but as I thought about my aim, I remembered that my dope was set to 500 yards. Searching the distance to the target reference points in my mind, I recalled these men were standing at about 350 yards. Excited at the chance of a kill,

I took my head off the rifle and quickly changed my scope to match the range instead of just lowering my aim. When I placed my face on the cheek piece I found that I was just in time to see the Iraqis' backs because they were quickly trotting away. The man who had held the mortar tube had it on his shoulder and was in the lead, followed by the one who had dropped the mortar. I questioned why they weren't running away. Then it occurred to me that anyone from the bridge wouldn't be able to see them, because a building was blocking their movement. But they hadn't noticed us.

I found the man with the expensive gun. It was still in his hand while he followed the other two, as if he were holding security. He didn't know it, but he became my new target and I quickly placed him in my sights. Knowing that he was almost in the alley and in a few moments he would be out of view, I lined him up and aimed for his upper back. Luckily he was moving in a straight line away from me so I wouldn't have to put a lead on him.

Easy kill, I thought while my crosshairs dissected his shoulder blades. Seconds after a firm squeeze of the trigger, the recoil settled and I watched the bullet impact the man's butt. I could tell it was in that area because his pelvis lunged forward, and he took one more step, before stumbling into the alley and out of view. Within seconds a white car stopped near the man, exposing only its hood and windshield. I knew immediately that I needed to disable the engine. I had already chambered another round and aimed high on the hood and fired, but the car was gone by the time I could focus on the area again. The whole situation lasted less than a minute.

"Damn it," I said. I wanted to see the kill. I knew the shot would be a little low because the man had been moving away from me, but didn't expect it to be that low. I looked at Stokley, and he was angry as well.

"What's wrong with you?" I asked.

He was furious that he hadn't been able to shoot. Instead of spotting for me, he had dropped the binos and got behind the 50 to take a shot. But the SASR was faced toward the city. When he finally adjusted the heavy rifle to where the men were, he had only had enough time to see the man that I shot get hit and fall out of view.

Still lingering on the fact that the shot was low, I checked my dope again, and it was on 350. I asked Stokley what the distance to the alley was.

"Four hundred yards," he replied. Not believing him, I ranged the alley and it was 400. Before I shot I was thinking of the distance to another alley just south of the field. It was 350 yards away. My heart sank. The shot was low because I had dialed on the wrong dope. I was disappointed that I had missed an easy kill because of a simple mistake.

I radioed the company and told them the situation. Soon, kids gathered in that same alley. They were taunting us. They knew what vicinity we were in and a few of them took off their sandals and waved the bottoms of them toward us, gesturing that we were nothing to them. Others pretended that their hands were pistols and shot in our direction. I watched this through the scope in my rifle and wondered how these kids would match up against the kids in the ghettos of America. But it was two different worlds.

Hours later a machine-gun burst went off at the bridge. We got information over the radio that a woman with binoculars was observing the company's position just before they had been mortared. A machine gun opened up on her as she ducked behind a wall. Now anyone observing us was fair game.

The platoon had security on the third story during the day, and marines also manned the weapons on the LAVs. If not on watch everyone else was in the house. The house had electricity, running water, showers, and a stove. There were over seven rooms in the house, making it easy to find a place to sleep. It was a nice house by Iraqi standards, but it wasn't like the house that our four-man team had found a month earlier while in Haditha during the elections. That house had four stories, stone and marble flooring, elegant paintings and furniture, gold silverware, and over 1,000 blankets. We even found a chrome-plated shotgun and AK-47.

Hours later, while I was watching television downstairs, a shot rang out from the roof. I rushed upstairs to see what had happened. Stokley and his observer had caught two men carrying a duffle bag with rifle barrels sticking out. They were dressed in all black and were walking toward the same alley I had shot into. Stokley had seconds to shoot before they made it into the alley. The Iraqis were moving fast and Stokley quickly put a lead on the front Iraqi and shot, but the bullet impacted the wall behind them. The two men dashed into the alley before he could get another shot off. Stokley was even angrier now. He knew that he shouldn't have taken the shot, but the temptation was just too great.

Stokley and I discussed moving because we had fired twice from that position, and usually we would have moved from the area. But because we were concealed behind the metal wall, we stayed in place.

During the night, Stokley and I held security with the other marines. We moved to a corner of the property where we could observe across the river and down an avenue of approach. I enjoyed this time because we mostly talked about home and what we were going to do when we got back to civilization.

On the third day while Stokley was on watch again, he received a single shot. The bullet hit on the wall behind him but it was high and closer to the third story. There had been other marines walking around on the top roof and the shot seemed to be meant for them. Stokley focused on the area where the shot originated. The angle of the impact led us to believe the shot came from the ruins just north of the bridge. Stokley also heard the thump from the enemy's rifle discharge. It sounded like it came from that direction as well. He and I both hawked that area for the next few hours. I was hoping for the classic sniper-on-sniper duel. All of the buildings in the ruins seemed to run together, and with so many spider holes and dead spaces, a sniper could lose his mind guessing where the enemy could be. Hardly anyone went into those areas—mostly dogs but occasionally a few men would wander back there and disappear into a building.

Soon afterward, another mortar fell a few hundred meters away from us, but it didn't cause any damage.

Later that day I was on watch with Bob. He was another sergeant and vehicle commander and squad leader for the platoon. The day was beautiful, similar to a Southern California spring day. During the afternoon, we focused on observing the ruins. There hadn't been any activity elsewhere, so we were hoping the person who had shot toward our position would make the mistake again. The city streets were empty, probably because marines held a position just north of the city. They planned to move through the city, once they were finished in the palm groves. Not many cars traveled the roads and even fewer people wandered outside. I had been scanning the ruins behind the sniper rifle when I came across someone climbing out of a hole in the ground. As he stood up, an object hung from his hands. I set the scope on him and could make out his T-shirt and black pants. The object in his hands was a pair of binoculars. He was in a secluded section that had three walls, much like a square except that the wall that should have been facing us was missing. At first the man crouched as if trying not to be seen, but then he stood up facing southeast. From our position, I could tell that he was observing the marines on the bridge. Bob was behind the spotting scope and I told him to look at what I was seeing to make sure that it was a pair of binoculars. As he searched, I reached for the range finder to laser the wall behind the Iraqi. It was 505 yards. I manipulated the scope and sighted in. As I did this, I asked Bob if it was binos that the Iraqi was holding, and he confirmed that it was. I told him I was going to shoot. But first I had to make a wind call. I tried to find anything around the man that would give me an idea as to what the wind was like where he was, but there was nothing. The wind was hardly a factor from where we were, but on the western banks the wind was blowing lightly right to left. I estimated that the wind would be a tad bit stronger farther up in the ruins where the man was, and I adjusted the scope to make the bullet impact to the right. I aimed at the man's ribs as he stood facing the bridge and slowly took a deep breath closing my eyes. When I exhaled and opened my eyes, the man had moved. He stepped toward the wall that I had lazed. With his back now toward us, Bob and I watched as he started to pee on the wall. I momentarily wondered if what I was about to do was wrong. It didn't seem right to shoot a man while he was taking a leak, but I knew that he would do the same thing to me, if he had the chance. I set the crosshairs on his upper back and was tempted to take a head shot but came to my senses. I wanted to get a first-round hit, and a 505-yard head shot wasn't easy, especially if you couldn't tell the wind. The rifle was stable now and I instinctively said, "On target," but got no reply. Then I remembered that Bob was spotting. I took a breath, exhaled, and then squeezed the trigger. After the rifle spit the bullet toward the man and settled, I had time to see its effect. I was shocked when the bullet slammed against the wall one foot to the right of the man's head.

I shouldn't have dialed right, but had to quickly forget about it because the man was on the move. He instinctively ducked after the bullet hit. He turned and looked around, and I could see he was scared. Moments later he jumped to grab the top of the wall that he had just urinated on. I had already chambered another round and was making an adjustment to fire again.

"You were high and to the right!" Bob said.

I was aiming low and to the left of the man's back as he climbed the wall. This forced my sights to be on the wall itself. Just as he was pulling himself up, I steadied the rifle and shot once more. The rifle came to a rest just as the man disappeared from the wall. He was out of sight.

"Did you see a hit?" I asked Bob.

"I couldn't really tell," he replied.

I knew the adjustment was perfect and I didn't jerk the trigger, either. I had to have hit him. But the truth was that I couldn't confirm anything, so I hesitantly informed the company what happened and told them that the shots appeared to be misses. I knew that everyone with a radio would be listening on the net to our situation, and I was embarrassed. It didn't help my pride when I had to call in a missed shot as a sniper.

Stokley took over watch as I retreated downstairs, only to explain the situation a couple more times.

Staying in the house was comfortable. The electricity made the time go by faster. We watched American movies dubbed in Arabic. I wondered how these people hated us so much but they watched our movies. Every night while on fire watch, I was with a different marine and heard a different story each night. Stories of conquests of the opposite sex, killing in Fallujah, and of wives and girlfriends waiting back home.

Later in the week, the other marines began the push through the city. From our side of the river we could see the occasional firefights. Machine guns went off sending tracers into the air, followed by Cobras swooping nose-first toward the palm groves. The helicopters poured destruction on targets not visible to us. But the sound of explosions and flashing of lights was enough to keep us satisfied. At night, we waited for attacks on our position. We had occupied the house for almost two weeks now, and sitting there for so long had made us vulnerable.

One night at 0300, the platoon was called to assist other marines that were miles away. They loaded up their vehicles and departed, but they left four men back to help hold security with our sniper team. With the house empty, we all went to the roof, because it was the best place to hold security. I couldn't help but think that an attack was imminent. On the roof, I pointed the 50-caliber sniper rifle down the stairs waiting for anyone trying to sneak up. We had traps set throughout the area leading to our house and had the drop on anyone trying to get at us. But nothing happened and the platoon came back a few hours later.

On the morning of the fifteenth day, it was time to leave. Stokley and I were glad to be through with this mission. We were one step closer to the States. The other sniper teams were already at the FOB. I was glad to hear that we would be traveling through the city to get back to base. It meant the ride would only be about thirty minutes, compared to the twelve-hour-plus drive it had taken for us to get there. Iraqis stood next to the road as we drove through town. The reception from them wasn't very friendly, but I didn't care. They could have thrown rocks and shown us the bottom of their sandals, but this would be the last time I would have to see this godforsaken country. Marines also took to the streets, except they were alert and held security for us as we passed through. The drive lasted twenty minutes. At base I couldn't wait for a shower and hot chow. I dropped off my gear in our berthing area and went with the lieutenant from the LAR platoon to debrief at the battalion headquarters. Only when we stepped inside did I notice our stench. The major who greeted us also noticed.

"Who killed the kid?" was his first question.

The lieutenant and I glanced at each other in confusion.

"What?" I asked.

"Who shot the kid in this sector?" he said, pointing to a map on the wall.

His finger landed on the ruins.

I remembered the man climbing the wall. "That was me," I said, elated that I hit him, but wondered what he meant by "kid."

"The man you shot was actually a fourteen-year-old. Another man claiming to be the kid's guardian approached the marines as they were sweeping through the city and wanted reparations for the death of his son," the major explained. "When marines went through that area they found a blood trail but no body. The kid died hours after the incident. What happened?" he asked.

I told him about how we had seen the Iraqi observing the marines on the bridge with binos, and that he had climbed out of a hiding place. I told him of how the mortar attacks on our side had stopped after that.

"Okay," he said and moved on.

During the debrief, I wondered why that kid was on the battlefield. I didn't really care that he was dead; he shouldn't have been out there. I knew when I arrived that there's no age limit on who wants to kill you in this country. But I put myself in his shoes. If someone had come to my town, seeming to be conquerors, I would probably help to fight them, too. It was all just an unfortunate consequence of war.

Endnote: The new unit arrived just days before we were to leave the FOB. They had been in country a week and at our base for two days. A new platoon was getting a tour of the surrounding areas outside the base. A few marines from the new platoon were crossing the highway outside the base when a suicide bomber drove toward them on the road. He detonated a car full of explosives, meters away from them. Miraculously, no one was killed, but there were major injuries. Minutes later, rockets set for airburst exploded near our buildings. The enemy was getting smart. They had observed that every time we received mortars, we took to the roof just in case of an attack. I wished the new guys luck. This was their official Iraqi welcoming.

Epilogue

CHAPTER 2—By the end of his tour, Romeo was known as "the Man, the Myth, the Legend" by his peers in 2/4. He left Iraq physically unharmed despite being in the most engagements in the scout/sniper platoon. He received an honorable discharge and is now a police officer in California.

CHAPTER 3—Clifton was honorably discharged and returned to Southern California. He has completed a fire academy, and is one step closer to his goal of becoming a fireman.

CHAPTER 4—Mulder's experience and knowledge proved to be invaluable, and when he returned to the States, he became an instructor at First Marine Division scout/sniper school.

CHAPTER 5—Cody returned home safely and successfully graduated the First Marine Division scout/sniper school. Months later he returned to Iraq as a team leader and one of the most senior HOGs in his platoon.

CHAPTER 6—Ethan was honorably discharged. Initially, for his actions in Fallujah, he was selected for the Bronze Star, but after review from his superiors, he was awarded the military's third-highest award for valor in combat, the Silver Star. Although it's known how many men he had killed, more important for him, it's unknown how many marines he saved. Later, an insurgent manual found in Iraq by U.S. forces stated the "seven duties of a sniper," referring to an insurgent sniper. In the writings, the number one duty was to "Target enemy snipers and surveillance teams because of lessons learned in Fallujah, where Mujahideen were handicapped more by U.S. marine snipers than by air raids or other artillery and cover fire." The reference to marine snipers was due in large part to Ethan and his team.

CHAPTER 7—Reyes stayed in Fallujah for a total of twenty-one days before returning to his original base. He returned to California and was given the opportunity to instruct others on his passion—sniping.

CHAPTER 8—Jack was honorably discharged and went to work for the State Department in Iraq. For his actions in An Najaf, his command put him in selection for a Silver Star. They recognized the importance of finding and disabling the 74 mm recoilless rifle. By doing so, Jack was able to save his fellow marines, the tanks in support of them that day, and other vehicles moving on the road that the weapon was fixed upon.

CHAPTER 9—Memo was awarded the Bronze Star with the combat distinguishing device for his actions that day. He made it home but returned to Iraq once more as a platoon sergeant for a scout/sniper platoon. He survived another horrific bombing on his second tour when an IED exploded feet away from him, while on a foot patrol. In two tours, he received four Purple Hearts.

CHAPTER 10—Since his discharge, Longoria moved back to Texas. He attends rehabilitation weekly. Although losing part of himself, he has no regrets about what happened. Before even going to Iraq, he fully accepted the consequences of war and would do the same over again.

CHAPTER 11—May received a Bronze Star with a V for Valor in Combat for his actions that night in Husaybah. Garcia also received a Bronze Star and Adams received the Silver Star for his courage under fire. May returned to Husaybah for his third tour, and made it back safely. He plans to receive an honorable discharge and become a police officer in Las Vegas, Nevada.

CHAPTER 12—The lasting effects of his tour in Husaybah forced CJ to make the decision to leave the military. He currently owns and operates Tactical Applications Group, located outside the main gates of Camp Lejeune, North Carolina. CJ has continued to serve his brothers in arms by dedicating himself and his company to training military and law enforcement, as well as manufacturing specialized equipment in hopes of saving lives.

CHAPTER 13—Afong received an honorable discharge and is currently living in Southern California, where he goes to school for business.

Acknowledgments

I'm very thankful to be given the opportunity to put this book together and it's a blessing to thank the people who have helped me.

All credit goes to my best friend for allowing me the opportunity; thank you, Jesus Christ.

Thanks to everyone directly involved who helped to accomplish the project.

To the men who have contributed, I'm truly grateful and I hope to have done you justice.

Thanks to the HOGs who instructed me and to Gunnery Sergeant Timothy Cooper for introducing me to the community.

Special thanks to the men who helped me to stay alive, my partners and teammates: Daniel Peterson, Jason "Cooper" Hill, Tom Eaton, Pablo Castellanos, Shawn Spitzer, Jorge Clynes, Stephen Johnson, Fimmie Rush, and Travis Stokley.

Thanks to all my brothers from the 00-03 2/4 SSP and the 04-05 1/23 SSP—this one's for you killers.

Very special thanks to Jeanne Barlow; your work is exceptional and I couldn't have done it without you. You truly made it all possible.

Lastly, to my family and friends who helped me along the way, thank you.